Recommendations

"The Netherlands is by any standard a global success story. A nation without significant natural resources and where most people live below the sea level has been a beacon of human development, peace and social justice throughout the centuries. *The Dutch Way* brings a much awaited story about the role of schools, teachers and education in general to be read by international audiences. This book is a must-read for anyone seriously interested in understanding global education issues today and it is especially enlightening to those looking for alternative routes to excellence and equity in education. Written by leading scholars and educators this book provides a eye-opening narrative that should be also heard by politicians and decision makers as well."

- Pasi Sahlberg, author of *Finnish Lessons 2.0:
What can the world learn from educational change in Finland.*

"Education is cultural and local. The quality of an education system cannot be simply measured by international test scores. The lessons drawn from simplistic comparisons can be misleading. Valuable and meaningful lessons should be based on thoughtful, critical, and nuanced examination of individual education systems within their own historical, societal, political, economical, and cultural contexts. *The Dutch Way* does just that. A thoughtful, critical, and nuanced examination of education in the Netherlands."

- Yong Zhao, author of *World Class Learners:
Educating Creative and Entrepreneurial Students.*

THE DUTCH WAY

IN EDUCATION

Teach, learn & lead the Dutch Way

Uitgeverij Onderwijs Maak Je Samen
Deurneseweg 13
5709 AH Helmond
The Netherlands

Translation: Eefke de Groot, vertaalbureau Thusana Talen
Copy editing: Nicol van den Hurk, Van den Hurk Vertalingen
Final editing: Jan Heijmans and Job Christians
Design & photography: Mark Verlijsdonk, Onderwijs Maak Je Samen

First edition, 2017

ISBN: 978-90-79336-22-7
www.onderwijsmaakjesamen.nl
www.thedutch-way.com

THE
DUTCH
WAY

IN EDUCATION

Teach, learn & lead the Dutch Way

Onderwijs Maak Je Samen

De Brink foundation

Table of contents

Acknowledgements

During her visit in February 2016, Professor Alma Harris inspired us to describe the unique aspects of our Dutch education system for the rest of the world. On many occasions during her keynote speeches in the Netherlands Alma has hailed our country as 'the best kept secret of education', often adding in a teasing tone that 'We are done with Finland!'.
This motivated us to put Dutch education on the international stage. On the one hand, to give worldwide teachers and school leaders the chance to become acquainted with a very successful education system and, on the other hand, to contribute to developing a sense of pride. Something we Dutch people are often too reticent about.

As we explain in the introductory chapter of this book, successful education policy is not achieved by gathering together successful policy interventions by well-performing governments all over the world, but by implementing an education policy that does justice to the national context and culture. This is something that we have successfully achieved in the Netherlands and therefore we believe it is very much worth sharing with the rest of the world.

From the autumn of 2016, we have energetically worked on the content and set-up of this publication, with the help of many people at various levels in our education system. It would be risky to attempt to individually thank everyone who contributed, as a great number of people were involved in supporting and carrying out the project. Yet there are a few people we wish to thank specifically.

First of all, we would like thank all the professors who took up the challenge of writing a chapter for *The Dutch Way*. Their contributions enabled us to bundle in one book both the puzzles and the pearls of our Dutch education. We would also like to thank Professor Alma Harris and her colleague Michelle S. Jones for their role as initiators and co-authors of this book. And we wish to thank our colleagues at De Brink foundation and Onderwijs Maak Je Samen for their help in finding the right people to make the right contributions, their valuable input on titles and topics and their support in proofreading and commenting on the text.

We would also like to thank Theo Camps and Henno Theisens for their advice on the set-up of this book. Our thanks also to the Ministry of Education, Culture and Science and Nuffic for their contributions to the publication of *The Dutch Way*.
And, last but not least, a special word of thanks and appreciation for all Dutch teachers and school leaders who every day make an invaluable contribution to the quality of our future.

Jan Heijmans   **Job Christians**
De Brink foundation   *Onderwijs Maak Je Samen*

Preface

Finally we have a book presenting Dutch education, in all its facets, to the rest of the world. It is high time, as the Netherlands also has a lot to offer in the field of education. In the OECD rankings, our primary and secondary education have been highly rated for decades, our vocational education is regarded as a world-class system and our higher education consistently scores well with respect to education participation. We rarely present our primary, secondary and senior secondary vocational education outside the Netherlands. We do advertise our higher education all around the world, primarily to attract international students. My organization, Nuffic, plays an important role in this. We promote the advantages of studying in the Netherlands, for example by emphasizing the fact that of any non-English-speaking country, the Netherlands has the highest number of study programmes taught in English.

Is there any point in drawing international attention to all aspects of Dutch education? I certainly believe so. Why? Because we need talent. To keep performing well as a country economically, culturally and socially. In various economically important sectors, we are crying out for good people, with technology being a good example. The quality and diversity of Dutch education, from primary school to PhD, is a factor in attracting talented people to come to the Netherlands. Expats are interested in the education available for their children. To some extent, this education is provided by international schools, but the number of foreign companies in the Netherlands is growing so rapidly at the moment that mainstream education needs to be considered as well. And the more this becomes internationally oriented, the more attractive it becomes to expats.

The good news is that primary, secondary and senior secondary vocational education are rapidly becoming more internationally oriented as well. Internationalization is receiving more political attention too. In 2016, the Onderwijsraad (Education Council, a key advisory body in the Netherlands) expressed its ambition that all pupils should acquire international competencies.
In primary education, we see this being implemented in early foreign-language learning, with pupils often learning English from their first year in primary school, preferably combined with a focus on knowledge about the world: the first steps towards world citizenship.
In many secondary schools, internationalization is a hot topic. It takes many forms: from projects on Germany or France to exchange weeks with schools in India or China. Around 130 secondary schools offer bilingual education, providing half of all lessons in English during the first two or three years. A few dozen schools have fully internationalized their curriculum.

Institutions for senior secondary vocational education (MBO) are also gaining experience with internationalization. In some sectors, this is an obvious step, such as in agricultural or catering training programmes. But it is also relevant in healthcare: particularly in cities, one can expect to work with an international and multicultural patient group. In MBO we see promising examples of cross-border cooperation, bilingualism and international internships.

Primary and secondary education and MBO training programmes are placing more emphasis on international orientation, but there is still a long way to go. Higher education has a more established tradition of internationalization. Our oldest university, Leiden University, had almost equal numbers of international and Dutch students as early as the 17th century. Today, almost 100,000 international students study in the Netherlands, following entire study programmes or participating in exchange programmes, such as the popular Erasmus programme.

The international talents we seek often come to the Netherlands as students. Recently, the Nobel Prize was won by a Dutchman for the first time in many years, the chemist Ben Feringa. When this was announced, various Dutch newspapers published a great photograph of him and his enthusiastic, diverse and international research team. A significant proportion of the team members came to the Netherlands to study, ultimately finding themselves in a research team working at Nobel Prize level.

If we succeed in holding on to international talent, this is good for our education. Good international students contribute to an international classroom. Particularly when the quality and ambitions in these classrooms are high, Dutch students also benefit from the diversity in this enormously stimulating environment.
Not only is internationalization good for our economy, our country also benefits when international students ultimately return to their home country or move to a new country. International alumni are often the best ambassadors for the Netherlands and can be excellent partners for trade or knowledge exchange. Dutch embassies have good reason to value a strong alumni network.

Internationalization is good for the individual and for our country. The Netherlands aims to be one of the world's leading knowledge economies. Only graduates entering the world with an open attitude will be able to contribute successfully. The Netherlands is small and depends on others. Even for this reason alone, it is important that the Netherlands is sufficiently attractive to foreign companies and workers. Our prime minister refers to the Netherlands as a 'great country' and not without justification. Our education can contribute to this. An extra reason for Dutch education to be open to international minds. So let's get to work!
But Dutch education already has lot to offer to the world around us. This story has not yet been widely told. *The Dutch Way* aims to change this. I hope you will enjoy reading it.

Freddy Weima
Freddy Weima is a director of Nuffic,
the Dutch organization for internalization at all levels of education.

THE NETHERLANDS
AT A GLANCE

AREA
41,543 km²
18.41% water

POPULATION
17,016,967

DENSITY
410/km²

OFFICIAL LANGUAGES
Dutch, Frisian *(only spoken in the province of Friesland)*

CAPITAL
Amsterdam
*population: **838,338** in 2016*

SEAT OF GOVERNMENT
The Hague
Parliamentary constitutional monarchy

HEAD OF STATE
King
Willem-Alexander

NATIONAL HOLIDAYS
April 27
King's Day

May 5
Liberation Day

RELIGION
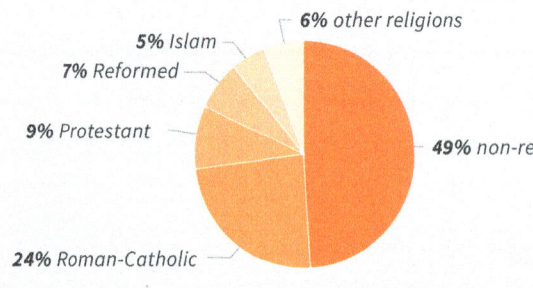
6% other religions
5% Islam
7% Reformed
9% Protestant
49% non-religious
24% Roman-Catholic

CURRENCY

Euro

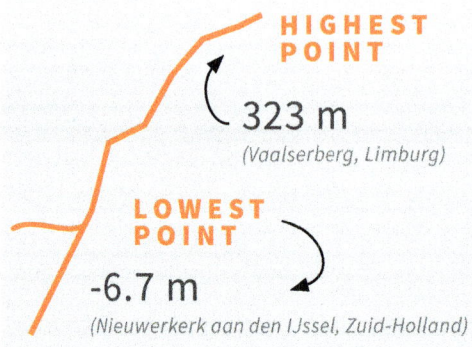
HIGHEST POINT
323 m
(Vaalserberg, Limburg)

LOWEST POINT
-6.7 m
(Nieuwerkerk aan den IJssel, Zuid-Holland)

AVERAGE TEMPERATURE
JULY
17.4 °C

JANUARY
2.8 °C

10 FACTS YOU HAVE TO KNOW ABOUT THE NETHERLANDS

1. THE NETHERLANDS IS THE LOWEST COUNTRY IN EUROPE.

2. ONE-FIFTH OF THE DUTCH POPULATION IS FOREIGN.

3. KING WILLEM-ALEXANDER IS THE FIRST DUTCH KING AFTER 123 YEARS.

4. THE NETHERLANDS HAS THE HIGHEST POPULATION DENSITY IN EUROPE.

5. DUTCH MEN ARE THE TALLEST IN THE WORLD.

6. THE FIRST MULTINATIONAL COMPANY, STOCKS AND STOCK EXCHANGE WERE DUTCH.

7. THE NETHERLANDS HAS THE HIGHEST ENGLISH-PROFICIENCY IN THE WORLD.

8. DUTCH ARTISTS ARE WORLD FAMOUS.

9. MORE THAN 60 PERCENT OF THE NETHERLANDS IS AGRICULTURE AND HORTICULTURE.

10. DISCOVERERS OF MICROBIOLOGY AND VIROLOGY.

Facts retrieved from: http://www.expatica.com.
Map of the Netherlands – Single Color by FreeVectorMaps.com

5 THINGS YOU HAVE TO KNOW ABOUT DUTCH HABITS

1. **WE ARE VERY HAPPY PEOPLE.**
Dutch kids are the happiest in the world. Researchers say that citizens in countries with a good health care system, a high GDP per capita and with good access to education are the happiest.

2. **GET THAT 'GEZELLIG' FEELING.**
You'll often hear "gezellig" referenced wherever Dutch people gather. The word roughly translates to cozy, quaint, familiar or friendly.

3. **DUTCH GLITTER AND GLAMOUR.**
This Calvinist attitude is all about modesty and being down-to-earth. Arrogance is considered not done in the Netherlands.

4. **ANYONE CAN CRITICIZE ANYONE.**
In general the Dutch are not ashamed when a mistake is pointed out to them. They see this as a chance to correct the mistake and to learn.

5. **THE DUTCH ARE CHEAP.**
"Let's go Dutch" is probably the most misunderstood phrase associated with the Netherlands. To really go Dutch, you should only pay for what you eat or drink rather than split the bill equally.

Facts retrieved from: http://www.expatica.com.
Map of the Netherlands – Single Color by FreeVectorMaps.com

The Dutch Way in Education
Teach, learn & lead the Dutch Way

Introduction

Jan Heijmans, De Brink foundation
Job Christians, Onderwijs Maak Je Samen

The Richards family from the United States arrives at Schiphol International Airport, one of the world's finest airports, with more than 50 million passengers each year. In the arrivals hall, the family is greeted by an array of clogs, miniature windmills, Delft blue china and reproductions of works by Van Gogh, Rembrandt and Vermeer. After picking up their luggage in record time, the family rents a car and heads for Keukenhof, the Dutch flower industry's celebrated show gardens. On the way, Dave suddenly calls out from the back seat: 'Hey, Dad, there's a boat going over our heads!' The whole family looks out of the windows and, yes, there really is a ship passing by on the elevated canal above them.

Figure I.1   *Aquaduct Harderwijk (Photo by Ekim Tan. [CC BY 2.0], via Wikimedia Commons).*

Welcome to the Netherlands. A small, idiosyncratic, low-lying, densely-populated country surrounded by water and located where several major rivers meet the sea; an access port for the European hinterland and international transport hub. The image of a boat passing over our heads illustrates the fact that the Dutch are able to achieve things that were believed to be impossible.

The instantly recognizable polder landscape that the Richards family is driving through, has been into development since the 10th century, the creation of citizens with a sense of urgency, specialist expertise and a flair for business. The limited space and the constant threat of flooding made the Dutch highly proficient in water management. Dikes, water mills, pumping stations, water management authorities, flood barriers and so on, are all products of the creativity, innovative zeal and perseverance of that industrious, Calvinistic people living on the edge of the North Sea. Education then ensured that the acquired knowledge was passed on and developed from generation to generation. Today, not only is the Netherlands a world leader in water management, it also has a place in the premier league in the agrifood sector, chemistry, creative industries, energy, the high-tech industry, life sciences and logistics. The Netherlands is a country driven by expertise and innovation and, more than anything, it's a great place to be.

> The wave of pessimism sweeping this country would make you think that the apocalypse cannot be far away. If it doesn't begin at midnight tonight, then surely within the next few months. Once again, the Downfall of the European Continent is imminent – and if that downfall doesn't materialize, another one will. The Netherlands is not lost yet, but it won't be long. Close the borders!
>
> This pessimism contrasts sharply with the hard facts as shown by international comparative research. This country is already doing very well and it looks as though things are only going to get better next year.
>
> Economic growth is predicted at 2.4% in 2017, unemployment will decrease further, the budget deficit will reach zero and consumer spending power is already the second highest in the EU. The Netherlands is among the top 10 countries, with a strong competitive position and one of the five most innovative economies in the world. We have the best health care in Europe and it's affordable too, our pensions are excellent, only three countries have better education, crime figures are low, we come fourth on the list of countries where children feel happiest and seventh on the list for happy adults, our citizens and press enjoy a large degree of freedom and we are also in the top 10 when it comes to democracy.
>
> These lists don't mean there is no room for improvement, but they do make it clear that we are fortunate to live in this country. Actually the only countries that are doing better are Denmark and Sweden, but they are doing so well that it's starting to get boring and you don't want that either. There has to be something to complain about, otherwise everyone will be unhappy.
>
> Bert Wagendorp (Column published in *de Volkskrant* newspaper on 31 December 2016)

Reasons for Publishing this Book

The immediate reason for bringing out *The Dutch Way* is the fact that the education system as we know it celebrates its centenary in 2017. In 1917, the Pacification brought an end to the battle between Protestant and Catholic schools over freedom of education and introduced equal funding for public (secular) and privately run (generally religious) education institutions (see Chapter 1 and 6).

There are also several other reasons. Worldwide discussion about education quality has for years been dominated by the PISA, TALIS, TIMSS and PIRLS studies and a dominant Anglo-Saxon management paradigm. The trend towards homogenization of the curriculum, emphasis on cognitive subjects, standardized tests and publication of ranking lists for schools in the media, can also be seen in the Netherlands. Pasi Sahlberg, the well-known Finnish educational theorist, recently aptly commented: 'If everyone wants to be the best or first in the rankings, the main effect is to create large numbers of losers' and this can never be the aim of education. He pointed out the dangers of the 'Global Education Reform Movement' (GERM) mentioned above, as a virus that is spreading rapidly among governments, policymakers and managers all over the world (Sahlberg, 2013). In 'Leading Futures' (2016), Professor Alma Harris and Dr Michelle Jones compare the dominant Anglo-Saxon paradigm with Asian and Eastern European alternatives. They point out the importance of context and culture in finding appropriate answers to the challenges of our time.

Governments and policymakers worldwide have limitless faith in comparative policy research, based on the assumption that what works in one country will work in another. Two main approaches can be identified:

1. The *promised land* approach. Researchers advocate an element of a system, without describing that element in its context. Recent examples of this include Finland, where it is claimed that teachers with a university education are the determining factor for success, and Singapore, where education in arithmetic and mathematics is identified as the determining factor for economic and technological progress.
2. The *statistical* approach taken by researchers such as the German econometrician Wößmann, which we often see in the form of conclusions based on 'what works'. This produces reasoning such as: a combination of decentralized curriculum content and centralized written final tests gives the best results. With this approach, statistics narrow the complex reality down to a few determining factors, when it is common knowledge that hundreds of factors and coincidences influence education every day.

The fundamental problem with this type of research is that it does not compare like with like. The multiplicity of different contexts and the cultural variety within those contexts can never be fully described in a study. The ability to generalize these conclusions and consequently to transpose the solutions to other contexts is the real problem.

Many countries deal with 'competition' in a different way from the U.S. This means that the Anglo-Saxon paradigm does not work everywhere. Many countries have a different attitude to 'obedience' from Eastern countries with a Confucian tradition. The way we 'deal with authority' is also determined by cultural variables. A typical feature of society in the Netherlands and Western Europe is that we want to have our 'individuality' as a unique person acknowledged and be allowed to express this. This, too, is determined by context and culture.

Anglo-Saxon approach	Rhineland approach
Anxiety governs: managing suspicion	Creating hope: trust in something
Rule-driven	Value-driven
Management decides (top-down approach)	Everyone involved in decision-making (bottom-up approach)
Emphasis on efficiency (fast management)	Emphasis on effectiveness (slow management)
Standardization	Customization
Measurable objectives	Noticeable change
Short-term profit maximization (more is better)	Continual reassessment and interpretation (human dimension)
Prioritize own interests	Organize community
Individual performance	Collective strength (team performance)
Job differentiation and specialization	All-round expertise
Free market competition	Balance between private and public
Money, money, money	People, planet, profit

Table I.1   *Anglo-Saxon approach versus Rhineland approach (Source: P. Bakker et al. (2005)).*

However much we might wish it to be the case, copying an approach that is successful in one country is no guarantee of the same result in another country. Every teacher, every school, every country must go their own way. This is essential to the learning process. If we give ourselves the time to look more closely, we discover that different contexts produce different answers to what are generally the same social challenges. Those answers can be placed within a historic perspective, do justice to cultural values and local attitudes and are appropriate for that context. The 'World Values Survey'[1], a study that has been carried out in almost a hundred countries since 1981, helps academics, governments and policymakers to track changes in people's attitudes, values and motivation for more than 90% of the world population. This makes this survey a valuable tool in developing satisfactory solutions and successful innovations for different contexts and cultures.

By examining the nuances with respect and talking to one another about them, we learn to appreciate diversity and respect variety. This puts us on the right track to find promising approaches for our own context. This is why professionals want to learn from colleagues in networks, why we participate in internationalization and why the worldwide discourse concerning good education is of vital importance for sustainable development in education and in our societies.

On a superficial consideration of the Netherlands, you will note there are not many areas in which we rank as the best in the world but that we perform very well in a great many areas. You could say that in line with our national character (epitomized by the well-known Dutch saying: just be normal, that's quite crazy enough), we're not so focused on getting to the top of the rankings, but the coherence in the system ensures that this is a good place to learn, live and work. Perhaps this the reason why the Netherlands does top the Unicef (2013) ranking list of the happiest children in the world.

Taking a closer look, we see, for example, that the Netherlands:
- has ranked in the top 10 in the PISA studies for the past twenty years;
- spends less than the OECD average on education and still ranks in the top 10% of best-performing countries;
- has good generally-accessible education and a high rate of participation in higher education;
- has 94% of its population speaking two or more languages.

With results like these, it's time the Netherlands took proper pride in showing the world what our education system has to offer. The Netherlands occupies a unique middle ground between West and East and offers the reader who is prepared to take a more detailed look some alternatives useful in the discussion about paradigms.

---

[1] http://www.worldvaluessurvey.org/wvs.jsp

This book aims to offer a perspective for the future, as we are still working towards an 'ideal' situation. For many developing countries and emerging economies, education is still a motor for emancipation. A way to guarantee yourself an income and climb up the social ladder. However, in more and more societies, education is increasingly becoming a motor for *participation*, an institution that not only qualifies you to enter the employment market but where you also learn how to participate in and contribute to a vigorous, sustainable society. This means that the socialization function of education (see Chapter 2) will become increasingly important in the future.

Under the Universal Declaration of Human Rights, every child has the right to education. To education aimed at the full development of the human personality and at reinforcing respect for human rights and fundamental freedoms. The dialogue between parents, teachers, principals, managers, policymakers and governments anywhere in the world, must offer children in any context and in any culture optimum development opportunities, so that together we are able to achieve the 'Global Goals for Sustainable Development'[2].

In short, the aim of this book is:

- To take proper pride in showing that the Dutch education system makes some original choices and has a great deal to offer;
- To make the context and culture of Dutch education accessible to anyone with an interest in the subject;
- To issue an invitation to collective learning with an international perspective;
- To position the Netherlands as an alternative in the discussion about paradigms;
- To contribute to the worldwide discourse on 'good' education.

What Does this Book Cover?

The Dutch Way is by no means a showcase for yet another education paradise. In this book, leading Dutch academics and educational theorists introduce you in nine accessible chapters to the unique aspects of our education system. The authors provide a realistic look at how Dutch education deals with the challenges of our time and the original responses it has developed to these challenges. Prepare to be surprised, they may even offer some new insights into your own context.

The different chapters provide an interesting mix of some general reflections on what constitutes 'good' education and the challenges for the system and a number of accounts describing the situation in various education sectors focused on a specific topic. To assist the reader, we provide a description of the various chapters.

[2]   http://www.globalgoals.org/

The Dutch education system is often praised internationally as a good example of significant freedom of education and a high degree of autonomy for parents, teachers and school management. The right to freedom of education was introduced to resolve a fierce political battle between schools that lasted more than a hundred years. It was originally intended to give parents and private organizations in society the right to establish their own schools based on religious or other beliefs. In Chapter 1, Professor Edith Hooge discusses freedom of education as a complex convergence of forces. She deals with the question of what autonomy parents, teachers and school management actually have by law and in practice, and explores two mechanisms that play a role in this today: the use of policy instruments other than legislation and the constraints on that freedom at management level.

Chapter 2 provides a more general analysis. In this chapter, Professor Gert Biesta speaks out in defence of the teacher's professional opinion. He shows us that the current 'language of learning' gets in the way of a proper understanding of the theory and practice of education and he highlights the need to refocus our attention on the normative question of what constitutes 'good' education. For this question to be answered, the 'objective' of education needs to be clear. He introduces three objective categories (qualification, socialization and subjectification). These categories are frequently referred to in the other authors' contributions. The objective categories enable us to give a multidimensional answer to the question of what constitutes 'good' education. In the second part of this chapter, Biesta discusses three trends in the professionalization of teachers: treating students as customers, methods of accountability and the replacement of the teacher's professional opinion with scientific evidence.

Chapter 3 focuses on young children (aged 0-6 years). In the Netherlands, there are a wide variety of models of cooperation between education, day care, after-school care and pre-school playgroups. In her contribution, Dr Jeannette Doornenbal describes inclusion as the task for the Integrated Child Centre (ICC). An inclusive ICC works to develop every child's talents regardless of its origins, religion, sexual orientation, disposition and ethnicity. In her contribution, she discusses four aspects that will assist in moving closer to this ultimate goal:

- First, she asserts that a sustainable learning infrastructure needs to be created at local level.
- Second, as revealed by the work of the pedagogue Genesis Ponti, there are five key aspects to optimum talent development: building a relationship of trust, the need to belong, having high expectations, the quality of the interaction and the professional as role model.
- Third, according to Doornenbal, working inclusively requires T-shaped professionals and teams.
- Fourth, she asserts that working inclusively in an ICC is still very much a 'work in progress' that requires further research.

In Chapter 4, Dr Marco Snoek describes the changing role and position of the teacher in education. He describes the phases in the teacher's professional development process: from a follower of system requirements and government policy, through professionalization of the individual teacher, to good education as a result of a cooperative culture within teams. This approach corresponds closely to the T-shaped teams described by Doornenbal in Chapter 3. For each phase, Snoek deals with the dilemmas encountered in that phase and the successful initiatives taken to develop on to the next phase. At the end of this chapter, he considers the phenomenon of 'teacher leadership' and the circumstances that make this possible.

Chapter 5 adopts a similar structure. Professor Inge Wolf et al. deal in their contribution with the changing role and position of the Inspectorate with respect to regulating education quality. The Dutch Inspectorate of Education has existed since 1801, making it the oldest regulator in the world. This chapter describes the development from uniform regulation, through risk-focused regulation, to management-focused regulation. The current 'assessment framework' involves answering three simple questions:

- Are pupils safe and what is the atmosphere like (school climate)?
- Are pupils learning enough (education results)?
- Are pupils being taught well (education process)?

The Inspectorate also assesses performance in the areas of education quality achievement and ambition and financial management as these are requirements for sustainable education quality. This chapter also considers annual reporting to parliament on the 'State of Education' and deals with some regulatory dilemmas.

Chapter 6 again presents a more general analysis. In their contribution, Professor Marc Vermeulen and Professor Sietske Waslander ask how successful the Dutch education system has been over the past hundred years in fulfilling the emancipation task given to it since the Pacification. Taking as their starting point the meritocratic ideal[3] in which one's social position is determined on the basis of qualifications, the authors explore the question of why even after hundred years the Dutch education system – despite being easily accessible – does not offer equal opportunities for all. They argue that we may even be heading towards the collapse of the meritocratic ideal. The authors introduce a thought-provoking model that clearly shows the segregation between the 'haves' and the 'have nots' at the lower end of the employment market. According to the authors, this leads to various forms of extremism. They then explain what education can mean for each group in the future. A visionary contribution that invites further intensification of the discourse on what constitutes 'good' education for different target groups.

In the next two chapters, we turn our attention to vocational education, in each case focusing on one of the key challenges. In Chapter 7, Dr Rick Wolff describes how the Netherlands deals with 'super-diversity'. Diversity refers to a situation with one ethnic majority group and various ethnic

---

[3]   A model for society in which each individual's socioeconomic position is based on his or her merits.

minority groups. Super-diversity is where the population consists of various ethnic groups, none of which makes up a significant majority. This is particularly the case in primary, secondary and higher education institutions in large cities. In itself, this is a positive sign. It shows that all levels of education and the various types of education provided at each level are in principle accessible to all young people. However, there are significant differences between the path through school towards higher education taken by young people with no migration background and young people with a non-Western migration background. This gives rise to the two key questions addressed in Wolf's contribution:

- Why are students with a non-Western origin less successful in their studies than students without a migration background?
- What changes are needed to give students with and without a migration background equal opportunities for study success in higher education?

He comes to the conclusion that a combination of a strong focus on supervising students, a personal approach by lecturers and supervisors and a small-scale educational institution provides a promising mix. Investing in internationalization strengthens the impact.

In Chapter 8, Dr Marc van der Meer discusses how further vocational education attempts to close the gap between theory and practice. Dutch vocational education has a good reputation internationally. One aspect of this success comes from the dual study routes (a combination school-based and work-based training). Youth unemployment is also relatively low by European standards and significant opportunities are available in the employment market for young people who complete a vocational training programme. At the same time, considerable challenges exist in view of the internal and external changes to the employment market and changes in student composition. In view of the far-reaching technological developments, Van der Meer believes that collaboration in innovative arrangements combining learning and work-based training (in the shape of a cohesive learning structure) provides the model for the future.

In Chapter 9, Professor Caroline Hummels discusses the innovative mindset of Dutch education. Her contribution divides into three parts. In the first section, she discusses the shifts in the social and educational paradigms that form the basis for her work. Her second section discusses the need to remain a 'lifelong self-managing learner', using ten parameters expressed in the form of opposites (or apparent opposites). Examples include self-managing versus guided learning, acting versus thinking, tied to a time and place versus independent of time and place, individual versus collective learning and online versus offline learning. In the third section, Hummels discusses four inspiring examples of innovative Dutch learning environments.

In Chapter 10, Professor Alma Harris and Dr Michelle Jones consider the developments in Dutch education from an international perspective.

Looking Forward

One of the aims of *The Dutch Way* is to make a contribution to the discourse about 'good' education and offer an alternative to the dominant paradigms in that discussion. Together, the ten chapters provide the reader with a good overview of the versatility and multiplicity of our unique education system. They also set out the challenges facing Dutch society and education in the coming years and the promising innovative solutions that are currently being adopted in all sectors.

In short, based on the contributions of the various authors, on behalf of Dutch education we would like to shape the discourse by introducing the following new insights:

* First, we would like to argue in favour of the distinction made by Professor Gert Biesta between three categories of educational objectives: qualification, socialization and subjectification. This model prevents governments and policymakers from developing an excessively one-sided focus when considering educational innovations and helps us to include all the relevant aspects in the discourse.
* Second, based on our rich educational tradition we would like to take a 'holistic' look at the question of what is good for the development of children/young people. From the perspective of the Dutch education system, this equates to equal opportunities for all children, targeted development of multi-faceted talents within the system and cultivation of excellence to preserve a position as one of the top education systems in the world in many areas.
* Third, we have a long tradition of dealing with 'diversity' in society and in education. Our famous 'polder model' with its consensus culture is a good example of how the Netherlands has for centuries shown itself capable of dealing productively with apparently insurmountable contradictions. In a time of worldwide polarization, this model could well be put to good service again.

The 'polder model'
The 'polder model' has its origins in the Middle Ages when farmers, noblemen and townspeople had to work together to build terps and dikes to stay dry. This was only possible with concerted efforts. It involves accepting that the higher purpose is more important than the interests of the individual. Employers, the government and the unions meet periodically to negotiate collective employment conditions and wages. In other sectors such as healthcare and education, the polder model is used in the discussions about policy and regulation between the government and the organizations representing the various sectors and interests. 'To polder' means to achieve a consensus in which the parties agree on a compromise such that all the interests involved are carefully balanced and a common higher purpose is served.

How Should You Use *The Dutch Way*?

The Dutch Way is a reference book containing a great deal of information and background, offering teachers, students, researchers, ministers, policymakers and anyone else who may be interested the opportunity to become quickly acquainted with the many facets of the unique Dutch education system.

In addition to this introduction, the book contains:

1. A range of 'infographics' providing the reader with factual information about the Netherlands and its education system.
2. Nine absorbing contributions from leading Dutch academics and educational theorists further illuminating various unique aspects of Dutch education. In their contributions, the authors describe the developments that have taken place in the Netherlands and in education with respect to the topic discussed. This enables the reader to understand the topic from the perspective of the Dutch context and culture and consequently to form a well-considered opinion on the subject discussed from an international perspective. Each chapter concludes with three questions relating to the topic that are currently engaging the author. This lays a foundation for dialogue and discourse.
3. A final international comparison chapter by Professor Alma Harris and Dr Michelle S. Jones containing a critical analysis of the topics considered from an international perspective.
4. Portraits of the education professionals who make Dutch education and give it colour. These portraits give the reader a glimpse of everyday education practice and paint a good picture of what these 'insiders' value so much about Dutch education.

We, the initiators of this book (Onderwijs Maak Je Samen and De Brink foundation), believe that it is time for the Netherlands to take a more active role in the worldwide discourse about 'good' education. We have compiled this book with the greatest possible care. We hope that by reading this book you will come to appreciate our country and our education system and that it will offer you new insights. We also hope that this book will help our Dutch readers to appreciate Dutch education more. Even though it rather goes against our nature, we Dutch people should be proud of our education!

The Dutch government, Nuffic, the authors and our schools would be happy to put you in touch with the right people, based on our firm conviction that only discourse will enable us to move forward. On our website, www.thedutch-way.com, we provide more examples, downloadable infographics and various contact details.

References

Bakker, P. et. al. (2005). Het Rijnlands model als inspiratiebron. *Holland Management Review 103*, pp. 72-81.

Harris, A & Jones, Michelle S. (2016). *Leading Futures, global perspectives on Educational Leadership*. Sage Publications India.

Sahlberg, P. (2013). *Finnish Lessons. Wat Nederland kan leren van het Finse onderwijs*. Helmond: Uitgeverij OMJS/Stichting De Brink.

Unicef Office of Research (2013). *Child well-being in Rich countries, a comparative overview*. Innocenti Report Card 11. Unicef Office of Research: Florence.

Infographics

About the Netherlands
and the Dutch

THE EDUCATIONAL SYSTEM IN THE NETHERLANDS IN 2017

Age
(estimate)

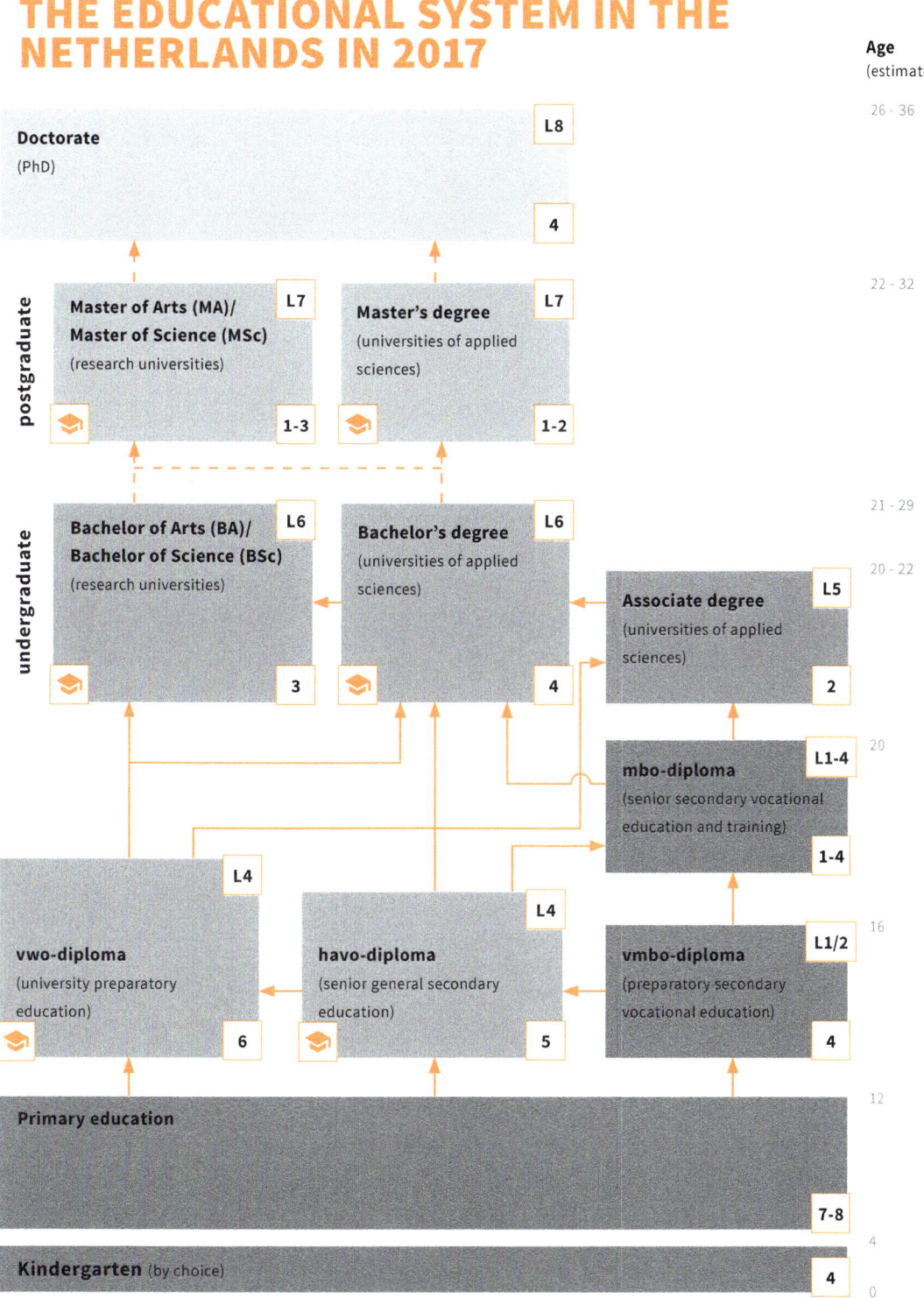

Doctorate (PhD)	**L8**	26 - 36
	4	

postgraduate

Master of Arts (MA)/ Master of Science (MSc) (research universities) — **L7** — **1-3**

Master's degree (universities of applied sciences) — **L7** — **1-2**

22 - 32

undergraduate

Bachelor of Arts (BA)/ Bachelor of Science (BSc) (research universities) — **L6** — **3**

Bachelor's degree (universities of applied sciences) — **L6** — **4**

Associate degree (universities of applied sciences) — **L5** — **2**

21 - 29

20 - 22

mbo-diploma (senior secondary vocational education and training) — **L1-4** — **1-4**

20

vwo-diploma (university preparatory education) — **L4** — **6**

havo-diploma (senior general secondary education) — **L4** — **5**

vmbo-diploma (preparatory secondary vocational education) — **L1/2** — **4**

16

Primary education — **7-8**

12

Kindergarten (by choice) — **4**

4

4

0

SCHOOLS PER DENOMINATION

PRIMARY EDUCATION

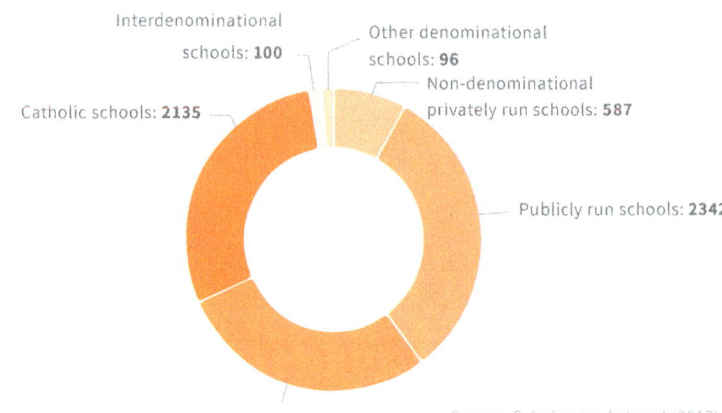

Interdenominational schools: **100**

Other denominational schools: **96**

Non-denominational privately run schools: **587**

Catholic schools: **2135**

Publicly run schools: **2342**

Protestant schools: **2083**

Source: Scholen op de kaart (2017)

SECONDARY EDUCATION

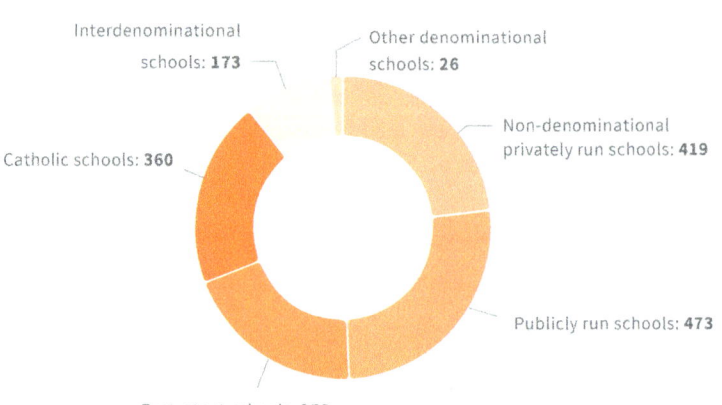

Interdenominational schools: **173**

Other denominational schools: **26**

Non-denominational privately run schools: **419**

Catholic schools: **360**

Publicly run schools: **473**

Protestant schools: **358**

Source: Scholen op de kaart (2017)

CONCEPT SCHOOLS IN PRIMARY EDUCATION

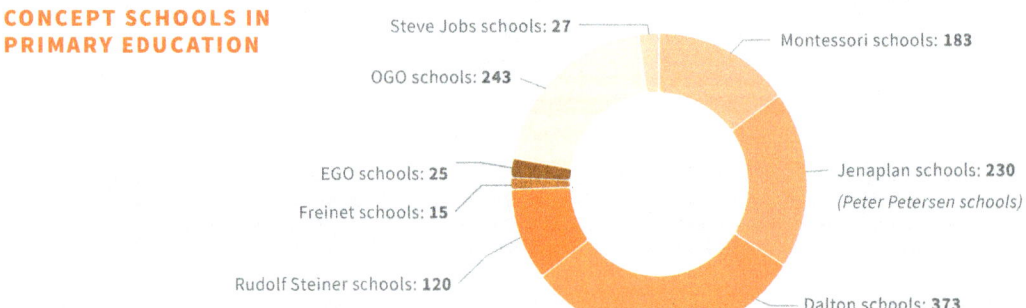

Steve Jobs schools: **27**

Montessori schools: **183**

OGO schools: **243**

EGO schools: **25**

Freinet schools: **15**

Jenaplan schools: **230**
(Peter Petersen schools)

Rudolf Steiner schools: **120**

Dalton schools: **373**
(Helen Panckhurst schools)

The Dutch Way in Education
Teach, learn & lead the Dutch Way

DUTCH GOVERNMENT SPENDING IN 2017

€ 264.4 billion total

Healthcare	Social affairs and employmenty	Education, culture and science
75.4	78.5	33.8

Foreign affairs	Safety and justice	Infrastructure and environment
10.8	10.5	8.0

Defense	Interest debt	Economic affairs
7.9	6.4	4.4

Other

6.3

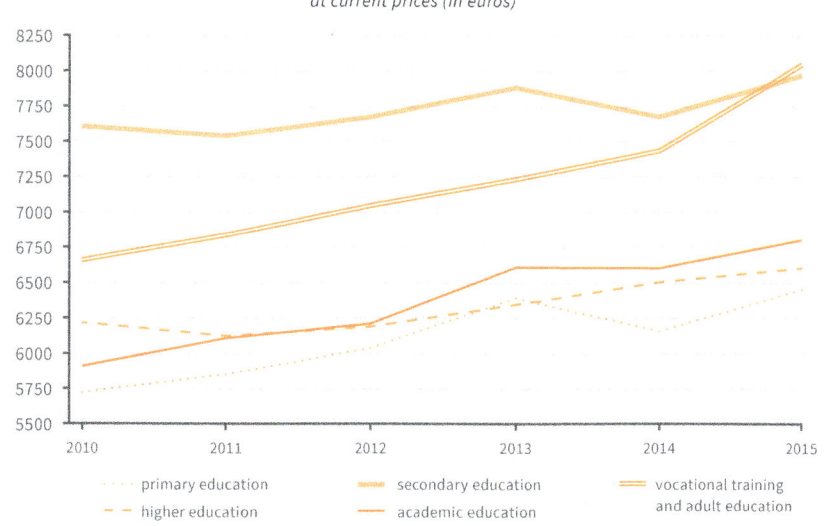

Government spending per sector
at current prices (in euros)

········· primary education
— secondary education
═══ vocational training and adult education
– – higher education
— academic education

Source: Ministry of Education, Culture and Science

WELLBEING OF DUTCH PUPILS

The table below ranks 29 developed countries according to the overall well-being of their children. Each country's overall rank is based on its average ranking for the five dimensions of child well-being considered in this review.

A light orange background indicates a place in the top third of the table, mid orange denotes the middle third, and dark orange the bottom third.

		Overall well-being	Dimension 1	Dimension 2	Dimension 3	Dimension 4	Dimension 5
		Average rank (all 5 dimensions) (rank)	Material well-being (rank)	Health and safety (rank)	Education (rank)	Behaviours and risks (rank)	Housing and environment (rank)
1	Netherlands	2.4	1	5	1	1	4
2	Norway	4.6	3	7	6	4	3
3	Iceland	5	4	1	10	3	7
4	Finland	5.4	2	3	4	12	6
5	Sweden	6.2	5	2	11	5	8
6	Germany	9	11	12	3	6	13
7	Luxembourg	9.2	6	4	22	9	5
8	Switzerland	9.6	9	11	16	11	1
9	Belgium	11.2	13	13	2	14	14
10	Ireland	11.6	17	15	17	7	2
11	Denmark	11.8	12	23	7	2	15
12	Slovenia	12	8	6	5	21	20
13	France	12.8	10	10	15	13	16
14	Czech Republic	15.2	16	8	12	22	18
15	Portugal	15.6	21	14	18	8	17
16	United Kingdom	15.8	14	16	24	15	10
17	Canada	16.6	15	27	14	16	11
18	Austria	17	7	26	23	17	12
19	Spain	17.6	24	9	26	20	9
20	Hungary	18.4	18	20	8	24	22
21	Poland	18.8	22	18	9	19	26
22	Italy	19.2	23	17	25	10	21
23	Estonia	20.8	19	22	13	26	24
23	Slovakia	20.8	25	21	21	18	19
25	Greece	23.4	20	19	28	25	25
26	United States	24.8	26	25	27	23	23
27	Lithuania	25.2	27	24	19	29	27
28	Latvia	26.4	28	28	20	28	28
29	Romania	28.6	29	29	29	27	29

Lack of data on a number of indicators means that the following countries, although OECD and/or EU members, could not be included in the league table of child well-being: Australia, Bulgaria, Chile, Cyprus, Israel, Japan, Malta, Mexico, New Zealand, the Republic of Korea, and Turkey.

Source: UNICEF Office of Research (2013). 'Child Well-being in Rich Countries: A comparative overview', Innocenti Report Cord 11, UNICEF Office of Research, Florence.

The Dutch Way in Education
Teach, learn & lead the Dutch Way

FACTSHEET PER SECTOR (1)

Primary and Secondary Education

| **Students** (Primary Education) **1,457,550** | **Students** (Secondary Education) **985,069** |

Schools/institutes (Primary Education)
6,714

Schools/institutes (Secondary Education)
636

Average school size (Primary Education)
224

Average school size (Secondary Education)
1,548
(Figures from own institute)

Full-time jobs (Primary Education)
101,544.5

Full-time jobs (Secondary Education)
85,383.3

Boards (DUO) (Primary Education)
1,085

Boards (DUO) (Secondary Education)
335

One-school boards (Primary Education)
472

Graduates (Secondary Education)
172,708 (91%)
CBS (Statistics Netherlands)
exam figures (2013-2014)

| **VMBO** (Secondary Education) **96,332** (93%) Preparatory vocational secondary education | **HAVO** (Secondary Education) **44,560** (87%) Senior general secondary education | **VWO** (Secondary Education) **31,816** (89%) University preparatory education |

CBS (2014-2015); DUO (2015);

DIVERSITY IN THE NETHERLANDS

Gender

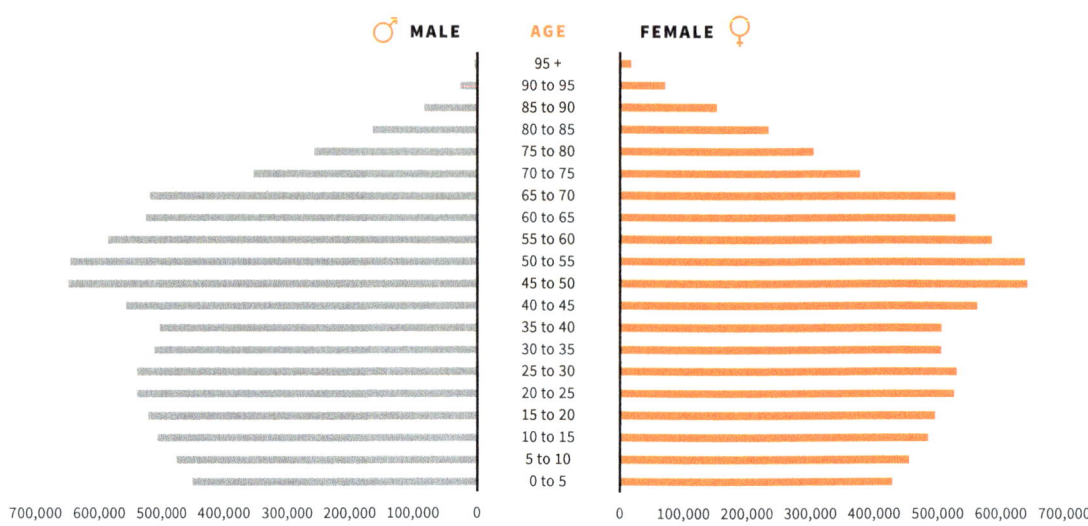

Source: CBS (2016)

Religion

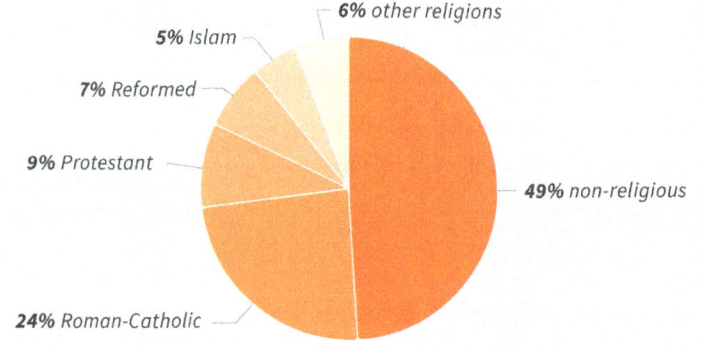

6% other religions
5% Islam
7% Reformed
9% Protestant
49% non-religious
24% Roman-Catholic

Source: CBS (2015)

Origin of birth

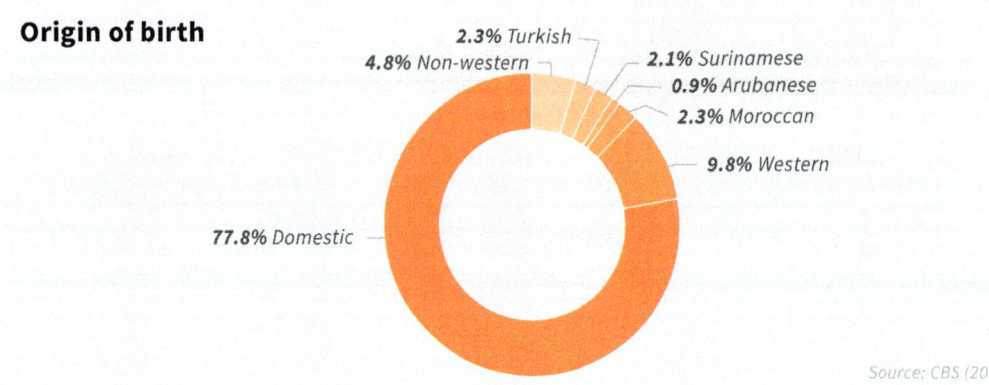

2.3% Turkish
4.8% Non-western
2.1% Surinamese
0.9% Arubanese
2.3% Moroccan
9.8% Western
77.8% Domestic

Source: CBS (2016)

The Dutch Way in Education
Teach, learn & lead the Dutch Way

FACTSHEET PER SECTOR (2)

Vocational and Higher Education

Students
(Vocational Education)
491,731

Students
(Higher Education)
699,572

Schools/institutes
(Vocational Education)
56

Schools/institutes
(Higher Education)
52

Universities
(Higher Education)
15

Average school size
(Vocational Education)
8,780
(Figures from own institute)

Average school size
(Higher Education)
1,818

Full-time jobs
(Vocational Education)
43,602.1

Full-time jobs
(Higher Education)
73,600
DUO (Dutch government's Executive
Agency for Education, 2014)

Graduates
(Vocational Education)
167,210

Graduates
(Higher Education)
94,571
CBS (Statistics Netherlands)
exam figures (2013-2014)

PhD
(Higher Education)
4,663

CBS (2014-2015); DUO (2015);

CHARTING 100 YEARS OF DUTCH EDUCATION POLICY

Harm Klifman

Over the past century, the Dutch education system of publicly and privately run schools has seen changes in which various relational and interactional patterns between the government (represented by the Ministry of Education, Culture and Science) and the field of education (schools and their governing and representative bodies) can be identified. The table below reflects the four dominant relational patterns, each of which is representative of a wider development in the relationship between government and social stakeholders.

Education politics[1]

	Distributive 1917-1962	Constructive 1962-1982	Effective 1982-1994/98	Economic 1994/98 to date
Coordination	Government as follower	Government in a steering role	Focus on relationship between objective and means	Focus on performance
Focus	Legal	Pedagogical	Administrative	Economic
Means	Legislation	Policy documents Debate	Appointment of intermediaries	Market forces Sanctions Performance agreements
School management	Classical model (school principal)	First among equals (team leader)	Integrated leader	Entrepreneur
Partner for ministry	Social 'pillars'	Umbrella organizations	Process management bodies	Sector councils
Approach	Non-intervention	Negotiation	Allurement	Sanctioning

Education politics (vertical axis label)

[1] The terms 'distributive' and 'constructive' education politics originate from the public administration theorist P.J. Idenburg, 'Naar een constructieve onderwijspolitiek' [Towards constructive education politics] *Pedagogische Studiën, 47*, 1979, pp. 1-18.

Legend 1: Relational aspects

Coordination: nature of the relationship between the ministry and the field of education

Focus: perspective in terms of dominant academic discipline

Means: dominant administrative instrument

School management: image of school leader

Partner for ministry: negotiating partner on behalf of the field of education

Approach: basic attitude of the ministry towards the field of education

Legend 2: Education politics

Distributive education policy (1917-1962):
1917 Education Pacification, development of social 'pillars' system, financial equality, decrease in publicly run schools, increase in privately run schools, distributive justice, legislation for public education = funding conditions for privately run schools, reproduction of social relationships, no upward mobility, relative peace, 19th-century school structure (higher civic school (HBS), girls' secondary school (MMS), technical school, domestic science school) reflects social positions.

Constructive education policy (1962-1982):
1963 Mammoetwet (Secondary Education Act), upward mobility, new types of schools, progression to higher school levels, Den Uyl cabinet, politicization of education, middle school debate, policy documents, modernization of special education, pedagogical approach, kindergarten merges with primary school, uninterrupted chain of development, intercultural education, religious movements, education plays a role in 'fair distribution of income, knowledge and power'.

Effective (and efficient) education policy (1982-1994/98):
HOAK (Higher Education Autonomy and Quality) policy document, 'De school op weg naar 2000' [The school heading towards 2000] (1988), administrative orientation, core objectives in primary and secondary education, scale-up, incentives, Scheveningen agreement, lump-sum financing, key tasks discussions, selectively active government, 'doing what works', New Public Management, introduction of market forces, government as business, international orientation, school as learning organization.

Economic education policy (1994/98 to date):
International core curricula, back to basics, short learning pathways, no certificate stacking, negative sanctions, neoliberal thought, market forces, personal budgets for special-needs students, performance agreements, output-directed policy, return-directed education, evidence-based, exact subjects prioritized over linguistic subjects, technical subjects prioritized over humanities subjects, education prioritized over healthcare, benchmarks, enterprising school.

Chapter 1

Freedom of Education as an Interplay of Forces

Prof. dr. Edith Hooge,
TIAS Tilburg University

ntroduction

The Dutch education system is often seen as a vivid example of great freedom of education and a high degree of autonomy for parents, teachers, and school boards. Freedom of education has long constituted the backbone of the Dutch education system. It is the outcome of a fierce, more than a hundred years long political battle along religious and social lines, referred to as the 'school struggle'. Freedom of education was originally intended to give parents and private communities/parties in society the right to establish and operate their own schools based on religious, ideological or educational convictions or on 'general interest'. It exists in the Netherlands in an ideal or theoretical sense until the present day. When education policy is implemented, freedom of education works out differently for the various parties involved. Two mechanisms are discussed that play a role in this. First, the use of policy instruments other than legislation and regulations to implement education policy. Second, the so-called 'substitution effects'; that is, the partial bureaucratization of this freedom at the intermediary level of governance between schools and the government. These mechanisms mean that in practice, the freedom of education involves a complex interplay of forces.

Historical Context

Freedom of education and equal financial footing of both publicly run and privately run and publicly funded schools lie at the heart of Article 23 of the Dutch Constitution, on which education legislation is based. They have their origin in the school struggle and the ensuing Pacification of 1917.

The school struggle took place during the formation and development of the Dutch nation state in the late 18th and 19th centuries. At that time, the Kingdom of the Netherlands was characterized by deep social and religious polarization. Initially, the school struggle played mainly between the prospering Protestant majority and the disadvantaged Catholic minority. In the middle of the 19th century, equal treatment of the Catholic minority and the dominant Protestants was gradually ensured in the Dutch nation state. The constitutional amendment in 1848 that established formal freedom of education, i.e. freedom to provide education, symbolized a compromise between the two religious parties.

From then onwards, the school struggle moved to the realization of the achieved formal freedom of education, i.e. the funding of schools. Also, 'neutral' public education became an issue, because until then, public schools were of Protestant character in line with the Protestant character of the Dutch royal house. To the annoyance of all non-Protestant parties, it proved difficult to turn the traditionally 'Protestant' public schools into genuinely 'neutral' public schools. The debate focused on the right to public funding of religious schools, claimed by religious parties, and the ideal of a single public school, articulated by liberal parties. With the creation of a constitutionally sanctioned system of publicly and privately operated schools that are all eligible for government funding in 1917, more than a century of school struggle was brought to an end.

Since freedom of education was laid down in Article 23 of the Constitution in 1917, about two-thirds of the schools are privately run, which means founded by private initiative, e.g. by parents and private communities/parties though publicly funded. About one third of the schools are public, i.e. founded by local government. Every local government is expected to provide public education in a sufficient number of schools, thus ensuring that every child is able to attend a publicly run school. The Netherlands has only a small number of privately operated schools that are privately funded (approximately 7% of all pupils in primary and secondary education attend private schools). Nevertheless, during the last decade, private education has grown substantially in the form of private schools and institutes providing homework supervision and exam training, and mentoring and guiding children with special education needs. The amount of private schools and institutes that provide schooling and training in addition to standard education, and therefore referred to as 'shadow education', has doubled in 2016 compared with 2009. The emergence of 'shadow education' is seen as evidence of the failure of the standard education system in the Netherlands and as a threat to overall accessibility of education and equal opportunities.

Tension between Freedom of Education and Government Intervention

Typically, Article 23 reflects tensions between freedom of education and government intervention, because it both protects against, and legitimates, government intervention in education. On the one hand, freedom of education is practiced according to the 'principle of the three freedoms', i.e. that freedom of education can only be achieved when the freedom to give schools a specific religious, ideological, educational or 'general interest' character (*vrijheid van richting*) is accompanied by the freedom to establish schools (*vrijheid van oprichting*) and educational and organizational autonomy (*vrijheid van inrichting*). This principle was intended to protect the educational rights of school organizations and those of parents and pupils against too far-reaching government intervention in education. On the other hand, Article 23 expresses the government's responsibility with respect to education, formulated as 'education being a subject of continued attention for the national government'. This legitimates government intervention, as it requires national government to set statutory requirements (*deugdelijkheidseisen*) to ensure a minimal level of educational quality, and as it demands that *all* schools are under the scrutiny of the Dutch Inspectorate of Education, which acts as a government agency. The government has the right to translate the statutory requirements into organizational requirements relating to school subjects, class schedules, final attainment levels and examination regulations. The requirements relating to the expertise, understanding, skills and professional attitude of teachers also fall under the organizational requirements, as do requirements relating to management and the internal organization of the education. In the Pacification of 1917, the statutory requirements were interpreted as minimum standards, whereby the government is bound to do 'that which is essential'. This basic-standards approach requires self-discipline from the state when interpreting the statutory requirements, as well as a sophisticated understanding of the meaning of Article 23 of the Dutch Constitution.

The above tension between freedom of education and government intervention can be interpreted as a tension between the freedom of groups and individuals on the one hand, and collective aims and aspirations in relation to education on the other. When designing educational policy and legislation, the desire to adjust the statutory requirements in line with political and social views and requirements may be in conflict with the interpretation of the freedom of education, something that continues to cause political and social controversy in the Netherlands repeatedly to this day. At present, important points of discussion are government measures with respect to, for example, public funding of Islamic schools and the issue of eliminating school segregation, or education governance and quality assurance interfering with school board autonomy[1]. With respect to the latter, it is noteworthy that over the last years, the legal powers of the Inspectorate of Education have been extended by introducing an integrated approach of monitoring school quality, financial management, compliance with rules and regulations and checking that schools ensure educational quality effectively. Since 2010, the law allows for government intervention if the Inspectorate finds schools to be at risk of underperformance (see Chapter 5).

Autonomy for Parents, Teachers and School Boards

A large amount of freedom of education implies a high degree of autonomy for parents, teachers and school boards. In this paragraph I'll address the question: What kind of autonomy does each actor have, and to which degree?

Parents

Although not explicitly mentioned in Article 23 of the Constitution, free parental choice of schools, and the major role parents play in the establishment and the governance of privately run and publicly funded schools, have long been significant consequences of the Dutch freedom of education.

From an international perspective, Dutch pupils and their parents enjoy a unique freedom, namely the freedom to choose a school. In the past, philosophical and religious preferences played a major role in this. In recent decades, however, quality-related considerations have become increasingly important. As it is difficult for parents to gauge the quality of a school, in

---

[1]   Waslander, 2010

practice their choice of school is determined by the school's image and reputation. The latter is partly dependent on the level of education and the social background of the pupils who attend the school, as well as that of their parents. In general, parents consider schools with a high concentration of disadvantaged and high-risk pupils to be less suitable for their children, and for middle and higher educated parents, it is important for a school to be in keeping with their ideas on education and upbringing.

The freedom to choose a school is sometimes limited by local arrangements that oblige parents and pupils to choose a school within their own postcode region, or to participate in a system of lottery or a matching system. In addition, the fact that parents have to choose from existing schools also limits their freedom of choice. Since the early 1990s, there have been very few real possibilities for founding and securing funding for new schools. Yearly, ten to twenty new primary schools are established out of 6,700, and one to three secondary schools out of 1,400[2]. If parents and/or other parties and groups in Dutch society wish to establish a new school, they must demonstrate the need of pupils and parents for a new school based on a specific religious, ideological, educational or 'general interest' approach, in the Dutch language referred to as *richting*. Today, there is a strong debate on what exactly can and should be understood as a specific *richting*, and which role *richting* should play in establishing new schools. A growing voice is calling for the abolishment of the concept of *richting*, as it is often experienced as an impediment to establish new innovative schools. The process from idea to effective start of a new school may take long, especially because local government has five years to offer suitable accommodation.

Historically, parents are both constituents and beneficiaries of privately run and publicly funded schools, and play a major role in the governance of 'their' schools as members of school boards, of governing bodies and through participation structures. However, parent participation has decreased over the last decades, partly due to processes of restructuring and professionalising school governance and the upscaling of school organizations, and also because parents are less willing to participate. In 1990, 80% of school boards of privately run and publicly funded schools consisted of parents, compared with 30% of school boards in primary education and 16% of school boards in secondary education twenty years later[3]. The Dutch Onderwijsraad (Education Council) has repeatedly voiced its concerns about the low degree of interest and expertise of parents and pupils regarding participation. Parents are not always seen as equal partners, and schools are not always able to involve parents who are difficult to reach, often parents from immigrant backgrounds or with a lower level of education.

In response to these developments, the position of pupils and their parents has been strengthened by various means. Schools are being forced to take greater account of pupils and their parents, because the transition from a reimbursement-financing model to lump-sum funding established a linear relationship between a school's finances and the number of pupils attending the

[2]   Klein, Waslander, Hooge, Imandt & Bisschop, 2014
[3]   De Bruin, van de Linden, van de Vegt & van der Aa, 2012; Honingh & Hooge, 2012

school. In addition, the school's obligation to account for its policy to parents, in the form of the school guide and the annual report, as well as the information on school quality provided by the Inspectorate of Education, have increased the onus on schools to take account of the users of education. In 2007, the Wet Medezeggenschap Onderwijs (Education Participation Act) was updated, requiring every school to have a council composed of employees, students and parents that is entitled to take part in governance processes. Very recently, in 2016, the Wet Versterking Bestuurskracht (Administrative Power Reinforcement Act) was introduced to further strengthen the position of the employee and student/parent council. Transparency and openness in the appointment and dismissal of education administrators, and the involvement of the council in these procedures, is one of the main proposals.

Teachers

From an international perspective, Dutch teachers, like parents, enjoy a unique freedom, namely, the freedom to choose their employer. Rather than being assigned to a school, as is the case in many other countries, they are free to apply to the school of their choice. This means that they can choose the school that best fits their preferred form of professional practice and – owing to the decentralization of fringe benefits – their preferred terms of employment. A shortage of teachers, especially in particular subjects or types of school, which occasionally occurs in the Netherlands, further strengthens this freedom to choose a school.

Another freedom that is enjoyed by teachers could be called the 'freedom to teach and educate'. Due to the freedom of education, central government has little direct control over teachers and their teaching practice. Traditionally, the Constitution only holds the Dutch State responsible for 'the ability and morality of those teaching (delivering education)'. In consultation with their colleagues and managers, teachers are free to organize their teaching by using methods and teaching aids at their own discretion. However, this freedom to teach and educate has always been limited. The government, school boards and – at the level of the school organization – managers, internal and external advisers, exercise what is known as 'professional oversight'. This oversight is manifest in the establishment of human resource policies, the development of the teaching profession and requirements relating to expertise. With the introduction of the Wet op Beroepen in het Onderwijs (Education Professions Act) in 2006, the control of central government over teachers, indirectly via school boards, has grown slightly. This act requires the Inspectorate of Education to check on school boards establishing human resource policies for their schools, keeping competency files for teachers, and ensuring that teachers' competencies are maintained. Regulations require regular performance interviews with all staff. However, there is little central guidance on *how* teacher performance should be evaluated. School boards have the power to design and implement strategies and policies to achieve objectives with regard to human resources, organizational development and the quality of education. It is also up to school boards to take measures to promote professionalization and the learning and collaboration of (teams of) teachers.

School Boards

All privately run and publicly funded schools are under the auspices of school boards which are structured in private legal forms. In the last few decades, local governments have set up separate entities to govern their public schools, so that they now seldom fall under the direct control of local government. However these separate entities operate schools with a public character on behalf of local government, in practice they act and look like school boards of privately run and publicly funded schools.

There is large variation in governance models. Today, the majority of school boards have provided for professional governors (receiving a salary), whilst the number of school boards that have voluntary governors (often parents and other laypersons receiving a honorarium) rapidly decreases. Professional governors are appointed by their internal supervisors. Since the introduction of the Wet Goed Onderwijs Goed Bestuur (Good Education, Good Governance Act) in 2010, all school boards are required to arrange for internal supervision and guarantee a clear separation between governing and supervising functions[4]. Internal supervision can be executed in various ways through either a two-tier or a one-tier structure. The two-tier structure encompasses two separate boards: a governing board that governs, and a supervisory board that executes the supervision function. The two-tier structure is a legal requirement for the entire Dutch private sector and it is widely accepted and approved of in the Netherlands. The one-tier structure, which is conventional worldwide, includes just one board in which the governing and supervision functions both are executed by respectively executives and non-executives. In the Netherlands, it is generally agreed that the internal supervisory function in the governance of public sector organizations involves three tasks: 1) decision control, 2) acting as the employer of the governors and 3) assisting with advice and acting as a sounding board. The internal supervisors are laypersons (parents, citizens, stakeholders, members of a religious or life philosophy community or professionals with specific expertise such as law, finance, HRM or education) who are appointed by cooptation, which means that the current internal supervisors jointly recruit and appoint a new board member in case of a vacancy.

Voluntary governors (parents) often delegate their executive tasks and responsibilities to the school director(s), and limit themselves to the broad outline when formulating and controlling policies. Voluntary governors are appointed by co-optation and obliged to provide for internal supervision.

Since they all are appointed either way, school board members in the Netherlands function as trustees rather than as representatives. In many other countries (e.g. the USA), members of school boards are elected officials and therefore operate in a political environment in which they are held accountable through such means as elections. Compared to this, school boards in the Netherlands lack democratic accountability mechanisms and operate at a relative distance from (the dynamics of) government.

[4] Hooge & Honingh, 2014

Dutch school boards have more autonomy than school boards anywhere else in the world. Data provided by the Organization for Economic Co-operation and Development (OECD) show[5] that, in the Netherlands, 85% of the decisions are taken by school boards and only 15% by central government, as can be seen in Figure 1.1. Compared to other European countries, we see that in England, Estonia and Belgium (FL), 70% or more of the decisions is also taken at school (board) level, whereas in Belgium (FR), Switzerland, Spain, Germany, Portugal, Norway, Luxembourg and Greece less than 30% is taken at this level.

Traditionally, school boards in the Netherlands enjoy all three types of freedom: the freedom to establish schools, the freedom to give schools a specific religious or philosophical character, and educational and organizational autonomy. The freedom of the school board to appoint teachers, shape the content and form of teaching in accordance with its own vision and choose its own teaching aids, are all important aspects of this autonomy. School boards in the Netherlands have a significant degree of autonomy concerning the allocation of resources, personnel matters, infrastructure of buildings, and curriculum and assessment. School boards' decision-making power has grown during the 1980–2000 period, as a result of decentralization and increased school autonomy policies. However, Figure 1.1 shows that since 2003 the degree of autonomy has decreased slightly. This is due to growing government control with respect to content of education, didactics and quality of education in general[6].

A large amount of freedom for school boards does not automatically mean that school directors and managers of schools that fall under their authority also enjoy greater freedom. School boards can claim considerable scope for policymaking, leaving little room for the levels below (individual schools or colleges).

[5] OECD, 2012
[6] Hooge, 2013

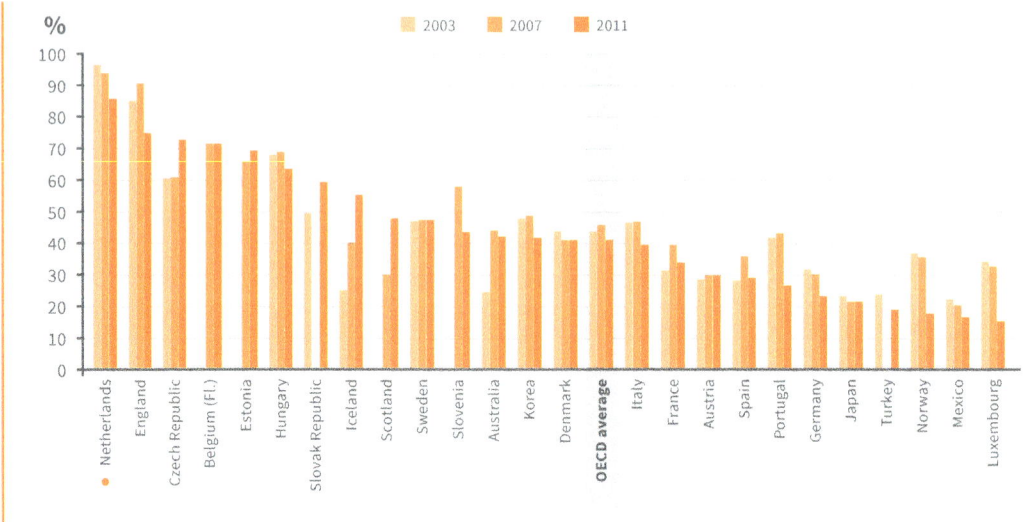

Figure 1.1   *Share of decisions taken at the school level. Countries are ranked in descending order of the percentage of decisions taken at the school level in 2011. (Source: OECD, 2012, p. 509.)*

Freedom of Education in Practice

In the preceding section, a general sketch is provided of the extent to which parents, teachers and school boards enjoy freedom of education. It shows that there is a difference between freedom *de jure* and *de facto*. We will now look in more detail at the differences between legal freedom and actual freedom. In practice, schools' educational and organizational autonomy is the outcome of a complex play of forces between the government, school boards, policymakers, school managers, teachers, parents and pupils and other stakeholders. Two mechanisms shape the legal freedom of education in practice. First, there are mechanisms other than legislation and regulation, referred to as soft governance. Second, apart from the government there are other influencers that determine the scope of the freedom. We will now outline these mechanisms.

Soft Governance

The dominant doctrine of freedom of education and autonomy runs like a thread through the Dutch practice of policymaking and steering in education. The Pacification of 1917 requires a self-disciplined central government that is only doing 'that which is essential'. To this day, the Dutch Ministry of Education is therefore walking a fine line, being very reluctant to steer education too ostentatiously or to control school boards too directly with law and regulation. If central government oversteps the mark, this draws heavy criticism and triggers controversy from religious and private political/societal parties.

As the development and introduction of education policy in the Netherlands is a complex undertaking, as suggested above, the government uses 'soft' policy instruments such as communication and incentives for this purpose rather than legislation and regulation. More flexible and less visible forms of steering and policymaking offer the Dutch government a way out of the constitutional tensions between educational freedom and state intervention. These forms, in literature referred to as 'soft governance', represent steering in or via networks and 'horizontal' non-hierarchical steering mechanisms such as using discourse that includes persuasion, negotiation, framing and sense giving, and that convinces, supports and empowers. Instead of command and control, Dutch government and other steering actors in networks make extensive use of soft governance modes while steering education. They do this in a variety of ways, including consulting, connecting parties, engaging in conversation and dialogue, listening, supporting, launching websites, videos, blogs and vlogs, reflecting, inspiring, connecting, giving examples, developing tools, models and frameworks, organizing networks, giving impulse, disclosing information.

This approach is used, for example, since central government has been aiming at improving language and numeracy education and raising achievement levels in secondary and vocational education and training (VET) schools from 2011[7]. As the freedom of education limits central governments' possibilities for formal steering of educational processes and content in schools, legislation has only been used to set reference levels as examination norms for language and numeracy proficiency of students. Steering the improvement of language and numeracy education is mostly done by means of soft governance. This includes the establishment of a national support centre specialized in 'language and numeracy education' (Steunpunten Taal en Rekenen), setting up independent committees to advise on how to operationalize and implement 'language and numeracy education improvement' policies in schools, and (financially) supporting and commissioning a tight network of educational consultancy and support centres to develop exemplary assignments, tests and exams, to launch websites providing teaching material and good practices, to advise schools on their language and numeracy education, to organize informational conferences and webinars, to develop frameworks and models to implement good quality language and numeracy education etc.

This example of how central government steers improvement of language and numeracy education and raising achievement levels illustrates that the government opts for policy instruments such as group pressure and the transfer of information, in addition to legislation, when introducing the substantive and educational-didactical aspects of educational improvement. Particularly striking, in this regard, is the use of an intermediary national support centre and independent committees, which are tasked with promoting, directing and administering the introduction of the improvement. The improvement of language and numeracy education and raising achievement levels thereby assumes a more compelling and specific nature than that set out in the legislation.

---

[7] Hooge, Waslanders, Theisens & Drewes, 2017

Other Influencers

School boards do not operate in a void, but in consultation and deliberation with a large number of organizations and institutions at the intermediate administrative levels. A great diversity of organization forms exists, such as independent administrative bodies with policy responsibilities or administrative tasks in education, regional administrative authorities, municipalities, sector organizations (representing employers in education), trade unions (representing employees in education), (associations of) occupational groups in education, consultancy and support organizations, process and project management organizations, platforms, think tanks and knowledge centres. In varying degrees, the parties at this intermediate administrative level engage in policymaking and steering in the education field, resulting in a great deal of activity and influence that affect school boards' autonomy and room for policy and decision making.

To develop and maintain legitimacy, school boards must take all legislative and regulatory conditions into account, whether or not central government is the source. This is leading to so-called 'substitution effects', whereby other institutions are assuming the regulatory role of government. The scope for policymaking for school boards vis-à-vis central government is indeed great, but a new layer of bureaucracy has emerged with rules and regulations and various soft governance modes at the intermediary level. The assessment frameworks and quality standards that are used by the Inspectorate of Education are one example of this substitution effect; they go further than the criteria that are set out in existing legislation. Another example is that of schools' dependence on educational publishers, product developers such as the Stichting Leerplan Ontwikkeling (a national expert centre on curriculum development), educational consultancy centres, education support services, process management and other advisory agencies for organizing, modernizing and improving the learning process in schools. The degree of dependence, of course, is determined by the so-called policymaking or innovative capacity of the schools themselves; schools differ in this respect. In addition, the delimitation of the scope of policymaking by intermediary organizations is not only seen as a constraint by school boards and school leaders, but also welcomed as a means of supporting schools' individual strategies and increasing support and commitment among the teaching staff.

Negotiated Freedom of Education

To this day, the tension between the principle of the freedom of education and government intervention is expressed at the level of national politics in the development and introduction of education policy. In practice, educational and organizational autonomy emerges as the result of a complex play of forces between the government, intermediary organizations, school boards, school managers, teachers, parents and pupils and other stakeholders. Its outcome – which actors enjoy educational and organizational autonomy, and the scope of this autonomy – is thus no simple matter. This means that the way in which the government interprets the statutory requirements is not the only important factor. Although the government, by virtue of the Constitution, does have the last word in conflicts over the interpretation of the freedom of education in the constitutional article, this last word is not always definitive when it comes to the introduction of education policy. Who ultimately enjoys educational and organizational autonomy depends, to a large extent, on their position, motivation, expertise and ability to utilize this autonomy. When parents, teachers and school boards do not, or are unable to, do so, other actors in the intermediary layer of governance will take advantage to make their own contributions.

Key Questions
- How can it be avoided that Dutch school administrators, educational staff and teachers use freedom of education as an excuse for backing out of education improvement and innovation?
- How, and by which parties, should school boards be held accountable for accessible and good quality education?
- How can modes of soft governance be justified from a transparent and democratic point of view?

About the author

Prof. dr. Edith Hooge is full professor of Boards and Governance in Education at TIAS, Tilburg University in the Netherlands. Her research activities revolve around governance and management in education systems and organizations, drawing on social network theory and the concept of governmentality. She teaches in the TIAS programmes for professionalization of (non-)executive board members, regularly presides in monitoring committees of governance codes and advises boards in different public sectors.

Contact: e.h.hooge@tias.edu

References

Braster, J.F.A., & Leune, J.M.G. (1986). Samenstelling en functioneren van schoolbesturen. [Composition and operation of school boards.] In: A.M.L. van Wieringen (1996). *Onderwijsbeleid in Nederland.* [Educational policy in the Netherlands.] Alphen aan den Rijn: Samsom H.D. Tjeenk Willink.

De Bruin, G., Van de Linden, J., Van de Vegt, A., & Van der Aa (2012). *Monitor ouderbetrokkenheid in het po, vo en mbo.* [Monitoring parent participation in primary, secondary and VET education.] Rotterdam: Ecorys.

Dijkstra, A.B., Dronkers, J., & Karsten, S. (2001). *Private schools as public provision of education: school choice and marketization in The Netherlands and elsewhere in Europe.* New York, NY: Columbia University, National Center for the Study of Privatization in Education.

Herweijer, L., Vogels, R., & Andriessen, I. (2013). *Samen scholen. Ouders en scholen over samenwerking in basisonderwijs, voortgezet onderwijs en middelbaar beroepsonderwijs.* [Education together. Parents' and schools' views on cooperation in primary and secondary education and in senior secondary vocational education and training.] The Hague: Sociaal en Cultureel Planbureau.

Honingh, M.E., & Hooge, E.H. (2012). *Goed Bestuur in het primair onderwijs. Eindverslag Monitor Goed Bestuur PO 2010-2011.* [Good governance in primary education. Final Report of the monitor research.] Amsterdam /Nijmegen: Hogeschool van Amsterdam/Radboud Universiteit Nijmegen.

Hooge, E.H. (2013). *Besturing van autonomie. Over de mythe van bestuurbare onderwijsorganisaties.* [Steering autonomy. On the myth of steerable educational organizations.] Oration. Tilburg: Tilburg University.

Hooge, E.H., & Honingh, M.E. (2014). Are school boards aware of the educational quality of their schools? *Educational Management Administration & Leadership, 42*(3), 1-16.

Hooge, E.H., Waslander, S., Theisens, H. C. & Drewes, T. (2017). *Raising standards. learning organisations and civic education: steering dynamics at the Dutch national level.* Paper presented at the annual meeting of the American Educational Research Association, April 27 – May 1, San Antonio, Texas.

Karsten, D., De Jong, U., Ledoux, G., & Sligte, H. (2006). *De positie van ouders en leerlingen in het governancebeleid.* [Parents' and students' positions in governance policy.] Amsterdam: SCO-Kohnstamminstituut, Universiteit van Amsterdam.

Karsten, S. (2006). Freedom of education and common civic values. *European Education, 38*(2), 23-35.

Karsten, S., Felix, C., Ledoux, G., Meijnen, W., Roeleveld, J., & Van Schooten, E. (2006). Choosing segregation or integration? The extent and effects of ethnic segregation in Dutch cities. *Education & Urban Society, 38*(2), 228-247.

Klein, T., Waslander, S., Hooge, E.H., Imandt, M., & Bisschop, P. (2014). *Nieuwe toetreders in het onderwijsstelsel: een verkenning naar de effecten van richtingvrije planning.* [Newcomers in the educational system: exploring the effects of orientation-free planning.] Utrecht: Utrecht/Tilburg, Amsterdam: Oberon, TIAS, SEO.

Mentink, C. (2008). Tien jaar later. Over pluriformiteit en identiteit, over grondwetgever en wetgever. [Ten years later. Pluriformity and identity, constitutional legislator and legislator.] *Nederlands Tijdschrift voor Onderwijsrecht en Beleid* [Dutch Journal on Educational Law and Policy], *20*(6), 10-50.

OECD (2012). *Education at a Glance 2012: OECD Indicators.* Paris: OECD Publishing.

Vermeulen, B.P., & Zoontjens, P.J.J. (2005). Artikel 23 Grondwet op de tocht? Naar een debat over betekenis en toekomst van de onderwijsvrijheid. [Article 23 of the constitution at risk? To a debate on the meaning and future of freedom of education.] In: E.M.H. Hirsch Ballin et al. (2005). *Getuigend Staatsrecht: Liber amicorum A.K. Koekkoek* [Constitutional law as witness: Liber amicorum A.K. Koekkoek] (pp. 431-468). Nijmegen: Wolf Legal Publishers.

Vermeulen, B.P. (2008). Waarheen met het onderwijsrecht? [Where to go with education law?] *Nederlands Tijdschrift voor Onderwijsrecht en Beleid*, Themanummer 'De stand van het onderwijsrecht' [Dutch Journal for Education Law and Policy, special issue on the status of education law], 39-56.

Vogels, R. (2002). *Ouders bij de les.* [Involving parents in educational matters.] The Hague: Sociaal en Cultureel Planbureau.

Waslander, S. (2010). Government, school autonomy and legitimacy: why the Dutch government is adopting an unprecedented level of interference with independent schools. *Journal of School Choice: Research, Theory and Reform*, *4*(4), 398-417.

Waslander, S., Hooge, E.H., & Drewes, T. (2016). Steering dynamics in the Dutch education system. *European Journal of Education: Research, Development and Policy*, *51*(4), 477-462.

DAISY MERTENS

TEACHER OF THE YEAR 2016

'EVERY MORNING WHEN I GO TO SCHOOL, I HAVE ONLY ONE AIM: TO BE THE BEST TEACHER EVER FOR MY CLASS'

Self-confidence, autonomy, connection, reflection and learning together by taking responsibility. If it were up to Teacher of the Year Daisy Mertens, this would be the focus in the Dutch education system for all teachers. For herself, she has only one aim every day: to be the best teacher ever for her class. But how does the best teacher in the Netherlands do that?

'Every child deserves high-quality education and a teacher who is fully committed to achieving this. As a teacher, you no longer stand out by imparting knowledge alone. You need to offer more. That's why I believe it's very important that I also pass on life lessons to the children in my class.

You need to teach them to think critically about their options and about the decisions they make. And this isn't just about learning, it's about dealing with situations that arise. I teach my class to analyse these situations so that they gain confidence in themselves. I teach them to surf on the waves of life: sometimes you wobble, sometimes you stand steady and sometimes you have to do everything you can to stay upright. As a teacher, it's important that you know what you can do to achieve this and have the skills to deal with this and to take your children along in it. Each child needs to learn lasting lessons about life. Of course, the knowledge and subject matter covered is very important as well.'

"It would be great to share in the expertise and strengths from other countries as well."

TAKING PRIDE IN SUCCESS

'Dutch children are the happiest in the world. Of course that's the best compliment we can get. The people who stand in front of the class and put all their energy into education, fight for this every day. I believe that we should be proud of this even though our successes are sometimes overshadowed by all kinds of peripheral issues.

What I am also really pleased about in our education system is that increasing emphasis is being placed on learning organizations. And that with the Teacher Register an increasing degree of control is being given to teachers. This gives them space and autonomy that they eagerly put to good use. As a teacher, I consider my primary role to be safeguarding the learning process by observing well. That's why together with my class I am constantly seeking to achieve connection and interaction on the basis of their genuine curiosity. This way, children learn to take responsibility themselves and have the courage to ask questions: they take ownership of their own learning process.'

LEARNING FROM EACH OTHER AROUND THE WORLD

'I therefore believe that it's a good thing that the Netherlands has so much diversity in education concepts, offering a lot of possibilities and opportunities. As far as I'm concerned, this goes beyond Dutch education. It would be great to share in the expertise and strengths from different countries as well: what works and what doesn't work? That way we develop our own vision as teachers and we know how we can facilitate our children's learning most effectively. Their whole lives long. So that they develop into harmonious citizens and are stimulated to develop social skills instead of focusing entirely on acquiring and imparting knowledge. It is up to us teachers to sense what action works best at a particular moment. Each day, we make choices about this as teachers. We learn to look through the eyes of our pupils.' ‹

"It is up to us teachers to sense what action works best at a particular moment."

Chapter 2

Back to the Basics:
On Good Education,
Teacher Judgement,
and Educational
Professionalism[1]

Prof. dr. Gert Biesta,
Brunel University London, UK & University of Humanistic Studies,
Utrecht, the Netherlands

This is a slightly updated version of a paper that appeared earlier as Biesta, G.J.J. (2015). What is Education For? On Good Education, Teacher Judgement, and Educational Professionalism. *European Journal of Education, 50*(1), 75-87.

n Praise of the Teacher?

Much of what has been happening recently in educational policy and research in many countries worldwide is having a profound impact on educational practice and more especially on the position of the teacher. Today, many voices from across the policy, research and practice spectrum claim that the teacher is the most important 'factor' in the educational process (Hay McBer, 2000; OECD, 2005; Sammons & Bakkum, 2012 and, for the European policy dimension, Stéger, 2014). While such claims do stem from a concern about the ways in which teaching and schools can 'make a difference', they are often linked to rather narrow views about what education is supposed to 'produce' – taking their cues from large-scale measurement systems such as PISA which continue to focus on academic achievement in a small and selective number of domains and subject areas. Claims about the importance of the teacher are also problematic because they tend to see the teacher as a 'factor' and believe that, in order to increase the 'performance' of the educational system, it is important to make sure that this 'factor' works in the most effective and efficient way possible. The fact that this 'factor' is a human being and, more importantly an educational professional who should have scope for judgement and discretion is all too often forgotten (Ball, 2003; Cowie, Taylor & Croxford, 2007; Keddie, Mills & Pendergast, 2011; Wilkins, 2011; Priestley et al., 2012; Priestley, Biesta & Robinson, 2015).

In this chapter, I seek first to indicate why I think that teacher judgement is essential in education and the kind of judgements teachers need to make. I do this in the context of a discussion about the problematic impact of the language of learning on the theory and practice of education. Here, I argue for the need to refocus the discussion on the normative question of *good* education, rather than on technical questions about effective education or competitive questions about excellent education. This requires that we focus above all on the question of the purpose of education and have an informed understanding of the particular character of how the question of purpose manifests itself in education, i.e. as a multi-dimensional question. It is only against this background that one can indicate what particular judgements are 'at stake' in education and what this implies for teaching and the teacher. Secondly, I discuss recent changes in the context in which teachers are supposed to enact their professionalism and act professionally. I argue that three tendencies that are often presented as developments in the ongoing professionalization of teaching and that can be found in different forms and guises in schools, colleges and universities – treating students as customers; being accountable; and replacing subjective judgement by scientific evidence – are undermining rather than enhancing opportunities for teacher professionalism. Taken together, the two lines of the chapter provide indications as to how teacher professionalism might be regained and reclaimed in the context of the discussion about education and its purpose.

The Learnification of Education

In the past decade, I have written about a phenomenon that I have referred to as the 'learnification' of educational discourse and practice (for the term see Biesta 2010; for the wider analysis, see Biesta 2004, 2006, 2013; see also Haugsbakk & Nordkvelle, 2007). 'Learnification' encompasses the impact of the rise of a 'new language of learning' on education. This is evident in a number of discursive shifts, such as the tendency to refer to pupils, students, children and even adults as 'learners'; to redefine teaching as 'facilitating learning', 'creating learning opportunities', or 'delivering learning experiences'; or to talk about the school as a 'learning environment' or 'place for learning'. It is also visible in the ways in which adult education has been transformed into lifelong learning in many countries (Field, 2000; Yang & Valdés-Cotera, 2011).

The rise of the language of learning is the outcome of a range of loosely connected developments in the theory, policy and practice of education. These include the critique of authoritarian forms of education that focus solely on the activities of the teacher and conceive of education as a form of control (see, e.g. Freire's critique of 'banking education'; Freire, 1970); the rise of new theories of learning, particularly constructivist theories (Richardson, 2003; Roth, 2011); and also – and this is particularly relevant in the shift towards lifelong learning, although it is not all that is at stake in this shift – the influence of neo-liberal policies that seek to burden individuals with tasks that used to be the responsibility of governments and the state (Biesta, 2006). The language of learning has not only impacted on research and policy, but has also become part of the everyday vocabulary of teachers in many countries and settings (Biesta, Priestley & Robinson, 2015).

What is the problem? Perhaps the briefest way to put it is to say that the point of education is *not* that students learn. Formulating the issue in this way is relevant because many discussions about education (in policy, research and practice) keep using the language of learning in this abstract and general sense.[2] In contrast I wish to suggest that the point of education is that students learn *something*, that they learn it for a *reason*, and that they learn it *from someone*. Whereas the language of learning is a process language that, at least in English, is an individual and individualizing language, education always needs to engage with questions of content, purpose and relationships. We must also bear in mind that the word 'learning' can refer to a very wide range of phenomena. Think, for example, of the difference between what it means to learn to ride a bike, to learn the second law of thermodynamics, to learn to be patient, to learn that you are not good at something, etc. This is another reason why the suggestion that education is simply about making students learn or about facilitating their learning is potentially misleading, both for students and teachers.

[2] It is difficult to give concrete examples, not because there are too few but because there are too many. Much research literature tends to refer to learning in a general and abstract sense, often implicitly bringing in assumptions about what good and desirable learning is without reflecting on them. There is a similar tendency in policy documents, and perhaps a telling example of the issue of the language of learning from policy close to teaching are the 'Standards for Registration' from the General Teaching Council for Scotland – see http://www.gtcs.org.uk/web/Files/the-standards/standards-for-registration-1212.pdf; last accessed 5 November 2014).

The problem with the language of learning – both the language itself and the ways in which it is used and contextualized in research, policy and practice – is that it tends to prevent people from asking the key educational questions of content, purpose and relationships. Rather, they talk in abstract terms about promoting learning, supporting learning, facilitating learning, about learning outcomes, student learning, etc., and too quickly forget to specify the what 'of what' and the 'for what' of the learning[3]. This indicates that the language of learning is *insufficient* to express what matters in education, just as *theories* of learning are insufficient to capture what education is about. At most, these theories provide us with insight into the dynamics of the learning that takes place in educational contexts and settings – provided they do not approach learning in an abstract and general sense, but are aware that learning the second law of thermodynamics is a very different thing from learning to be patient. But such theories in themselves do not give us access to and insight into the construction and justification of these contexts and settings themselves. For this, we need theories of educa*tion* and educa*ting*.

The Threefold Question of Purpose

Of the three questions, i.e. content, purpose and relationships, that are at stake when we try to capture what education is about, the question of purpose is the most fundamental for the simple reason that, if we do not know what it is we are seeking to achieve with our educational arrangements and endeavours, we cannot make any decisions about the content that is most appropriate and the kind of relationships that is most conducive. Some authors have even gone so far as to say that the purpose is *constitutive* of education, which means that education *necessarily* needs a (sense of) purpose. In more technical terms, this means that education is a teleological practice, i.e. a practice constituted by a 'telos' – the Greek word for the 'point' and purpose of a practice (Carr, 2003, p.10).

There is, however, something special about education – which, if I understand correctly, distinguishes it from many other human practices.[4] This is the fact that, in education, the question of purpose is a *multidimensional* question because education tends to function in relation to a number of domains. In my own work I have suggested that three domains can be found, viz., qualification, socialization and subjectification (Biesta, 2010, chapter 1). Qualification has to do with the transmission and acquisition of knowledge, skills and dispositions. This is important because this allows children and young people to 'do' something – it qualifies them. This 'doing'

---

[3] An additional problem with the word 'learning' – at least in the English language but not only there – is that it can refer both to an activity and to the outcome of the activity. This is why several authors have suggested using different terms for the activity, such as 'studying', 'practising', 'making an effort', and the like, or also Fenstermacher's suggestion to refer to student activity as 'studenting' (Fenstermacher, 1986).

[4] I would suggest that practices such as medicine and law are also characterized by a telos, but in these cases the telos is one-dimensional such as, in the case of medicine, a focus on the promotion of health and, in the case of law, a focus on the promotion of justice (which does not mean that there are no discussions about the meaning of health and justice or the question of what it means to promote them and how this can be done best).

can be very specific, such as in the field of vocational and professional education, or it can be conceived more widely, such as in general education that seeks to prepare children and young people for their lives in complex modern societies. But education is not just about knowledge, skills and dispositions. Through education we also represent and initiate children and young people in traditions and ways of being and doing, such as cultural, professional, political, religious traditions, etc. This is the socialization dimension which is partly an explicit aim of education but, as research in the sociology of education has shown, also works behind the backs of students and teachers, for example in the ways in which education reproduces existing social structures, divisions and inequalities. In addition to qualification and socialization, education also impacts positively or negatively on the student as a person. This is what I have referred to as the domain of subjectification, which is the way in which children and young people come to exist as subjects of initiative and responsibility (rather than as objects of the actions of others)[5].

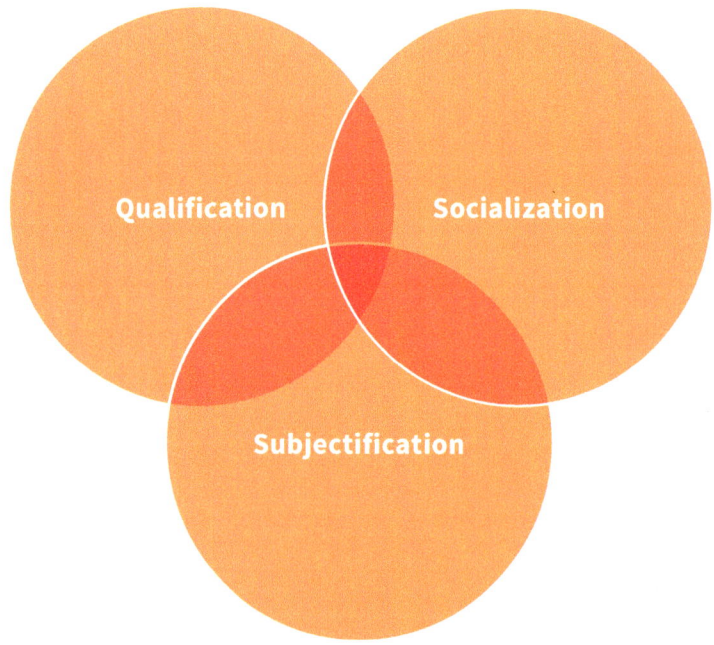

Figure 2.1 *The three functions of education and the three domains of educational purpose.*

---

[5] I have chosen the term 'subjectification' partly to distinguish it from the question of identity, which, in my view, belongs to the domain of socialization, as it has to do with the ways in which we identify with and are identified by existing traditions and practices. Subjectifcation, on the other hand, concerns the qualities of being a subject – qualities that in modern educational thought are often captured in such notions as autonomy, independence, responsibility, criticality and the capacity for judgement.

If education always functions within these three domains or if education always *impacts* on these three domains, then it means that, as educators, we must take responsibility for what it is we seek to achieve in each of these domains. Hence, they not only appear as three *functions* of education, but also as three *domains of educational purpose*. I prefer to refer to them as *domains of educational purpose* in order to highlight that in each domain there can be widely different views about what knowledge is and how it can be acquired, or about what it means to exist as a human being. Although we can distinguish between the three domains of purpose, they cannot really be separated. Even if we are 'just' trying to give our students some knowledge, we are also impacting on them as persons – to have knowledge will, after all, potentially empower them – and, in doing so, we are also representing particular traditions, for example by communicating that this particular knowledge is more useful or valuable or true than other knowledge.

Looking at education provides us with a broad conception of what it is for, i.e. one acknowledges that we always need to engage with content, tradition *and* the person. This also makes it possible to see the problem with one-sided conceptions of education. The issue here is not only that such conceptions are out of balance in that they only pay attention to one of the three dimensions, but also that a one-sided emphasis can often damage one or more of the other domains (for an early 'warning' on this problem see Kohn, 1999). This is what we are witnessing with the current emphasis on achievement in the domain of qualification where excessive pressure on students (and teachers, for that matter) to perform in that domain (and within that domain in a very small number of subjects) is beginning to have a significantly negative impact in the domain of subjectification. To put it bluntly: excessive emphasis on academic achievement causes severe stress for young people, particularly in cultures where failure is not really an option.

The Central Role of Judgement

If we look at education from the angle of purpose and acknowledge that this poses itself as a three-dimensional question, then this has a number of important implications for the design, enactment and justification of education – implications that I suggest are mainly relevant for the work of the teacher. And what this makes visible is the essential role of *judgement* in education.

There is a need for judgement about what we seek to achieve in each of the three domains and about how we can keep these in an educationally meaningful balance. This is not just an abstract question that can be resolved at the highest level of policy or curriculum development. It is a concrete question that comes back again and again in the educational context, not only in a general sense, but also in relation to each individual student. To speak about a possible balance between the three domains should not make us blind to the fact that, although there are possibilities for synergy between qualification, socialization and subjectification, the three domains can be in conflict. This means that a second judgement that needs to be made – again not only at a general level, but also in relation to each student at each point in time – is how we deal with the 'trade-offs' between the three domains, i.e. what we are willing to temporarily give up in one or two of the domains in order to focus on one of the other domains. It is, after all, legitimate to focus our educational endeavours and the educational efforts of our students for a limited period of time on one particular dimension of the educational spectrum. Sometimes we do want our students to focus on mastering particular knowledge or skills and pay less attention to the domains of socialization and subjectification. In other cases, we can judge that what matters most for a particular student at a particular point in time is their formation as human beings – and there are reasons why this should sometimes prevail in our educational efforts and practices. But one-sidedness always comes at a price, the price we are willing to pay for a temporary emphasis on one of the dimensions. I wish to highlight once more that the current emphasis in many countries and settings on just enhancing academic achievement – i.e. performance in the domain of qualification – comes at a very high price.

In addition to the domains, their balance and the trade-offs, teachers also need to make judgements about appropriate pedagogy, curriculum, organization of the classroom, and so on. The reason for this – and this is another peculiarity of the practice of education – is that the means of education are not indifferent in relation to the ends, but are constitutive of them (Carr, 1992). In plainer language, this means that students not only learn from what we say, but also from how we do. They often focus more on how we do than on what we say, particularly if there is a (performative) contradiction between the two. Teachers therefore also need to make a judgement about the appropriateness of the ways they teach and organize their education. This raises an important issue for the idea of educational effectiveness, as, in education, there is not only the question of whether particular ways of doing are the most effective to reach certain 'outcomes', but also the question of whether they are the most educational ways. Or to put it differently: we need not only to judge the impact of our ways of doing – in the wide sense – on their effectiveness, but also on their educative potential. After all, it may well be that we can increase our students' performance in a particular domain by threatening them with punishment if they do not perform well or by promising them money if they perform well. The question is whether the messages we convey with this are those we deem desirable for the education of our students.

This shows the central role of judgement in teaching – and such judgements are crucially 'of the teacher' (Heilbronn, 2008) because they must be made in new, unique and concrete situations. I also wish to highlight that judgement about balance, trade-offs, and educational forms are entirely *pragmatic* in the technical sense, i.e. we can only come to a judgement about how to proceed in relation to what it is we are seeking to achieve. This is an important antidote against educational fashions and categorical statements, such as the idea that education should always be flexible, or that students should always have transparent knowledge about what is expected of them. This is not something we can say categorically, but depends on what we are seeking and what we intend our students to be seeking. Sometimes education needs to be flexible, personalized, and tailored to the individual students, but sometimes it is important for education to be strict, structured, and general, for example when we want to teach our students that, in some domains, it is important to get things 'right' or to act in a prescribed way (think, for example, of teaching pilots to fly an aircraft, or instructing nurses and doctors about how to wash their hands). In some cases, education needs to be centred on the student – for example when we want to promote creative action and generative thinking –, but sometimes it needs to be centred on the teacher or the curriculum – again when it matters to get things right or when it matters for children to experience what authority represents. In some cases, everything we expect from students should be visible and clear to them from the outset, but in other cases it is important to work with a sense of openness and mystery, for example in those domains where we, as teachers, are not in possession of clear insights about how to be or about what is to be done, such as in domains of moral, political or spiritual education.

Pragmatism, Normativity and the Question of Good Education

The need to think of all these judgements as pragmatic judgements – i.e. as necessarily connected to what it is we are seeking to achieve – highlights the problem with notions of evidence-based education that seem to suggest that research evidence can tell teachers what they should do on the assumption that particular forms of research can provide clear and unambiguous knowledge about 'what works'. The issue here is that something never 'works' in the abstract sense, but always in relation to a particular purpose or set of purposes. To say, for example, that homework is of no use – a claim apparently supported by research, as reported by Hattie (2008) – is a meaningless statement if we do not specify what it is not useful *for* (see also Biesta, 2016). And while there may be no positive evidence that homework impacts significantly on academic achievement (which could also be because there may not be meaningful research available), this does not mean that we should just abolish it, because it could well be that homework has significance and meaning for other domains of educational purpose. After all, to make students responsible for a task outside the controlling 'gaze' of the teacher may be very important if we want to help them to become responsible subjects, rather than entirely driven and controlled from the outside and thus remain objects. In this sense, I am surprised by Hattie's suggestion – partly made in response to my critique of evidence-based education (Biesta, 2007; 2015) – that, although there is more to education than academic achievement, in the end it is what matters most (Hattie, 2008, pp. 245-255), thus reinforcing a one-dimensional view of education in which only qualification seems to count.

All this also shows – and this is perhaps the most important point – that in the design, enactment and justification of education we must engage with normative questions. This is why I have emphasized that it is of crucial importance that we engage with the question of *good* education and do not make the mistake to think that it suffices to talk about *effective* education. The point here is that, although 'effectiveness' is a value that only refers to the degree to which a particular course of action is able to bring about a desired result, it does not say anything about the desirability of the result. For this, we need to embed questions about effectiveness within a large discourse about what is educationally desirable – in other words, what makes education *good*. To speak about *good* education also provides an alternative for another trend in contemporary education discussions, which is the idea of 'excellent' education. The problem with excellence is that it very quickly entails a competitive mind-set, where some schools or some educational systems are supposed to be more excellent than others. In my view, the educational duty is to ensure that there is good education for everyone everywhere.

Judgement and the Democratization of the Professions

So far, I have suggested that education is a teleological practice; that the *telos* of education is three-dimensional; and that, because of this, there is a need for judgement with regard to the three domains of purpose of education, their balance, the 'trade-offs', and the educational 'forms'. I have also suggested that these judgements are first and foremost 'of the teacher', because the teacher is confronted with situations that, in some respects, are always new and hence call for judgement rather than the application of protocols or the enactment of abstract evidence about what allegedly 'works'. If education requires judgement, and if this judgement is 'of the teacher', then it would follow that teachers have ample space and opportunity to exercise their professional judgement. Yet it is here that we encounter problems in the ways in which the professional space for teachers is constructed and 'policed'. They often limit rather than enhance the scope for teacher professional judgement. This is, of course, a complex area about which much has been written (Gleeson & Gunter, 2001; Gewirtz, 2002; Leander & Osborne, 2008; Priestley et al., 2012; Leat, 2014; Pyhältö, Pietarinen & Soini 2014). I nonetheless wish to make several observations that are meant to help to gain a better insight into the ways in which the space for teacher judgement has changed in recent years, some of the pitfalls that teachers may face and which direction we might need to take in order to reclaim and restore a space in which teacher judgement can occur.

To understand how the conditions for teacher professionalism have changed over time, it might be useful to start with a 'classic' definition of professions and professionalism (e.g. Freidson, 1994) in which it is argued that professions are special domains because they promote human wellbeing; they need highly specialized knowledge and skills; and they work in relationships of authority and trust. These three aspects not only provide a *definition* of the professions – particularly the 'traditional' professions (doctors, lawyers, priests) –, but also justify why professions need to regulate themselves rather than be ruled from the 'outside'. But this particular account of the professions can easily be abused, not only with regard to their internal regulation, but also, and more importantly to the relationships between professionals and their clients (and there are many examples of abuse of professional self-regulation and professional trust). It is, after all, quite easy for professional authority to turn into authoritarian ways of operating where 'the doctor knows best' and where clients become the objects of the power exercised by professionals rather than legitimate partners in the professional relationship.

Authoritarian forms of professionalism and even more so the abuse of professional power were the main targets of the emancipation movements that emerged in the 1960s and 1970s, such as the student revolts of 1968, first in psychiatry, but also in mainstream health care. This was one way in which the professions were 'broken up' from the outside by the challenge to develop more transparent, equitable and democratic ways of working. A similar impetus also came from the incorporation of the professions in the 'project' of the welfare state, where the services offered by many professions were seen as central to welfare state provision. This not only opened up the professions to wider questions about public health and the common good, but also – because the professions were to a large extent funded by the public purse – involved the professions in the process of public and democratic accountability. Although these developments did not resolve all the problems at once, they did help to make professions more democratic and more accountable and in this regard did help to steer professions away from authoritarian modes of operation. Hence, they also set a standard for developments in other fields of work (that often sought to claim professional status themselves as well), including the field of education.

Post-Democratic Distortions: The Erosion of Professionality

If these developments helped to push the professions towards less authoritarian and more democratic and accountable ways of working, then it seems reasonable to expect that further developments along these lines will strengthen the democratization of the professions. Seen from this angle, it would appear that we should welcome and embrace recent developments that emphasize the importance of seeing patients or students as customers who need to be served and satisfied; of making the operation of the professions entirely transparent so that they can be even more accountable; and of basing professional activity on scientific evidence about 'what works' rather than on subjective judgements of individual professionals. While at first sight this may sound plausible and desirable – and demands for a focus on the customer, for transparency and for evidence-based ways of working are often 'sold' in this way – I wish to suggest that these developments run the risk of doing the opposite of what they claim to do and thus result in the erosion of responsible, accountable and democratic professionalism. To give an indication of why this might be, I will briefly discuss each of these developments in relation to the domain of education (although similar arguments can be made in relation to other professional domains).[6]

---

[6] The discussion must be brief and can therefore not be as sophisticated as I would like it to be. For more detail I refer the reader to Biesta (in press).

Is it indeed a good idea to treat students as customers and give them what they want? Does this give them a much needed 'voice' in the educational process and does it therefore enhance the overall quality of the educational endeavour? I do not think so because there is a fundamental difference between economic transactions and professional transactions such as education.[7] Whereas in economic transactions we start from the assumption that customers know what they want, so that the main task of providers is to give them what they want, either at the lowest cost or, more realistically, the best price-quality ratio, the whole point of professional practices such as education is that they do not just service the needs of their clients, but also play a crucial role in the definition of those needs (Feinberg, 2001). We go to the doctor because we do not feel well, but trust that the doctor will find the reason and suggest a treatment based on this. Similarly, we go to school not to get what we already know that we want but because we want to receive an education. Here, we would expect teachers not just give students what they know they want or say they want or are able to identify what they want but to move them *beyond* what they already know that they want. We want teachers to open up new vistas, new opportunities, and help children and young people to interrogate whether what they say they want or desire is actually what they should desire.[8] To turn the student into a customer, and just work on the assumption that education should do what the customer wants is therefore a distortion of what education is about, a distortion that significantly undermines the ability of teachers to be teachers and of schools, colleges and universities to be educational institutions (rather than shops). This is, of course, not to suggest that students should have no voice in what goes on – as this would turn education (back) into authoritarian modes of operation –, but it is crucial to see that the voice of the student and the voice of the teacher are very different voices that come with different responsibilities and expectations.

I do not want to dwell on the second development that has been going on in education for quite some time now, i.e. the rise of a culture of accountability (see Chapter 5) or, to be more precise, of a bureaucratic rather than a democratic culture of accountability (Biesta, 2010). While accountability in itself is a good and important idea – professionals need to be accountable both to the immediate clientele they serve and to the wider public –, there is a crucial difference between democratic forms of accountability that engage in substantive exchanges between professionals and their 'stakeholders' about what, in the case of teaching, is good education and what the parameters for identifying good education are and the bureaucratic forms of accountability that significantly 'trouble' contemporary education (Sahlberg, 2010). If democratic accountability focuses on what makes education good, bureaucratic accountability has transformed the practice of providing data in order to show how education meets certain pre-defined standards into an aim in itself, where questions about whether the standards that are being applied are accurate and meaningful expressions of what good education is supposed to be are no longer at the centre of the process.

[7]   Feinberg's 2001-essay on choice, need-definition and educational reform, provides an extremely clear analysis of what the problem is here.
[8]   On the educational importance of the transformation of what is desired into what is desirable – a question that has to do with the educational theme of a 'grown up' or mature existence – see Biesta 2014; see also Meirieu 2008.

Onara O'Neill's 2002 Reith lectures still provide a highly insightful account of what is wrong with the contemporary culture of accountability. One problem she highlights is that while in theory 'the new culture of accountability and audit makes professionals and institutions more accountable to the public', in practice 'the real requirements are for accountability to regulators, to departments of government, to funders, to legal standards' (O'Neill, 2002). A second problem she highlights is that, while again in theory 'the new culture of accountability and audit makes professionals and institutions more accountable *for good performance*', in practice 'the real focus is on performance indicators chosen for ease of measurement and control rather than because they measure accurately what the quality of performance is' (O'Neill, 2002). The predicament here is whether we are measuring and assessing what we consider valuable, or whether bureaucratic accountability systems have created a situation in which we are valuing what is being measured, i.e. a situation where measurement has become an end in itself rather than a means to achieve good education in the fullest and broadest sense of the term.

The slightly more recent demand that professional practices should be based on scientific evidence about 'what works' rather than on professional judgement entails a similar distortion of professional practices such as education. There are two reasons for this. One is, as I have tried to show in the first part of this chapter, that the question of 'what works' is an empty question if we do not ask what something is supposed to work *for*. Without explicit engagement with the question of purpose, the idea that there can be evidence about 'what works' remains a rather empty suggestion – or, and this is more likely to be the case, with the push to base professional practice on evidence about 'what works' a particular idea of what education is supposed to work for is already assumed, either implicitly or explicitly (and more often than not, as I have indicated above, the assumption is that education should work for academic achievement rather than across the full spectrum of educational purposes).

That education needs to 'work' with reference to a number of domains, that what may 'work' for one domain may not necessarily also 'work' for the other domains and may actually create an adverse impact, and that even strategies that are proven to 'work' need to be judged on their educational 'quality' (see what I have said above about punishment and bribes) are not regularly considered when it is suggested that education should become evidence-based (Biesta, 2007). The logic of making education 'work' is often based on quasi-causal assumptions of the dynamics of educational processes and practices – that there are variables and factors that impact on certain outcomes – rather than on the acknowledgement that education 'works' through language and interpretation, meaning-giving and meaning-making, and thus through processes of communication and encounter. Also for these reasons the suggestion that education should be based on scientific evidence about 'what works' comes with assumptions that may be valid in such domains as medicine and agriculture – Slavin's favourite examples (Slavin, 2002) – but not in the field of education.

Reclaiming Teacher Professionalism

If we wish to reclaim a space for teacher professionalism and educational professionalism more generally, it is important to see current developments in the field of education for what they are and not for what they pretend to be. It is important to see – and make visible to the profession and the wider public – that these developments do not enhance teacher professionalism or good education, but constitute a threat to the strive for good education and meaningful professional conduct. While part of the strategy for reclaiming professionalism in education requires a detailed analysis and critique of the ways in which the space for professional judgement is being constructed and confined, it is also of crucial importance that teachers and the educational profession more widely have a clear sense of what their profession is actually about. That is why we also need a robust and thoughtful account of the specific character of education which needs to go beyond the fashionable but nonetheless problematic idea that education is about learning and that teaching is about the facilitation of learning. Rather, one needs to acknowledge the teleological character of education – the fact that education always raises the question of its purpose – and account for the fact that the question of educational purpose always poses itself in relation to three different domains. Hence, the ongoing challenge is to maintain an educationally meaningful balance between these domains. This challenge lies at the heart of accountable teacher professionalism.

Key Questions
- It has been encouraging to see that many people nowadays think about the question of good education in a broader sense, and that they find the distinction between qualification, socialization and subjectification a useful framework for doing so. What concerns me is that much that is said about subjectification, often interpreted in the broad sense of 'formation of the person' is actually about socialization, that is, about fitting children and young people into pre-defined views of what a good person is or of what kind of qualities they should possess. (Character education is an example of this, as is the focus on personality development.) How education engages with the question of human freedom, the real issue behind the notion of subjectification, remains little discussed.
- In my view Dutch education and Dutch society more generally is remarkably child-friendly. But being friendly for children and young people is not in itself good pedagogy or good education. Also, and this is my real concern, many situations where children and young people are given more control and ownership over their education may look child- and student-friendly but are often just more refined ways of control, ways in which children and young people are 'asked' to exert such control over themselves. The rise of such 'governmentality' in Dutch education is something that concerns me.

- It has also been interesting to see how teachers in the Netherlands have raised their voice and have tried to reclaim their profession. My concern is that this is often (still) done with reference to the language of learning rather than the language of education and the particular role teachers have to play in the educational endeavour. In my view, there are therefore further steps to take in reclaiming teacher professionalism.

About the author

Prof. dr. Gert Biesta is currently Professor of Education and Director of Research in the Department of Education of Brunel University London, UK, and NIVOZ Professor for Education at the University of Humanistic Studies, Utrecht, the Netherlands. In addition he is Visiting Professor at NLA University College Bergen, Norway, and an associate member of the Onderwijsraad (Education Council) of the Netherlands. His work focuses on the theory and policy of education and the theory and philosophy of educational and social research and has so far appeared in 16 different languages.

Contact: gert.biesta@brunel.ac.uk.

References

Ball, S.J. (2003). The teacher's soul and the terrors of performativity. *Journal of Education Policy, 18*(2), 215-228.

Biesta, G.J.J, Priestley, M., & Robinson, S. (2015). The role of beliefs in teacher agency. *Teachers and Teaching: Theory and Practice 21*(6), 624-640.

Biesta, G.J.J. (2004). Against learning. Reclaiming a language for education in an age of learning. *Nordisk Pedagogik, 25*, 54-66.

Biesta, G.J.J. (2006). *Beyond Learning. Democratic Education for a Human Future*. Boulder: Paradigm Publishers.

Biesta, G.J.J. (2006). What's the point of lifelong learning if lifelong learning has no point? On the democratic deficit of policies for lifelong learning. *European Educational Research Journal, 5*(3-4), 169-180.

Biesta, G.J.J. (2007). Why 'what works' won't work. Evidence-based practice and the democratic deficit of educational research. *Educational Theory, 57*(1), 1-22.

Biesta, G.J.J. (2010). *Good Education in an Age of Measurement*. Boulder: Paradigm Publishers.

Biesta, G.J.J. (2013). Interrupting the politics of learning. *Power and Education*, *5*(1), 4-15.

Biesta, G.J.J. (2014). *The Beautiful Risk of Education*. Boulder: Paradigm Publishers.

Biesta, G.J.J. (2015). On the two cultures of educational research and how we might move ahead: Reconsidering the ontology axiology and praxeology of education. *European Educational Research Journal, 14*(1), 11-22.

Biesta, G.J.J. (2016). Improving education through research? From effectiveness, causality and technology, to purpose, complexity and culture. *Policy Futures in Education 14*(2), 194-210.

Biesta, G.J.J. (2017). Education, measurement and the professions: Reclaiming a space for democratic professionality in education. *Educational Philosophy and Theory 49*(4), 315-330.

Carr, D. (1992). Practical enquiry, values and the problem of educational theory. *Oxford Review of Education*, *18*(3), 241-251.

Carr, D. (2003). *Making Sense of Education. An Introduction to the Philosophy and Theory of Education and Teaching*. London/New York: RoutledgeFalmer.

Cowie, M., Taylor, D., & Croxford, L. (2007). 'Tough, intelligent accountability' in Scottish secondary schools and the role of Standard Tables and Charts (STACS): a critical appraisal. *Scottish Educational Review, 39*(1), 29-50.

Feinberg, W. (2001). Choice, autonomy, need-definition and educational reform. *Studies in Philosophy and Education*, *20*(5), 402-409.

Fenstermacher, G.D. (1986). Philosophy of research on teaching: Three aspects. In: Merlin C. Wittrock (Ed.). *Handbook of Research on Teaching. Third Edition*. New York: Macmillan; London: Collier Macmillan.

Field, J. (2000). *Lifelong Learning and the New Educational Order*. Stoke-on-Trent: Trentham.

Freidson, E. (1994). *Professionalism Reborn: Theory, Prophecy, and Policy.* Chicago: University of Chicago Press.

Freire, P. (1970). *Pedagogy of the Oppressed.* New York: Continuum.

Gewirtz, S. (2002). *The Managerial School: Post-Welfarism and Social Justice in Education.* London/ New York: Routledge.

Gleeson, D., & Gunter, H. (2001). The performing school and the modernisation of teachers. In: D. Gleeson & C. Husbands (Eds.). *The Performing School: Managing, Teaching and Learning in a Performance Culture.* London: RoutledgeFalmer.

Hattie, J. (2008). *Visible Learning.* London/New York: Routledge.

Haugsbakk, G., & Nordkvelle, Y. (2007). The rhetoric of ICT and the new language of learning. A critical analysis of the use of ICT in the curricular field. *European Educational Research Journal, 6*(1), 1-12.

Heilbronn, R. (2008). *Teacher Education and the Development of Practical Judgement.* London: Continuum.

Keddie, A., Mills, M., & Pendergast, D. (2011). Fabricating and identity in neo-liberal times: performing schooling as 'number one'. *Oxford Review of Education, 37*(1), 75-92.

Kohn, A. (1999). The costs of overemphasizing achievement. *School Administrator, 56*(10), 40-42; 44-46.

Leander, K.M., & Osborne, M.D. (2008). Complex positioning: teachers as agents of curricular and pedagogical reform. *Journal of Curriculum Studies, 40*(1), 23-46.

Leat, D. (2014). Curriculum regulation in England: giving with one hand and taking away with the other, *European Journal of Curriculum Studies,* 1, 69-74.

McBer, H. (2000). *Research into Teacher Effectiveness: a Model of Teacher Effectiveness. Report by Hay McBer to the Department for Education & Employment June 2000.* London: DfEE.

Meirieu, P. (2008). Pédagogie: Le Devoir de Résister. 2e édition. [Education: The duty to resist. Second edition.] Issy-les-Moulineaux: ESF.

O'Neill, O. (2002). *BBC Reith Lectures 2002. A Question of Trust.* Available at: http://www.bbc.co.uk/radio4/reith2002.

OECD (2005). *Teachers Matter: Attracting, Developing and Retaining Effective Teachers.* Paris: OECD.

Priestley, M., Biesta, G.J.J., & Robinson, S. (2015). *Teacher agency: an Ecological Approach.* London: Bloomsbury.

Priestley, M., Edwards, R., Priestley, A., & Miller, K. (2012). Teacher agency in curriculum making: agents of change and spaces for manoeuvre. *Curriculum Inquiry, 42*(2), 191-214.

Pyhältö, K., Pietarinen, J., & Soini, T. (2014). Comprehensive school teachers' professional agency in large-scale educational change. *Journal of Educational Change, 15*(3), 303-325.

Richardson, V. (2003). Constructivist pedagogy. *Teachers College Record, 105*(9), 1623-1640.

Roth, W.-M. (2011). *Passability: At the Limits of the Constructivist Metaphor.* Dordrecht: Springer.

Sahlberg, P. (2010). Rethinking accountability in a knowledge society. *Journal of Educational Change, 11*(1), 45-61.

Sammons, P., & Bakkum, L. (2012). Effective schools, equity and teacher effectiveness: a review of the literature. *Profesorado Revista de curriculum y formación del profesorado, 15*(3), 9-26.

Slavin, R. (2002). Evidence-based educational policies: transforming educational practice and research. *Educational Researcher, 31*(7), 15-21.

Stéger, C. (2014). Review and analysis of the EU teacher-related policies and activities. *European Journal of Education, 49*(3), 332-347.

Wilkins, C. (2011). Professionalism and the post-performative teacher: new teachers reflect on autonomy and accountability in the English school system. *Professional Development in Education, 37*(3), 389-409.

Yang, J., & Valdés-Cotera, R. (Eds.) (2011). *Conceptual Evolution and Policy Developments in Lifelong Learning*. Hamburg: UNESCO Institute for Lifelong Learning.

BARTJAN COMMISSARIS
SCHOOL LEADER

'I FEEL PRIVILEGED TO SHARE MY TALENTS WITH PROUD CITIZENS OF THE WORLD WHO LATER RETURN TO SHOW ME THEIR CERTIFICATES'

Simply filling a child's head with knowledge doesn't work any longer. That's why school leader BartJan Commissaris is looking for a musical, cultural civic education that prioritizes children's humanity. The word 'trust' is crucial here: trust in children who by nature want to develop; and in teachers who want to put in maximum effort to achieve this.

"Sometimes a little civil disobedience is required to achieve your objective."

'The Dutch education system is reasonably effective: with very limited means we achieve optimum results. We primarily focus on the whole child development and the way we can add to this as a school. Children themselves let you know what is possible and what's not, and how they want to learn. For example, one child may be very visually oriented, while another works from a spatial or cognitive approach. As a school, we therefore offer more and more methodologies and learning styles to get closer to the child's development and educational needs. I think I can safely say that the Netherlands is very advanced, open and unique in doing this.'

MINISTRY OF THE CHILD

'I am unbelievably proud when I see how everyone at school shares in this process. It is not just the teachers, but the other staff and parents as well who are of key importance for the whole development of the child. And don't forget the people operating in the background, volunteers and the municipality: a whole network of people working on a daily basis for the benefit of Dutch education. An integral focus on the child is really important to this. I prefer to call it the 'Ministry of the Child'.

Besides the curriculum, our school offers offer all kinds of extras, from speech therapy and dyslexia coaching to physiotherapy. I believe that this supports the child and has a preventive effect. Why wait until something is broken before doing repair work? Fortunately, 'total solutions' of this kind are gaining more attention. And, increasingly, children are becoming closely involved in the design of these new solutions. We could take this even further in the Netherlands by forging even better links with day care centres, sports organizations, health and welfare authorities and out-of-school childcare facilities. That would enable us to stimulate children's social development even from a very early age by giving them the right support. This way, we can offer equal opportunities for all children: the primary objective of our education system.'

PROUD CITIZENS OF THE WORLD

'You shouldn't tell a story, you should be the story. I believe that a teacher needs to learn to see the world through the eyes of the child, so I need to look through the teacher's eyes. What does he need? Sometimes answers are difficult to find, and in some cases a little civil disobedience is required to achieve your objective. I would like to see a lot more entrepreneurial spirit looking out for opportunities. Of course, certain basic requirements need to be met and we need to ensure that we achieve something, but whatever the outcome, by trying we are at least creating something new.

"It feels fantastic to witness the connection with youngsters and thus with our future."

For me anyway, each day it feels fantastic to witness the connection with youngsters and thus with our future. When I look out of my office window, I see children from all layers of society and many different cultures playing together and learning from one another. It is this diversity that makes our country so rich. It is a joy to me to be able to work with parents, children and the entire school team to find the right environment in which to guide our children. Being able to share my talents with proud citizens of the world who later return to show their certificates, that is a real privilege.'

Chapter 3

A Place for Every Child: Inclusion as a Community School's Task[1]

Dr. Jeannette Doornenbal,
Hanze University of Applied Sciences Groningen

A version of this chapter was also published as *Plek voor ieder kind. Inclusie als opdracht voor brede scholen en kindcentra*. PACT (2017): www.pedagogischpact.nl

ntroduction

The International Convention on the Rights of the Child (United Nations, 1989) establishes every child's right to participate, to be of importance and to learn. Every right-minded person will support these rights, but what do they mean in real terms and are we successful in putting them into practice here in the Netherlands? Guaranteeing every child these rights is no simple matter. Children differ from one another in myriad ways. This is a complex task that cannot possibly be the sole responsibility of the education sector. It is a shared obligation, a fact well expressed in the African proverb, much used in recent times, that 'it takes a village to raise a child'.

For this reason, primary schools, day care centres and pre-school playgroups, after-school facilities (childcare and after-school activities) and local child welfare authorities in the Netherlands have been working together since 1995 to form 'brede scholen', literally 'broad schools', in other countries known as 'community schools' or 'Ganztagsschulen' (Doornenbal, Pols & Van Oenen, 2012). This cooperation was a novelty in 1995; now they are standard practice. Today, almost all primary schools in the Netherlands work in cooperation with one or more pre-school, day care or after-school facilities (Kieft, Van der Grinten & De Geus, 2016). The primary reason for working together originates in educational theory. The motivation most frequently cited is the need to provide children with uninterrupted learning lines and optimal opportunities for development. In practice, the extent to which teachers and childcarers (or day care professionals) work together, varies considerably across community schools. There are four distinct forms of cooperation: stand-alone; face-to-face; hand-in-hand, and all-in-one. The most common form of cooperation appears to be the hand-in-hand model, a systematic method of cooperation; followed by a method in which cooperation is generally incidental (the face-to-face model). The all-in-one cooperation model is rare. This form is known as the Integrated Child Centre (ICC), which was first introduced into the Dutch community school landscape in 2012 (Doornenbal, 2012). ICCs know the highest level of cooperation. There are no dividing lines at all between the sectors; for children aged 0 to 12, there is one single team providing education, childcare, and in some cases even health and welfare services, working under a single management and with combined funding. It also provides a single point of contact for parents. This kind of cooperation demands considerable efforts. Approximately half the principals of community schools and managers of child centres report difficulties. The most commonly cited problem concerns cultural differences between the organizations, as education and childcare are two distinct worlds, each with their own visions, ambitions and training programmes. Problems with legislation and regulations and with funding have also been reported (Kieft et al, 2016).

As described, there are many different forms of cooperation between schools, day care, after-school care and pre-school play groups in the Netherlands. But in all cases, cooperation between the different sectors is expected to improve children's opportunities for finding their place in society later on. This chapter is based on the knowledge and experience we have acquired with the development of community schools and ICCs in the Netherlands (Doornenbal, Pols & Van Oenen, 2012; Doornenbal, 2012; Doornenbal & De Kruiter, 2016). It starts with a message to the reader and then I pose a key question, to which I formulate an answer in four steps.

One Message

We have all gazed in amazement at a flock of starlings flying in formation. At the way the flock is constantly changing shape without disintegrating and the way every starling remains part of the flock. Even though the flock does not fly to a plan, has no centre, nothing directing it, no leader. The starlings simply improvise. The idea of a flock flying in formation appeals to me because the starlings seem to know instinctively how to deal with differences, with diversity. No bird is excluded, inclusivity seems to be a given. But people are not starlings. We don't form a flock instinctively. Therefore, if we want to do justice to children's rights to participate, to be of importance and to learn in everyday life, then we will need to work on diversity and inclusion. So my message is: we must work towards an inclusive ICC where there is a place for every child. Where every child is allowed to participate, to be of importance and to learn. Or, to use the words of Dutch pedagogue Gert Biesta (2013), where every child is given a chance of qualification, socialization *and* subjectification. If we adopt these aims as our frame of reference, this means that the ICC must ensure that every child:

1. is able to obtain the qualifications matching its abilities, to follow the curriculum best suited to increase its opportunities in the employment market;
2. is raised to be a democratic citizen participating in an open society; and
3. discovers who it wants to be and what it wants to contribute, and how its identity takes shape.

Achieving these three functions together results in children 'coming into the world' (Biesta, 2013; Pols, 2016). This is also my interpretation of the concept of talent development.

Talent development is interpreted in many different ways. It is often limited to cognitive development and specifically that of pupils with outstanding performance in cognitive tasks. In this view, talent development, giftedness and excellence are closely related terms. That is not what I mean by talent development. The approach I advocate is the one developed by the Dutch knowledge network TalentenKracht (see www.talentenkracht.nl), in which talent is regarded as every child's ability to develop itself optimally when it is stimulated by adults in a talented way. The TalentenKracht approach is based on every child's innate curiosity and teachers' and other educational professionals' task to recognise that curiosity and respond adequately to it. Talent, therefore, is not something one simply has, but something that professionals are able to bring out and stimulate, and that may lie in many different areas: art, culture, music, movement, programming, caring, building, gardening, etcetera. When we define talent development in this way, it is the school's task to ensure that every child is able to develop itself with talent regardless of its abilities.

That implies that an inclusive ICC aims to develop every child's talents regardless of its origins, religion, sexual orientation, disposition and ethnicity. From the perspective of inclusion, diversity is more than a starting principle. It goes deeper than that. We actually need to engage with those differences. Diversity then becomes a moral duty, a call to connect with differences (Kramer, 2013; Kramer, 2014). Precisely this engagement is the most difficult aspect. It is something that has to be worked at, because it goes to the core of your own standards and values, your own opinions, beliefs and convictions.

The rights of every child to be of importance, participate and learn are not adequately respected in the Dutch education system. Evidence for this is found in the fact that, compared with other countries, the educational system in the Netherlands is highly segregated. This can be seen in the table below, provided by the OECD (2012, p. 59). In the first place, the table shows that the Netherlands has the highest number of special educational facilities for different 'target groups', children who for various reasons require extra care. So, in both absolute and relative terms, many children fall outside the scope of basic educational services. Inclusion of children with different care needs is certainly not a given in the Netherlands.

In the second place, the table shows that, compared to other countries, selection for the different types of higher or secondary education happens relatively early in the Netherlands. Around the age of twelve, at the end of primary school, children are admitted to a secondary school on the basis of their performance in a national final examination (CITO) and the advice of their primary school teacher. This selection is a key predictor for their further school career. Once allocated to a particular education level, it is difficult for pupils to move to a different level (Dutch Inspectorate of Education, 2016). There are various reasons for this, including the performance pressure schools are dealing with.[2] Due to this, secondary schools do well not to admit the most demanding pupils. Relatively, they cost more time and energy, and bring down the final results. For this reason, downstreaming to lower types of secondary education has become easier than upstreaming to higher types, also called 'stacking'[3]. The fact that upstreaming to higher forms of education is becoming more difficult, has primarily a negative effect on the educational progress of children from deprived backgrounds. These children often need more time to develop and now their perspective at rising socially via stacking, has been reduced.

[2] Performance means that schools are successful in having as many students as possible pass their final examinations with good marks within the shortest possible period.
[3] Stacking means that pupils move on from pre-vocational secondary education to senior general secondary education or pre-university secondary education. That way, they can obtain a higher secondary education diploma that will give them access to higher professional education or university education respectively.

	Age of first selection	Number of school types or distinct educational programmes available to 15-year-old students	Percentage of students in schools where students' record of academic performance are considered for admittance (1)	Percentage of students in schools that group students by ability (1)
Australia	16	1	60	95
Austria	10	4	74	46
Belgium	12	4	52	46
Canada	16	1	53	90
Chile	16	1	70	65
Czech Republic	11	5	69	69
Denmark	16	1	24	50
Estonia	15	1	73	56
Finland	16	1	18	58
France	16	1	w	w
Germany	10	4	77	51
Greece	15	2	27	15
Hungary	11	3	90	68
Iceland	16	1	8	75
Ireland	15	4	24	96
Israel	15	2	78	97
Italy	14	3	55	56
Japan	15	2	99	67
Korea	14	3	61	90
Luxembourg	13	4	95	71
Mexico	15	3	59	69
Netherlands	12	7	97	80
New Zealand	16	1	43	98
Norway	16	1	7	73
Poland	16	1	49	46
Portugal	15	3	16	32
Slovak Republic	11	5	73	73
Slovenia	14	3	68	55
Spain	16	1	11	60
Sweden	16	1	5	74
Switzerland	12	4	70	75
Turkey	11	3	66	62
United Kingdom	16	1	20	99
United States	16	1	45	91

Table 3.1 *Types of differentiation in lower secondary education across countries.*

In this context, I would also like to mention that children in pre-school care or day care are already categorised children at the age of two into target group children and non-target group children.[4] Target group children are children who are raised by parents with low socio-economic status and who run a high risk of delayed language development. To ensure that target group children catch up in this area at the earliest possible age, they are offered programmes for pre-school and early-school education (*Voor- en Vroegschoolse Educatie* or VVE). Although early investment in the language development of children growing up in families where the use of 'school language' is less usual is very important, the VVE policy does result in children, as early as two-year olds, being categorised into target group children and non-target group children. This means that the VVE policy is a target group policy rather than an inclusive policy.

The inequality in opportunities in Dutch education has therefore grown rather than decreased, and the gap between privileged and underprivileged children (high and low) has become wider rather than narrower. With a view to narrowing this gap, we would therefore do well to prevent early selection and reduce the number of special education facilities by working on a basic inclusive childcare/educational facility in which differences between children are respected. Moreover, there is a good pedagogical reason for taking a more inclusive approach. Recent research by Annika de Haan (2015) shows that mixed groups have a positive effect on young children with delayed language development (and the evidence is reassuring for high-fliers: children with advanced language development are not adversely affected). According to De Haan, the positive effect of mixed groups is primarily achieved through the interaction with peers. Children learn from one another. We should not deprive them of that opportunity.

[4] The current pre-school system consists of various facilities with differing objectives, target groups and funding. All children can go to pre-school play groups to prepare them for primary school. For children of working parents, a day care subsidy is provided so that parents are able to combine work with childcare. For disadvantaged children, targeted intervention is provided in the form of pre-school education.

One Key Question

In short, inclusion still has a long way to go in the Netherlands. This is why a breakthrough is needed to create an inclusive ICC. Which brings me to the key question: how does one do this? How can we move closer to this appealing goal? I shall attempt to answer this question in four steps: *where* should *what* be done by *whom* and *how*?

The answer

Step 1: Where?

The first step is to ask oneself *where* inclusion needs to be worked at.

Of course, the place for this is the community school or ICC, which can be regarded as a miniature society (Dewey talks about an embryonic society, 1999) in which children prepare for their future in a safe environment. However, this miniature society is not an island. The ICC forms part of a local environment; of a community, town or neighbourhood. For this reason, it is important that the ICC is familiar with the local context. It should know who the parents and children are, what the issues are, what facilities are available, what volunteer initiatives and so on. It would be helpful for the ICC and the other organizations in the community to work together towards a common result, based on this analysis of the local area. University professor and expert on cooperation in networks Patrick Kenis (2015) talks about result with a capital R. According to Kenis, for effective cooperation in a network it is crucial to agree on a common Result that all parties (a) understand the necessity and urgency of and (b) commit themselves to by contributing to it based on their own role.

Practice has shown that agreeing on a common result at local level or cooperating to achieve this in a network is difficult. Particularly in deprived neighbourhoods, many government agencies are involved and energy and funds are fragmented.

The multicultural, deprived neighbourhood of Selwerd Paddepoel Tuinwijk (SPT) in the town of Groningen is a good example. I know this neighbourhood well due to the research we are carrying out there. In relative and absolute terms, many children grow up in poverty there, raised by young single mothers and/or unemployed parents. Core funding for education is not sufficient to provide the children in SPT with what they need to 'come into the world'. For this reason, there are all kinds of compensatory projects: isolated short-term projects carried out simultaneously, well-intended initiatives that come to an end because the money has run out. Such random projects result in very little. These children would benefit more from sufficient systematic core funding and a stable pedagogical and educational infrastructure so that they are also able to participate, be of importance and get ahead. In some places in the Netherlands, such as Stedenwijk in the town of Almere, efforts are being made to prevent this fragmentation. All the relevant parties in the community are working together to create and implement a pedagogical community plan. But this is still in the early stages. It was only

> with the introduction of the new Jeugdwet (Dutch Youth Act) in 2015 that local authorities, in this case the municipalities, were given responsibility for child welfare services including prevention and minor assistance (Dutch Youth Act, 2014). Previously, responsibility for child welfare lay with national government. Coordination of this system intervention has therefore been decentralised to rest with municipalities.

Step 2: What?

The second step involves the important question of *what* children need in an ICC. By way of introduction to this issue, I would like to mention 'The Dark Horse', a beautiful, moving, profound film, which I saw at the International Film Festival in Rotterdam in 2015. The Dark Horse is set in New Zealand and is based on a true story. The main protagonist is Genesis Potini, a chess champion. He suffers from bipolar disorder and has spent time in a psychiatric institution. The film begins when he is discharged from the institution and goes in search of a meaningful life. He wants to participate and integrate into society. An opportunity arises when he meets a group of underprivileged Maori children and decides he wants to do something for them. He will teach them to play chess, so that they can take part in a national chess tournament six weeks later. I mention The Dark Horse because Genesis Potini is a great teacher, who does five important things that enable every child to come into the world and develop its talents.

First, Potini builds a relationship of trust with the children, who have had little positive attention, by believing in them. He has absolute confidence that every one of them can learn to play chess. Belief in a child's development potential creates an affective relationship between the child and the adult, which is an essential prerequisite for development and learning. This basic confidence is precisely what vulnerable children lack, as the American science journalist Paul Tough (2013) shows in the convincing study How Children Succeed.

In the second place, Potini acknowledges the children's need for relationships, for joining in, for belonging. He places a large chess board by the door with all the pieces on it and on arrival, each child takes the piece that has been allocated to it from the board. This symbolises that they are all part of the game, of the community, each with its own position. I would like to look at this more closely. Paying attention to diversity is not the same as each individual getting what he wants. Children also need to learn that they are part of a group. That boundaries are necessary in the interests of the group, of society. Derksen, a Dutch psychiatrist, pointed out in Het Narcistisch Ideaal (The Narcistic Ideal, 2009) that bonding does not imply that parents and other adults need to respond to every signal given by the child. On the contrary. Children need to learn that their impulses cannot always be satisfied immediately, here and now. They need to develop tolerance for frustration, in the interests of other people and the group. And even more importantly, to experience that you can do something for another person that does not benefit yourself but the group.

Thirdly, Potini sets high expectations: learning to play chess to competition level within six weeks. It is well-known that high expectations stimulate development. However, research shows that teachers in the Netherlands often have lower expectations of children from underprivileged backgrounds and/or with different ethnic origins than of children who grow up in opportunity-rich families. In academic literature, this is referred to as the Pygmalion effect (Rosenthal & Jacobson, 1968), which leads to referral to lower-level secondary education programmes and underuse of talent (Timmerman, De Boer & Van der Werf, 2016). High expectations induce development, at least this is the case if children receive maximum support to achieve that high aim. And that is exactly what Potini does.

In the fourth place, his interactions in guiding the children to learn to play chess are of high quality. Much can be said on the subject of quality of interactions. What do high-value interactions consist of and how do you achieve them when working with different children? For now, I will simply give an example. Young children appear to develop more quickly in groups where many stimulating activities are offered, for example in enriched play, than in groups where professionals offer fewer activities of this type (Veen & Leseman, 2015). Scaffolding (Van Geert & Steenbeek, 2005), which literally means creating supportive structures for learning purposes, such as providing feedback and feed-forward, is also an important factor for success that is currently underused in educational practice.

Finally, children need an expert, a master in the subject, who will introduce them to the culture, in this case the rules of chess. It is therefore important that Potini himself is a good chess player. Children need stand on the shoulders of the previous generation, so that they can build on 'old' knowledge to create a 'new' world (Arendt, 1974; Dasberg, 1975). The importance of old knowledge, of mastery of a subject, is often underestimated these days as a result of the information society we live in. This has, for instance, been pointed out by the British educational researcher Daisy Christadoulou in her book Seven Myths of Education (2014). One of the seven myths is that children no longer need knowledge. After all, they can look everything up. But you really need knowledge, such as the meaning of terms (lower-order skills), in order to acquire higher-order skills (reasoning). For example, children were unable to get to grips with an assignment on global warming because they did not know what a glacier was. To put it metaphorically, don't send children into the woods (ask them to do something complicated like carry out an assignment) until they're able to recognise enough trees. They need teachers who teach them basic skills and concepts, which they can use as a basis for acquiring more skills.

In step 1, we saw that the coordinating role about the 'where' of inclusion lies with the municipalities. The coordinating role in establishing a common vision on the development, raising and education of children, and a warm educational climate, emphatically rests with the ICC principal responsible for implementation in the ICC. In the Netherlands this is often the school principal, who in addition to coordinating the educational facilities is also in charge of childcare and, in some cases, child welfare.

Step 3: Who?

This brings us to the third step: *who* should work towards an inclusive ICC and, in particular, what this requires of professionals. In the discussion of cooperation competencies of professionals in a network, a recognised tool is the image of the *T-shaped professional* (Doornenbal, Pols & Van Oenen, 2012; Doornenbal & De Leve, 2014). The T-shaped professional is someone who is good at his job, who understands how to implement the 'what' (see step 2) to a high standard. But the complex task of working to achieve inclusion with a diverse group of children cannot be carried out by a teacher alone. The doors and windows of the classroom need to be opened. In the first place, various professionals are needed (the vertical axis of the T) to complete this complex task. Not just teachers, subject teachers and day care professionals, but also welfare workers, specialists and generalists from child health and welfare and family support services. Working in an integrated team does not imply that everyone does the same thing. On the contrary: complementary areas of expertise are needed. Plus connecting powers (the horizontal axis of the T), so that the various areas of expertise are utilised in such a way that they add value. Key aspects are the necessity for a shared vision on inclusion and diversity and for generic horizontal skills, particularly in the areas of cooperation and of design, reflection and learning.

What does an interprofessional dialogue look like in a T-shaped team of this kind? It should be noted that by dialogue, I do not mean a one-off conversation, but a continuous dialogue in both formal and informal settings, starting with the following questions: What is our objective in forming a team? What values do we share? What is our common ambition and what aim are we seeking to achieve? We have already mentioned (in step 2) that the ultimate aim of the ICC is to bring children into the world through qualification, socialization and subjectivization. These are complex terms to which professionals bring their own associations, partly derived from their professional socialization. A discussion about the associations this aim evokes in them is preferably conducted on the basis of specific case examples (children). Discussion based on case examples has proven very useful in revealing underlying patterns of thought and action. Once there is clarity about the team's aims for this child (or group of children), what objective they would like to achieve, the next question is how each of the team members can contribute to this from their own expertise. For this, each professional needs to be capable of voicing his own expertise, recognising and acknowledging its limitations and actively seeking complementary expertise. If the team establishes that insufficient expertise is available to respond to the complex needs of a child or group of children, the team will need to develop an innovative solution: what other ways are there to help, who is going to be in charge, how will we monitor implementation and how will we discuss its results? Conducting this type of dialogue in a T-shaped team is not easy, certainly in the Netherlands where the teacher's autonomy as an educational professional is highly valued and teachers are not yet used to having these kind of discussions with one another. So professionals will need to leave their comfort zone. It is therefore essential that discussions of this type are supervised – in some cases supplemented with advice from researchers – certainly in the early stages when no routine has yet been developed for such discussions.

The dialogue should not only take place between professionals but also always with *parents*. I will discuss this in more detail, as parental involvement is generally found to be difficult. Bé Poolman carried out doctoral research into delayed language development in young children in North-East Groningen (2016). A key finding was that parents' socio-economic background was not the primary predictor for a child's language development. It turned out that parents' expectations and views with respect to child-raising and education were more important (Poolman, Minnaert, Leseman & Doornenbal, 2015; Poolman, 2016). That's why programmes are carried out in the Netherlands, such as 'Op Stap' and 'Opstapje', to support parents in raising their children at home: what can they do at home to support their children, such as reading to them in the evenings? This is not always effective, probably because it does not fit with parents' social environment and habits, as the following example shows.

Each Tuesday morning, from eight o'clock to half past eight, I read with Nathaniel as part of what is called a 'reading breakfast'. Nathaniel is seven and a half and this is the second time that he is doing the third year of primary school. As many children at his school have delayed language development, the school puts a lot of effort into language development. They offer all kinds of stimulating activities such as the reading breakfast. Two mornings a week, parents are offered the chance to read with their child in the third and fourth year before school starts – between eight o'clock and half past eight – while having breakfast at school. Nathaniel's mother organises this. She makes tea and coffee and sandwiches. Parents are also asked to read with their child at bed time (or better still: to get their child to read to them from a book called *Mees* and talk about the story based on the questions provided with the book: see www. successforall-nederland.nl). Nathaniel's mother regularly asks me: 'Would you get Nathaniel to read *Mees* with you and fill in the questions? I didn't get round to it yesterday evening because I read two stories from the Children's Bible.' But did she really fail in her duty to her son? I don't think so. Reading aloud from the Children's Bible creates a bond between mother and child and makes him part of the Christian family culture. Yet we have an opinion about her actions based on our own perspectives. For example, personally I am critical of the breakfast put in front of Nathaniel: a soggy roll with a sweet spread and an unidentifiable drink in a sachet with a straw. How do we deal with differences in lifestyles and the values they are based on? Because I'm quite certain that Nathaniel's mother has the best intentions for his wellbeing. That is a moral challenge for me – how do I engage with people in situations that summon up a negative judgment/emotion in me? Being with others, presence (Baart, 2001), meeting them, making contact and building a relationship with other people who are different from ourselves is a challenge, also from a moral point of view.

Professionalization can contribute to raising the quality of implementation in the ICC. Recent research into quality in day care centres (Slot, Leseman, Verhagen & Mulder, 2015) shows that continual professionalization in the workplace is a good predictor of quality. This involves more than refresher courses and extra training for individual employees, the effects of which are limited. In April 2016, Trouw newspaper ran the headline 'School hardly benefits from extra training for teachers'. This was shown by a research study that teachers themselves had carried out among their colleagues. For example, a teacher following a master's course, will not be able to use his newly gained knowledge if he is the only one with this training in a school that is not innovative.

So, professionalization is an important aspect when developing an ICC, by which I don't mean with colleagues in your own subject area or on your own. Instead, I promote continual professionalization in the workplace in T-shaped teams in order to achieve effective learning together. Those learning T-shaped teams include not just staff from childcare centres and schools, but also from child welfare and support services. In the Netherlands, we usually pass issues relating to special needs pupils on to welfare advice teams. From the viewpoint of inclusion, however, it is preferable to add youth care specialists to the implementing teams, right where the children play and learn (see also Hermanns, 2009). That way, the youth care specialists can immediately put their expertise to work in the workplace, as part of the basic facilities provided. This enables them to support teachers and day care professionals to deal with diversity in an inclusive way.

T-shaped working in learning teams demands leadership. A good leader is a key factor for success. The ICC principal is the person in charge of this professionalization process. But, here again, he cannot achieve this without the support and facilitation of the governing bodies for schools, childcare and child health and welfare services. Ideally, this should happen in cooperation with local government, which after all bears responsibility for all its citizens growing up into adulthood.

Step 4: How?
Finally, step 4 deals with the ICC as a concept in development (Van Aken & Andriessen, 2011). The inclusive ICC that has a place for every child is a work in progress. Concepts need to be monitored and studied: what is going well, what isn't, what could be improved, what should be discontinued? Such questions can only be answered after thorough evaluation. In the Netherlands, ICCs are now trying out different applications of the ICC concept in different contexts. This offers opportunities to join forces to discover effective mechanisms for these concepts in different contexts.

No exhaustive list of all the ICCs and community schools in the Netherlands exists. There are descriptions of good practices, such as the pilot projects by PACT. In the PACT pilot projects, primary schools, day care centres and healthcare facilities work together to provide all children with high quality childcare/educational services, with the objective to reduce referrals to child welfare services and offer every child a development programme that matches its abilities. Although the pilot projects work towards the same objectives, practical implementation varies.

In Middelburg, De Aventurijn is developing continuous learning lines by increasing cooperation and team development for pre-school and first- and second-year primary education; and by having the primary school special needs coordinator work with pre-school children as well, so that alarming behaviour can be identified and acted on more quickly.

In Apeldoorn, the Sterrenschool is expanding the existing integrated cooperation between professionals in childcare and education to include child health and youth care professionals. The school is also setting up a health and welfare system for children from 0 to 12 years.

In Lent, primary school Het Talent is working towards a continuous learning line for children from 0 to 6 years, together with the parents of children who give cause for concern. Child support workers provide child-focused, staff-focused and parent-focused support. This project is being carried out in cooperation with the municipality.

In the Amsterdam neighbourhood of IJburg, integrated child centre Laterna Magica is working to reinforce the expertise of coaches (teachers and day care professionals) in dealing with issues relating to the development of young children. For this, they use flexible child support workers from the local health and welfare system as co-teachers. This project is being carried out in cooperation with the municipality.

Finally

If we seriously want inclusive ICCs in the Netherlands that offer every child the space it needs to develop its talents whatever its abilities and limitations, the pedagogical educational system needs to be expanded in three important ways:
- Creation of a sustainable local pedagogical infrastructure in communities and towns, for which local government is responsible.
- Creation of adaptive organizations and governing bodies for schools, childcare and child health and welfare services that go beyond the sectoral interests of their organizations and facilitate the ICC principals and their interprofessional teams in the complex task of including every child.
- Investment in human childcare/educational capital for the benefit of learning T-shaped professionals and T-shaped teams.

The good examples we see (such as the initiatives by PACT (www.pedagogischpact.nl) and Kindcentra 2020 (www.kindcentra2020.nl)) show that we are working to achieve this in the Netherlands, in order to make sure that every child matters, belongs, participates and learns.

Key Questions
- My ultimate goal is inclusion of every child (from 0 to 12 years) in the basic educational facilities. But how much inclusion can we handle in a community school or ICC? Is there a limit to inclusion or are we only restricted by the limitations of our (current) expertise in dealing with diversity?
- How can we achieve effective interprofessional learning in the workplace so that every child receives appropriate support to develop its talents (qualification, socialization and subjectivization)? Do other countries have effective methods for achieving this?
- I have advocated a system innovation in which professionals in the workplace, organizations' governing bodies and local authorities work together to make a sustainable difference to children's opportunities as they grow up. What are successful strategies for a sustainable system innovation of this kind? Are there any useful examples, documented success and failure factors?

About the author

Dr. Jeannette Doornenbal is professor of Integrated Youth Policy at Hanze University of Applied Sciences Groningen and chair of the research team at PACT, an organization promoting cooperation between the various educational institutions working with young children.

Contact: j.m.doornenbal@pl.hanze.nl.

References

Aken, A., & Andriessen, D. (2011). *Handboek ontwerpgericht wetenschappelijk onderzoek. Wetenschap met effect.* [Handbook for design-oriented scientific research. Science with effect.] Utrecht: Lemma.

Arendt, H. (1994). *Tussen verleden en toekomst.* [Between the past and the future.] Antwerpen/ Apeldoorn: Garant.

Baart, A. (2001). *Een theorie van de presentie.* [A theory of presence.] Assen: Boom.

Biesta, G. (2013). *A beautiful risk of education.* Boulder: Paradigm Publishers.

Christadoulou, D. (2014). *Seven myths of education.* Abingdon/New York: Routledge.

CPB & SCP (2015). *De onderkant van de arbeidsmarkt in 2025.* [The lower end of the employment market in 2025.] The Hague: CPB & SCP.

Dasberg, L. (1975). *Grootbrengen door kleinhouden als historisch verschijnsel.* [Raising children by keeping them down as a historical phenomenon.] Amsterdam: Boom

De Haan, A. (2015). *Effects of preschool education in mixed and targeted classrooms.* Utrecht: Utrecht University (doctoral thesis).

Derksen, J. (2009). *Het narcistisch ideaal. Opvoeden in een tijd van zelfverheerlijking.* [The narcissistic ideal. Raising children in a time of self-worship.] Amsterdam: Bert Bakker.

Dewey, J. (1999). *Ervaring en opvoeding* [Experience and education] (translation and introduction by S. Miedema and G. Biesta). Houten/Diemen: Bohn Stafleu Van Loghum. [Originally published in America in 1938]

Doornenbal, J. (2012). *Opgroeien doe je maar één keer. Pedagogisch ontwerp voor het kindcentrum.* [You only grow up once. Pedagogical design for the child centre.] Groningen: Hanze University of Applied Sciences, Groningen on behalf of the project 'Andere tijden'.

Doornenbal, J., Pols, W., & Van Oenen, S. (2012). *Werken in de brede school. Een pedagogische benadering.* [Working in the broad school. A pedagogical approach.] Baarn: Coutinho.

Doornenbal, J., & De Leve, C. (2014). *De pedagogische professional van de toekomst. 21st century skills professionals 0- tot 6-jarigen.* [The pedagogical professional of the future. 21st century skills professionals 0- to 6-year-olds.] PACT; available at: http://www. pedagogischpact.nl/sites/default/files/files/21st-century-skills-13-6-HR(1).pdf.

Doornenbal, J., & De Kruiter, J. (2016). Twenty years of community schools in Groningen: A Dutch Case Study. In: H. Lawson & D. van Veen (Eds.). *Developing Community Schools, Community Learning Centers, Extended-Service Schools and Multi-Service Schools (pp. 229-253).* Cham, Heidelberg, New York, Dordrecht, London: Springer.

Inspectorate of Education (2016). *De staat van het onderwijs. Onderwijsverslag 2014/2015.* [The state of education in the Netherlands. 2014/2015 education report 2014/2015.] Utrecht: Inspectie van het onderwijs.

Jeugdwet (Dutch Youth Act) (2014). Dutch Ministry of Health, Welfare & Sport and Security & Justice Dutch State Gazette 14-3-2014.

Hermanns, J. (2009). *Het opvoeden verleerd*. [The forgotten art of raising children.] Oration. Amsterdam: Vossiuspers University of Amsterdam.

Kenis, P. (2015). *Over samen werken en netwerk opbouwen.* [On cooperation and network building.] Masterclass in Amsterdam in January 2015 for PACT. Available at: https://www.google.nl/search?hl=en&q=P+Kenis+samenwerken+netwerken+resultaat&gws_rd=cr,ssl&ei=yDm8V4uTHOyRgAbizIOgAg.

Kieft, M., Van der Grinten, M., & De Geus, W. (2016). *Samenwerking in beeld.* [Focus on working together.] Utrecht: Oberon on behalf of the Dutch Ministries of Education, Culture & Science and Social Affairs & Employment.

Kramer, J. (2013). *Wow! Wat een verschil! Diversiteit werkt*. [Wow! What a difference! Diversity works.] Zaltbommel: Thema.

Kramer, J. (2014). *Deep democracy.* Zaltbommel: Thema.

Landelijk Steunpunt Brede Scholen (Dutch Coalition for Community Schools) (2014). *Op weg naar een IKC.* [Heading towards an ICC.] Available at: http://toolkit.bredeschool.nl/PDF/Op%20weg%20naar%20een%20IKC.pdf.

Masschelein, J. (Ed.). *De lichtheid van het opvoeden. Een oefening in kijken, lezen en denken.* [The lightness of raising children. An exercise in watching, reading and thinking.] Leuven: Lannoo Campus.

OECD (2012). *Equity and quality in education; supporting disadvantaged students and schools.* Available at: https://www.oecd.org/education/school/50293148.pdf.

Pols, W. (2016). *In de wereld komen. Een studie naar de pedagogische betekenissen van opvoeding, onderwijs en het leraarschap.* [Coming into the world. A study of the pedagogical significance of upbringing, education and teaching.] Antwerpen/Apeldoorn: Garant (doctoral thesis at Vrije Universiteit Amsterdam).

Poolman, B.G. (2016). *Differences in language development among young children in the northeast of the Netherlands.* Groningen: University of Groningen (dissertation).

Poolman, B., Minnaert, A., Leseman, P., & Doornenbal, J. (2015). Achtergronden van taalachterstanden bij jonge kinderen in Oost-Groningen. [Backgrounds to delayed language development in young children in East Groningen.] *Pedagogische Studien, 92*(4), 150-169.

Rosenthal, R., & Jacobson, L. (1968). *Pygmalion in the classroom; teacher expectation and pupils' intellectual development.* New York: Holt.

Slot, P., Leseman, P., Verhagen, J., & Mulder, H. (2015). Associations between structural quality aspects and process quality in Dutch early childhood education and care settings. *Early Childhood Research Quarterly, 33*(4), 64-76.

Ten Doesschate, S., & Van der Pol, M. (2013). *Een IKC dat staat als een huis. Hoe bouw je een duurzaam integraal kindcentrum?* [A solidly built ICC. How to construct a sustainable integrated child centre?] Utrecht: APS.

Timmerman, A., De Boer, H., & Van der Werf, M. (2016). An investigation of the relationship between teachers' expectations and teachers' perceptions of student attributes. *Social Psychology of Education, 19*(2), 217-240.

Tough, P. (2013). *How children succeed. Grit, curiosity and the hidden power of character.* London: Random House.

United Nations (1989). *Convention on the rights of the child.* United Nations.

Van Geert, P.L.C., & Steenbeek, H.W. (2005). The dynamics of scaffolding. *New Ideas in Psychology. 23*(3), 115-128.

Veen, A., & Leseman, P. (Ed.) (2015). *Pre-COOL cohortonderzoek. Resultaten over de voorschoolse periode.* [Pre-COOL cohort study. Results during the pre-school period.] Amsterdam: Kohnstamm Instituut. (Report 932, project number 20541.)

WESLEY VAN DER HEIJDEN
TEACHER TRAINING STUDENT

**'PUPILS OFTEN FIND INFORMATION
FASTER THAN THEIR TEACHER'**

Fourth-year teacher training college student Wesley van der Heijden wants to teach young children things that will be useful to them throughout their lives. This future teacher believes that education should be more than just the transfer of knowledge. 'Teaching standards and values are really important because without this foundation, you won't be successful in our society.'

'I don't think primary education is primarily based on transfer of knowledge. You're preparing children for the society they will be entering. And you can't achieve this with knowledge alone. I would rather teach pupils at a young age to participate in our society, for example by getting them to play together. Teaching them how to interact with one another. The fact is that if you don't have this foundation, you can't function properly at school either. Today, a school is a miniature version of society where you profit from these social skills every day. Subjects should therefore interact with one another as well so that 'learning in the class' resembles the real world.'

TAILOR-MADE EDUCATION

'Nowadays, the job of the teacher is more about coaching and giving guidance than imparting knowledge. I think that education is currently

"Lifelong learning isn't just for the children, it applies to the teacher too!"

moving away from the notion that teachers have to know everything. After all, the world is changing so fast. Moreover, children often find the information they are looking for faster than you do. As a teacher I try to stimulate my class and every individual to bring out the best in themselves. I also teach them to look at themselves critically. For example, what do they still want to learn? What knowledge do they need for this? And where can they find that information?

I do this by asking questions and getting the child to think. That way it discovers what things it is already able to do and what questions it still has. You do notice when doing this

"I don't think primary education is primarily based on transfer of knowledge."

that we are going through a transition from whole-class teaching to learning in smaller groups. In my view, there are even smarter ways of responding to the children's needs. For example, by personalizing education or preparing tailor-made education.'

PRACTISE WHAT YOU PREACH

'As a teacher you need to keep up with the times. That means that you need to be pro-active about taking continuous professional development offers if you want to be able to relate to your pupils' perception of the world. After all, an inquiring approach should not be limited to your pupils, you need to practise what you preach. If I take my teacher training institution as an example, luckily there are increasing numbers of refresher courses on offer. And there are also many independent educational consultancies in the Netherlands offering courses for teachers. I can't imagine myself stopping learning any time soon: I'm quite sure I will keep encountering problems in practice that I need to tackle. So lifelong learning isn't just what we aspire to for the children, it applies to teachers too!' ‹

Chapter 4

The Teaching Profession in the Netherlands: From Regulative Structures to Collaborative Cultures

Dr. Marco Snoek,
Amsterdam University of Applied Sciences

ntroduction

In the Netherlands, as in every country in the world, the quality of education is an issue of major concern, as education is a key factor in maintaining and developing the economic and social stability of a country. It is a key responsibility of the government to maintain and develop that quality. After all, educational quality is not a static concept, as education needs to adapt itself continuously to changes and new needs in society.

This chapter focuses on the way in which educational quality and development are supported in the Netherlands and the role teachers play in these. Three perspectives on that role are presented, one in which teachers are recipients from government measures and follow system structures and regulations, one in which individual teachers are seen as the key actors in defining and realizing educational quality and one in which educational quality is considered the result of close collaboration of teams of teachers.

The chapter shows how government and local policies in the Netherlands have moved from the first to the second perspective and are now, slowly, evolving to the third perspective.

Educational Quality and Innovation as a Result of System Structures

The governmental responsibility to guarantee the quality of the educational system and, through this, to safeguard the education of every pupil in the Netherlands is a complicated responsibility. It raises the question whether and how the ministry can control the educational practices provided by 234,000 teachers in 7700 schools for primary, secondary and vocational education.

In the 70s and 80s, the general policy of the government was based on quality control by regulations issued by the ministry. Educational quality was regulated by a policy of central laws and detailed regulations, with little room for decisions made by schools and teachers. These laws and regulations focused on the finances and personnel policies of the schools, on general demands regarding the quality of education and on centralized conditions of employment. Governmental control dealt with the goals and exam criteria and with the number of teaching hours per subject. Curriculum innovations were initiated by the government using the RDD model (Research-Development-Diffusion). In this model, research has the task to develop knowledge that can be applied in realistic educational situations, this knowledge is translated into teaching practices through mediators like curriculum experts and educational publishers who develop teaching materials and curricula, and finally the results are diffused to teachers who are supported in the use of the materials through teaching guidelines and in-service training (Broekkamp & Van Hout-Wolters, 2007).

In the 80s and 90s, quality control based on government regulations was considered ineffective, as this approach reduced school principals to administrative managers with little influence on the quality of education in their schools, it slowed down educational innovation and it hindered schools to be flexible and adapt their teaching to local needs. In the 90s, a process of deregulation was started in which responsibility for the quality of teaching, finances and organization of education was shifted to the school authorities (local authorities or independent school boards). Basic idea is that decisions on the process and organization of teaching in a school need to be taken at institutional level, to enable adaptation to local circumstances. Within the governance of education, a shift was made from steering by rules and regulations to steering by goals and accountability on outcomes. In this shift towards accountability of school authorities, a stronger role was given to the Inspectorate of Education.

This change increased the responsibility of school authorities to set up innovation, finance and personnel policies. Educational policies became based on the understanding that the government was responsible for the 'what of education' – the aims and content of the curriculum – through curriculum and exam guidelines, and that schools were responsible for the 'how of education' – the pedagogics, didactics and logistics of teaching (Commissie Parlementair Onderzoek Onderwijsvernieuwingen, 2008).

This shift in responsibilities and division of tasks created an increase of the autonomy of school authorities, it made the schools the focal point of educational policies, it created space for more variation and diversity between schools, and it inspired schools to be more competitive and innovative. At the same time, it increased the responsibilities of school boards to find answers to societal needs and to adapt to changing circumstances. This shift fitted well within the development of the 'Polder Model', the social-economic strategy that was dominant in the Netherlands in the 90s and the first decennium of 2000, in which developments in society were seen as a collaborative responsibility of the government and social partners. The Polder Model is characterized by *'organized and autonomous groups that are embedded in political structures that recognise – even depend upon – the legitimacy of these particularistic institutions and provide a political space for negation and compromise between sovereign authority and subsidiary institutions'* (De Vries, 2014, p. 101). With the increased autonomy of school boards, national bodies of school leaders and school boards were created and strengthened that could act as counterparts for the ministry in finding consensus on national education policies. In this way, safeguarding educational quality became a shared responsibility for the ministry and schoolboards.

This shared responsibility was also applied to the quality of teachers. The quality of initial teacher education was a main responsibility of the teacher education institutes (universities and universities of applied sciences), but in the 90s and first decennium of 2000, school boards became partners in school-based teacher education, while the ministry kept close supervision on the quality of newly qualified teachers graduating from teacher education and initiated several improvement measures regarding the quality of teacher education programmes. The quality of teachers after graduation became the full responsibility of school boards: to create support programmes for novice teachers, to stimulate continuous professional development, to organize teacher appraisal, etcetera.

However, despite this process of deregulation – with a reduced role of the ministry to control the work of teachers – many teachers felt that their autonomy actually decreased. Given the fact that school boards were held accountable for the outcomes of the learning processes within their schools, the boards felt a responsibility to intervene in educational processes within their schools and to control the work of teachers. The same steering paradigm that was used by the government was now being used by the school authorities. This also impacted in-service professional development of teachers. School boards tried to align professional development activities to processes of school development and set up school-wide professional development strategies and programmes. On the one hand, these strategies and programmes aimed to strengthen coherence within the school and alignment with school development, while on the other hand, again, individual teachers felt that their autonomy regarding their professional development was reduced.

The government, too, intervened with the work of teachers. To stimulate and safeguard the quality of teaching at system level, the ministry stimulated the use of regular performance testing of pupils based on standardized tests, so teachers could work more data-driven and compare the results of their students to results of students in other schools. A national policy was introduced to stimulate school authorities to promote 'learning outcome oriented' teaching in their schools (Ministry of Education, 2007, 2011).

As the RDD model was no longer officially used, schools had more freedom to experiment with new innovative approaches in teaching, shifting responsibility to pupils. Sometimes, these experiments were teacher-driven, sometimes school board-driven to increase the competitive attractiveness of the school for parents and students. In response to the sometimes 'wild' experiments, some universities[1] started to promote the notion of 'evidence-based teaching'. They wanted teaching and innovations in teaching to be based on empirical evidence of effective practices that resulted from educational research based on high academic standards according to the golden standard of randomized control tests (CPB, 2016). This focus on evidence-based teaching could be considered a revival of the RDD model, where the outcomes of academic research define the work of teachers in the classroom (Biesta, 2007).

Dilemmas
In this perspective, the quality of education is mainly considered as something that is defined by national policy makers at ministries, by local policy makers within school boards or by educational researchers. Teachers are expected to meet external standards in their work with pupils. In the opinion of many, this lead to a 'deprofessionalization' of the teaching profession, as teachers were reduced to deliverers of ready-made curricula, written down in school methods and controlled by standardized tests.

---

[1] E.g. the Top Institute for Evidence Based Education Research of Maastricht University, University of Amsterdam and University of Groningen.

In response to this approach, a group of critical teachers was formed in the 90s[2], voicing complaints about the reduced autonomy of teachers, and criticizing authoritarian school boards and the way in which they used educational specialists from outside to develop curriculum concepts and neglected the professionalism of teachers (Verbrugge & Verbrugge-Breeuwsma, 2006).

This critical response from teachers to national and local policies that focused on system structures fits into the Dutch anti-hierarchical and individual culture. In the Netherlands, there is little respect for hierarchical authority. A higher position does not automatically lead to respect from people lower in the hierarchy, and many teachers were suspicious of the introduction of independent school boards led by CEOs. The introduction of company cars with chauffeurs for CEOs in some very large school boards didn't fit in a country where the prime minister takes a bike to the Parliament buildings and where a king tries to mingle with the people as often as possible. As a result, decisions are often criticized and teachers who disagree with them, tend to simply ignore them, using a practical veto within their own individual and isolated teaching practices.

Educational Quality and Innovation as a Result of Professionalism of Individual Teachers

Renewed Attention for the Role and Quality of Teachers

The focus on structures and control led to many complaints from teachers. The call of teachers to restore their professional freedom and to be regarded as the key professionals in teaching and learning was heard widely from 2006, leading to a report on the teaching profession (Commissie Leraren, 2007).

According to the report, the professional role and authority of teachers should be restored by raising salaries, stimulating further professional development of teachers and connecting that professional development to career steps. Additionally, the profession as a whole needed to be strengthened by the creation of one professional body that could represent the voice of the teachers both to the outside world – e.g. as a formal partner in negotiations with the ministry – and to the inside world of the profession – by setting professional standards for the members of the profession.

The proposals from the report were picked up by the government and translated into a number of initiatives (Ministry of Education, 2007). Salaries were raised and new career steps were introduced. A bursary system was introduced in 2008 (the 'Lerarenbeurs'), in which every teacher could apply for a one-time subsidy to do an in-service post-graduation course, mostly at master's level. This subsidy covered study costs and study time (up to one day a week), with a maximum duration of three years.

[2]   Beter Onderwijs Nederland, Better Education Netherlands.

In 2010, a professional teachers' body was created (the 'Onderwijscoöperatie'[3]), in which several teacher collectives (teacher unions and professional associations of subject teachers) collaborated. The Onderwijscoöperatie had four main aims: to represent the profession in meetings with other stakeholders like the government and educational employers (on other issues than employment conditions), to strengthen the self-awareness of the profession, to safeguard the quality of its members, to strengthen its public image. By creating the Onderwijscoöperatie, the Ministry stimulated the introduction of a new stakeholder within the debates on the teaching profession, representing the voice of teachers. In addition to the teacher unions, mainly concerned with working conditions for teachers, the Onderwijscoöperatie was developed as a body of, by and for teachers focused on the content and the development of the profession.

From the start, two formal tasks were given to the Onderwijscoöperatie: to propose standards for the teacher profession ('bekwaamheidseisen'), and to create a professional register for teachers, based on their professional development activities ('Lerarenregister').

Additionally, the government initiated a programme to stimulate the establishment of academic development schools ('academische opleidingsscholen'). The academic development schools are partner schools to teacher education institutes and engage in a combination of educating teacher training students, involvement in practice-oriented research and stimulating professional development of their teachers. As such, the academic development schools are similar to the concept of PDS, professional development schools (Darling-Hammond, 1994).

These initiatives had a strong impact on the teaching profession in the Netherlands. Through the Lerarenbeurs, the number of master-qualified teachers and, as a result, the number of teachers that had basic research skills and an inquiring mindset, increased. Several academic development schools set up their own research agenda and initiated studies on topics that were connected to dilemmas teachers encountered within their daily practices or to the innovation agendas of the schools. Even though most academic development schools collaborated closely with universities and teacher education institutes, research was no longer the exclusive domain of researchers. Through the Lerarenbeurs, the autonomy of teachers regarding their professional development was restored: teachers could apply for a subsidy, and the school was expected to facilitate this by reducing the teacher's teaching hours.

A Focus on the Individual Professional
As a whole, the call to strengthen the autonomy and quality of the profession was translated into initiatives that supported the autonomy and quality of the individual professional. Teachers could only apply for the Lerarenbeurs as an individual, which resulted mostly in individually motivated choices for a specific master's programme without much consultation with colleagues or school principals. As a consequence, teachers in master's programmes often initiated individual graduation research projects which were to a limited extent embedded within the school (Snoek

[3] www.onderwijscooperatie.nl

& Volman, 2014). Within some academic development schools, research was seen as one of the possible specialization areas within a teacher's career, and therefore considered as an individual task. The Lerarenbeurs also gave teachers the chance to think about their individual career tracks, as it created opportunities to gain access to higher salary scales.

Moreover, the teacher register strengthened the focus on the individual professional. From the start, it has been set up as an instrument to account for individual professional development. The teacher register has no relation to school development processes and the main focus is on keeping track of individual participation in formal continuous professional development (CPD) activities like courses, trainings and conferences. Powerful informal collaborative learning activities like lesson study (in which teachers collaboratively plan, observe and evaluate lesson designs with a strong focus on the activities and the learning outcomes of pupils), peer feedback or other collaborative activities of teams of teachers that stimulate professional development were more difficult to register.

Teachers with innovative ideas who wanted to redesign teaching and learning processes within their classes and school, often depended on support from their school principals. Many teachers felt that this support was limited, leading to frustration. This was recognized by the ministry and the Onderwijscoöperatie, who set up an innovation programme ('Onderwijspioniers') which enabled teachers with innovative ideas to apply for grants to put those ideas to practice. The main aim of the program was to strengthen the profession as an innovative profession, to foster innovative ideas of individual teachers and to stimulate innovation within schools.

Dilemmas

With more focus on the professional quality and the professional autonomy of teachers, many teachers felt recognized. The profession became more attractive through the possibility of career steps, opportunities for further education at master's level, a stronger diversification of teacher tasks, including practice-based and teacher-led research, and opportunities to engage in the development of the profession by joining activities of the Onderwijscoöperatie. Teachers who felt constricted by the limited opportunities that were offered by their schools, could engage in activities for professional development and innovation outside their schools. Through master's programmes, teachers could develop their teacher leadership capacities. Many teachers felt challenged to publicly account for their professional quality through the Lerarenregister[4].

At the same time, this created tensions. The focus on system and school structures had frustrated collaborative professional cultures in schools. In many schools, individual accountability for teaching and for learning outcomes dominated. This individual accountability easily led to professional uncertainty where interference by other teachers was felt as threatening. In many schools, teachers were not used to interventions in their teaching by other teachers.

---

[4] In 2014, 18,000 teachers voluntarily registered. In 2016, 33,000 teachers were registered (Visser, 2016).

A proposal from the Dutch Education Council to recognize excellent teachers in schools, give them a temporary salary raise and reduce their number of teaching hours so they could support colleagues (Onderwijsraad 2011), was met with cynicism and criticism by the unions and many teachers. In their opinion, it would divide teacher teams and, as there were no clear criteria available to define 'excellence', it would create arbitrariness within schools. This illustrated the Dutch non-hierarchical culture in which people react allergically to people standing out. This allergy was strengthened by the top-down structures of the system approach, which has led to a strong division between 'us' (teachers) and 'them' (management). Many teachers had become very sensitive to anything that could come close to professional scrutiny, either by the school principal or by colleagues. This allergy to interference in the practice of teaching, often lead to professional loneliness of teachers (cf. Vermeulen, 2009).

The possibility as an individual teacher to apply for a Lerarenbeurs to start a master's study, strengthened the opportunity to follow personal ambitions and learning needs, but also led to professional development that was disconnected from school or team ambitions and school policies (Snoek & Volman, 2014). The same disconnection exists for the Lerarenregister, as it was only designed as an instrument for keeping track of personal professional development, not linked to teams or schools.

With the lack of collaborative professional cultures, the development of individual professionalism of teachers through master's programmes and through engagement in teacher inquiry and research and in innovation projects had limited impact and created new problems. Often, teachers could only impact their own practice and not reach into the practice of colleagues. Teachers who developed their teacher-leadership capacities and felt that they could contribute to school- or department-wide innovations, often lacked a position to do so within the school. In schools without a culture of shared leadership, they didn't feel recognized and lacked opportunities to put their leadership qualities to practice. As a result, the increased focus on teacher professionalism sometimes led to frustration, as school cultures didn't change (Snoek, 2014).

Educational Quality as a Result of Collaborative Cultures

Towards Collaborative Professional Cultures in Schools

The dilemmas around the isolated role of teachers within schools became gradually recognized. The awareness that on the one hand, effective development and innovation in schools should not be externally imposed, but should be initiated and adopted from within the school, while on the other hand, effective development and innovation in schools could not be a matter of individual teachers, led to a stronger focus on collaborative professional cultures within schools. At several levels, activities were initiated to strengthen collaborative professional cultures in schools and to initiate and support teacher-driven school development and innovation.

The support program Onderwijspioniers recognized that innovative plans of teachers could only be successfully implemented within schools with the help of the school principal and colleagues. Within this programme, more attention was given to engaging school principals (by inviting them to programme sessions) and to the development of teacher leadership qualities (e.g. on implementation issues like how to gain grass root support from colleagues, how to engage colleagues, and how to get support from school principals). In the follow-up of Onderwijspioniers, the Teacher Development Fund (the 'LerarenOntwikkelFonds') founded in 2015, it is also possible for teams of teachers to send in innovation proposals. Alongside Onderwijspioniers, the Onderwijscoöperatie initiated pilots on peer feedback, in which teachers visit each other's lessons to analyse and discuss the quality of teaching, to give feedback or to develop lessons collaboratively.

With the implementation of the Bachelor-Master structure in higher education, new master's programmes have been introduced in the area of education. The most prominent one was the master's programme on Learning and Innovation. Since 2008, this programme has been offered at several universities of applied sciences. Key aim is to support teachers to become leaders of innovation and change within their schools. The curriculum covers not only topics concerning students' teaching and learning and research skills, but also theories on organization, change, innovation and on collaborative teacher learning. But most importantly, the programme contributes to a change in the professional identity of teachers, shifting their mind set from being an individual subject teacher to being a member of a wider community and a change agent in schools. Through this master's programme, a strong impulse was given to the creation of collaborative and innovative school cultures.

Within such post-initial master's programmes, initiatives are taken to involve school principals more intensively in the master's programmes and professional development of their teachers. Meetings are being organized for teachers in the master's programme and their school principals, school principals are engaged in the thesis research projects, schools are stimulated to enrol several teachers as a group into the programme, and educational institutes are experimenting with tailor-made master's programmes that are adapted to the context and needs of a specific school or school board (Snoek, Enthoven, Kessels & Volman, 2017). Through these initiatives, stronger connections are made between the aims of the master's programme, the individual aims of the participating teachers and the development agenda of the school as a whole.

To stimulate school principals to link professional development of individual teachers more closely to the development and innovation in the school as a whole, several support programmes have been started, focusing on professional development of school principals on issues such as human resources, teacher development, innovation theories, and collaborative cultures.

This has resulted in many school-level initiatives to stimulate collaborative professional cultures in schools. Almost 500 schools have joined an initiative to create innovative cultures in schools ('Stichting Leerkracht'[5]) by teams focusing on clear and shared goals, collaborative preparation of lessons, peer observation and feedback, and feedback from pupils. 150 schools joined a government-supported innovation programme ('InnovatieImpuls Onderwijs'[6]) in which the teaching process was defined as a collaborative process with forms of team teaching, the use of teaching assistants, the use of teacher development teams in which teachers from different schools took shared responsibility for the preparation of learning materials, and co-teaching by pupils (Snoek, Sligte, van Eck, Schriemer & Emmelot, 2014). Within academic development schools, post-initial master's programmes and initial teacher education programmes, research is increasingly seen as an intervention within a school, leading to a stronger focus on quality criteria for research projects that include quality criteria for effective system interventions, rather than quality criteria solely for academic research (cf. Anderson & Herr, 1999). As a way of collaborative professional development, lesson study has become increasingly popular, in which teachers collaboratively plan, observe and evaluate lesson designs with a strong focus on the activities and the learning outcomes of pupils.

The Voice of Teachers
Maybe the most important impulse for the development of collaborative professional cultures came from teachers themselves. While the focus on national or local structures to safeguard quality of education had alienated many teachers and led to a lot of complaining and frustration, it also created room for dissenting voices of teachers who recognized their own agency and responsibility to contribute to improvement in schools. Some of these teachers had the opportunity within their own schools to initiate new approaches or to create new cross-curricular subjects together with colleagues. Others, who felt isolated in their schools, looked for likeminded colleagues outside their schools and created national movements like Teachers with Guts ('Leraren met Lef'[7]) or professional associations for teachers in vocational schools. Although these groups represented much smaller groups than the traditional teacher unions, they voiced a different message, emphasizing the positive contributions that teachers could and should give to improving teaching and learning in schools. Because of this different message, several of these movements have been recognized by the ministry of education as important voices in the debate on improving the teaching profession and improving education.

Within the process of strengthening the voice of teachers, social media such as blogs and twitter, played an important role. Especially through twitter, a small but growing group of teachers have become important representatives and role models for the profession and are widely heard by colleagues, politicians and the minister. Some of them became national spokespersons, appearing at conferences and TV-shows or publishing books (e.g. Evers & Kneyber, 2015).

[5]   www.stichting-leerkracht.nl
[6]   www.innovatieimpulsonderwijs.nl
[7]   www.lerarenmetlef.nl

Through social media, teachers organized events where teachers from different schools could meet. Local groups of teachers started to organize professional development events, to which they invited colleagues with interesting initiatives, to share innovations and to inspire fellow teachers. Without the need for support from school principals or school boards, teacher education institutes or in-service training providers, teachers in Rotterdam started regular local meet-ups which are gradually copied by teachers in other cities (Pijl, 2017). In Amsterdam, a local group of primary school teachers[8] organized local debates with school principals and local politicians, through which they became recognized as important stakeholders in the development of local education strategies.

Towards a Moral Profession

One of the issues that keeps coming up in teacher-politician debates is the complaint that teachers feel restricted in their professionalism by a regime of educational standards, exams and testing. This regime leaves little room to deviate from the curriculum, to adapt to the needs and interests of pupils, or to bring issues from current events to the classroom. Moreover, it leads to 'teaching to the test'. This general discontentedness with the focus on measuring educational outcomes became more focused through the work of Gert Biesta who emphasized three key domains for education: qualification, socialization and subjectification (Biesta, 2014, see also Chapter 2 in this book). The work of Biesta resonated strongly in the Netherlands, as many teachers felt that he gave them the words and concepts to voice their concerns more effectively and to start to formulate alternatives. Concepts like Bildung, the moral purpose of teachers, and child-centred pedagogies are fuelling debates amongst teachers. These concepts give teachers tools to rethink their daily work, to re-evaluate their main purpose as teachers and to start looking for ways that are more closely connected to their passion for their jobs as teachers. At the same time, many teachers and schools realize that creating a more balanced curriculum – recognizing aims regarding qualification, socialization and subjectification – cannot be a task for individual teachers, but needs to be taken up collectively and school-wide. The Dutch freedom of education and the open system of school choice make it possible for schools to redefine their curricula and to develop new educational paradigms that try to strike a new balance between the three aims of education. Several experimental schools in which teachers try to reshape education collaboratively, have opened their doors to pupils and parents emphasizing the development of individual talents, creativity, collaborative skills, curiosity, 21st century skills, etcetera[9]. In such schools, pupils are given more freedom to set out their own challenges, and the development of social community and the fostering of individual talent are emphasized.

[8] www.meesterschappers.nl

The Development of Teacher Leadership in the Netherlands

In the past five years, there has been a strong shift in the image of the teaching profession, both in the outside world and within the profession itself. The self-awareness of teachers has grown and the voice of teachers is heard. This has led to many new initiatives by teachers within schools and across schools. This shift is not yet system-wide and varies between schools, but it is growing. Several policy initiatives that have been mentioned in this chapter have reinforced these developments.

The Lerarenbeurs has been an important mechanism to increase the number of master's qualified teachers in schools. These teachers have– to a greater or lesser extent –developed skills for teacher leadership and have strengthened their moral understanding of the profession. They often act as initiators of innovation and of networks in and across schools.

Many European countries have chosen to increase the quality of the teaching profession by raising the initial qualification level of teachers to the master's level. Compared to this, the strategy of the Netherlands to focus on stimulating post-initial master's programmes for teachers seems rather weak. However, the combination of these programmes and the Lerarenbeurs has been highly effective. First of all, post-initial master's programmes define the teaching profession as a profession of lifelong learning. Teachers can– or are expected to– follow new qualification courses after a number of years of teaching. Secondly, the impact of post-initial master's programmes can be very strong. Within these programmes, participants can combine new insights on educational concepts and theories with five, ten or even more years of experience, creating a powerful mixture to initiate changes in school practice. As these teachers have already an acclaimed position within the school hierarchy, they are able to use their thesis research as an intervention that can reach beyond their own subject and classroom (Snoek, 2009).

The LerarenOntwikkelFonds creates opportunities for teachers to get support, both financially and in time, for new initiatives. Through this, the teaching profession becomes more creative, innovative and attractive, and new impulses for school improvement are initiated.

The Lerarenregister is still somewhat problematic. On the one hand, it creates opportunities for teachers to develop a stronger professional identity and professional pride by making their professional development more explicit to the outside world. On the other hand, many teachers are suspicious of the register and feel that it is a new government initiated and imposed mechanism to exert external control over the profession. For this sentiment to be reduced, the register needs to be changed from a tool for recognizing individual professional development to a tool for collaborative professional dialogue and development, so that it can be more meaningful for teams of teachers.

[9]   See for example www.schoolofunderstanding.nl, www.agoraroermond.nl, www.vinseschool.nl, www.spinoza20first.nl.

All these initiatives contribute to the development of teacher leadership, not to be interpreted as formal hierarchical leadership or as leadership based on individual roles or positions, but as community-based leadership, which is embedded in a team of teachers, with roles of leaders and followers possibly changing over time (Murphy, 2005). Within several schools in the Netherlands, teachers and school principals explore the implications of this type of shared leadership for their schools. At the same time, this teacher leadership requires a new identity and new qualities of teachers. This need is recognized in teacher policies, in teacher support programmes and in master's programmes in the Netherlands. And the challenge to develop that new identity and those new qualities is taken up by many teachers, individually and collectively.

Educational Quality and Innovation as a Shared Responsibility

In this chapter, I have shown how the understanding of the dynamics of educational quality and change, and of the role of teachers in this, has developed over the years in the Netherlands. In the deregulation process in the 80s and 90s, responsibility for educational quality and innovation was shared between the ministry and school boards. From the 90s, the crucial role of teachers was acknowledged as key players in safeguarding quality and initiating and designing innovation. And finally after 2000, the recognition grew that this process cannot be a task for individual teachers, but requires collaborative cultures in and across schools.

This development has led to a strong belief that educational quality and innovation cannot be defined or directed by the government, but that they need the intense involvement and commitment of all key stakeholders – government, school boards and teachers. As a consequence, the governance structure in education needs to be based on collaborative governance, characterized by dialogue, consensus and collaboration between the key stakeholders (Working Group Schools, 2015).

Although the government has a constitutional responsibility to safeguard the quality of education, there is a strong realisation that this cannot be imposed top-down. It can only be realized when the ministry, schoolboards and teachers individually and collectively, understand that they all have a role and responsibility in this process. In the Netherlands, this awareness has grown in the past twenty years but still needs strengthening. The awareness of mutual interdependency of ministry, school boards and teachers and the willingness to take and share responsibility might be one of the key secrets of 'the Dutch way in education'.

Key Questions

- How can we create a system of collaborative governance within education in which each stakeholder is committed and responsible; and what does this require from each stakeholder?
- How can teachers be prepared and supported to be leaders of a curriculum which extends beyond the 'measurable' and includes the 'valuable'?
- How can leadership of teachers be developed and strengthened and what does this require from school cultures and structures?

About the author

Dr. Marco Snoek is professor of Teacher Development and School Innovation at the Centre of Applied Research in Education of the Amsterdam University of Applied Sciences in the Netherlands. He has been involved in many innovation projects in teacher education in the Netherlands and has published various publications in Dutch and English on teacher education, teacher development, and teacher leadership. From 2005, he has been a member of the European Commission working groups on teachers and teacher education as part of the Education & Training 2010/2020 agendas, representing the Netherlands.

Contact: M.Snoek@hva.nl.

References

Anderson, G.L., & Herr, K. (1999). The new paradigm wars: Is there room for rigorous practitioner knowledge in schools and universities? *Educational Researcher, 28*(5), 12-40.

Biesta, G. (2007). Why 'what works' won't work: Evidence-based practice and the democratic deficit in educational research. *Educational Theory, 57*(1), 1-22.

Biesta, G. (2014). *The beautiful risk of education*. London: Paradigm.

Broekkamp, H., & Van Hout-Wolters, B. (2007). The gap between educational research and practice: A literature review, symposium, and questionnaire. *Educational Research and Evaluation, 13*(3), 203-220.

Commissie Leraren (2007). Leerkracht! [Teacher Force.] The Hague: Ministerie van OCW.

Commissie Parlementair Onderzoek Onderwijsvernieuwingen (2008). *Tijd voor onderwijs. Eindrapport van de Commissie Dijsselbloem.* [Time for education. Final report of the Dijsselbloem Committee.] Den Haag: SDU.

CPB (2016). *Kansrijk Onderwijsbeleid.* [Promising education policies.] The Hague: CPB.

Darling-Hammond, L. (1994). *Professional development schools: Schools for developing a profession.* New York: Teachers College Press.

De Vries, J. (2014). The Netherlands and the polder model: Questioning the polder model concept. *Low Countries Historical Review, 129*(1), 99-111.

Evers, J., & Kneyber, R. (2015). *Flip the system: Changing education from the ground up.* London: Routledge.

Ministry of Education (2007). *Scholen voor morgen.* [Schools for Tomorrow.] The Hague: Ministerie van OCW.

Ministry of Education (2007). *Actieplan Leerkracht van Nederland.* [Action plan Teacher force of the Netherlands.] Den Haag: Ministerie van OCW.

Ministry of Education (2011). *Actieplan Beter Presteren. Opbrengstgericht en ambitieus.* [Action plan Improved performance: outcome-oriented and ambitious.] The Hague: Ministerie van OCW.

Onderwijsraad [Educational Council of the Netherlands] (2011). *Excellente leraren als inspirerend voorbeeld.* [Excellent teachers as inspiring role models.] The Hague: Onderwijsraad.

Pijl, M. (2017). Informele 'Meet-up' brengt kracht en inspiratie. [Informal meet-up brings power and inspiration.] *Onderwijsblad, 17*(2), 36-39.

Snoek, M. (2009). Initieel of niet-initieel – that's the question. Masteropleidingen in Europees perspectief. [Initial or not-initial – that's the question. Master's programs in European perspective.] *Onderwijsvernieuwing – MesoConsult, 2009* (8), 29-38.

Snoek, M. (2014). *Developing teacher leadership and its impact in schools.* Amsterdam: Hogeschool van Amsterdam.

Snoek, M., & Volman, M. (2014). The impact of the organizational transfer climate on the use of teacher leadership competences developed in a post-initial master's programme. *Teaching and Teacher Education, 37*(1), 91-100.

Snoek, M., Enthoven, M., Kessels, J., & Volman, M. (2017). Increasing the impact of a master's programme on teacher leadership and school development by means of boundary crossing. *International Journal of Leadership in Education, 20*(1), 26-56.

Snoek, M., Sligte, H.W., van Eck, E., Schriemer, M.P., & Emmelot, Y.W. (2014). *Impulsen voor vernieuw(en)d onderwijs. Eindrapport kwalitatief onderzoek InnovatieImpuls Onderwijs.* Rapport 926. [Impulses for innovative education. Final report on the qualitative evaluation of the project Innovation Impulse Education] Amsterdam: Kohnstamm Instituut.

Verbrugge, A., & Verbrugge-Breeuwsma, M. (2006). Help! Het onderwijs verzuipt! [Help! The educational system is drowning.] *NRC Handelsblad*, 3 June 2006.

Vermeulen, M. (2009). Vrijheid, gelijkheid en eenzaamheid. [Freedom, equity and loneliness.] In: D. van den Berg (Eds.). *Onderwijsinnovatie: geen verzegelde lippen meer*. [Innovation in education: no sealed lips anymore]. Leuven: Garant.

Visser, J. (2016). Factcheck: 60.000 leraren hebben zich ingeschreven in het Lerarenregister. [Fact check: 60.000 teachers have registered in the teacher register.] *De Correspondent*, 11 October 2016. Available at: https://decorrespondent.nl/5410/factcheck-60-000-leraren-hebben-zich-ingeschreven-in-het-lerarenregister/429840730-816490b3 (last accessed on: 23 March 2017).

Working Group Schools (2015). *Shaping career-long perspectives on teaching. A guide on policies to improve teacher education.* Brussels: European Commission.

FONS DINGELSTAD
POLICY MAKER

'FOR OUR FUTURE'S SAKE, WE NEED TO WORK TOGETHER TO MAINTAIN A HIGH-QUALITY EDUCATION SYSTEM'

Fons Dingelstad has spent his entire career working in the education sector. As Director of Primary Education at the Ministry of Education, Culture and Science, he is keen to discuss the changes and developments in Dutch education. 'After all, we're educating our children for tomorrow, not for today. So you always need to keep developing.'

'At the Ministry of Education, we're constantly focused on one specific task: ensuring that children are receiving a good education. We don't just make sure that we are able to pay for good education, it's also our job to guarantee that it is reliable and of high quality. Because high-quality education is about the future of our society. But it's also about ideals and political choices. We have expectations when it comes to children at school. You try to prepare them for tomorrow in the best possible way. It is this focus on the future that excites me about the education sector.'

ADAPTING TO CHANGES

'You see education adapting to significant social changes. In that sense, the Dutch education system is never stable or static. Fundamentally, there is always room for this kind of change. Already in the 19th century, this freedom of education was laid down in our constitution. As long as you have enough pupils and comply with legal requirements, you can establish a school based on your own educational principles. Internationally, our system stands out: two thirds of Dutch primary education is privately run but publicly funded. Of course, it means constantly finding a good balance between this freedom and the legal rules. Freedom means bearing responsibility for the education you provide, in a situation where the rules do not always guarantee quality. Schools and governing bodies sometimes seem to be insufficiently aware of this manoeuvring room.'

FUTURE-PROOF

'To be well prepared for our future, we need to work together to maintain a high-quality education system. After all, the importance of knowledge in society is undisputed. And knowledge is more than just study material. It also involves communication skills, 21st century skills and what it means to live in and be a citizen of present-day society. Society is simply becoming more complex and there is an increasing number of processes that you cannot contribute to without a proper knowledge base. Therefore, it is very important for a country to have a well-educated population. This starts even before primary education, with pre-school education. From the age of two-and-a-half, children with delayed language development are stimulated to learn Dutch. As a result, these children can perform at the required level during their first year at primary school and we can make sure that they are also better equipped when they leave school.'

"As government, we look to see where we can create the right framework or offer financial support."

NEW TECHNOLOGIES

'There are studies showing that pupils sometimes feel bored in our education system: it could do with a little more excitement. Especially after all the developments in ICT. Life outside school and online offers a lot more exciting challenges. The developments in technology enable us to improve the quality of education, but also to respond better to differences between pupils. The changes needed to make our education more challenging should be properly organized, across several academic years. They require good cooperation between schools, government and the various commercial organizations. As government, we look to see where we can create the right framework or offer financial support. But we may also need to adapt rules so that our education continues to reflect children's needs. This is only possible if all parties involved work together to see how we can achieve it.' ❮

Chapter 5

Supervision and Accountability in the Dutch Education System

Prof. dr. Inge de Wolf, Dr. Jos Verkroost, Drs. Herman Franssen,
Inspectorate of Education

ntroduction

Dutch schools and educational institutions are highly autonomous. They are allowed to make their own decisions about the use of funds from the government and from other sources, and they are responsible for the content and quality of the education they provide. This large degree of autonomy is offset by a strong Inspectorate of Education, which takes action if schools do not meet the required quality standards or make the right financial choices. The Inspectorate also monitors developments in the Dutch education system. It was recently given the additional task of stimulating quality improvements in all schools and programmes. This chapter deals with education supervision in the Netherlands as carried out by the Inspectorate of Education. First, we describe the way in which the Inspectorate operates and the key aspects of supervision. We then discuss three issues relating to supervision and accountability in the Dutch education system.

The Dutch Inspectorate of Education was founded in 1801, when the Netherlands was still known as the Batavian Republic. This makes the Inspectorate the oldest education regulator in the world and one of the oldest national regulators in the Netherlands. Since 2002, the powers of the Inspectorate itself have been laid down in legislation, along with instructions on how it should carry out its duties. This legislation is called the *Wet op het onderwijstoezicht* (WOT, Act on the Inspectorate of Education). The Inspectorate is the only regulator in the Netherlands with its own separate legislation.

The Inspectorate's Mode of Operation

The Inspection Framework

The inspection framework forms the core of the Inspectorate's work and is a coherent framework of quality standards for Dutch education. It is made up of legal requirements for schools, academic insights into what constitutes good education (see Scheerens et al., 2005) and educational best practices. The Inspectorate drafts the inspection framework in consultation with relevant parties in the education sector. This ensures that supervision is focused on issues that the legislator, academics and expert practitioners all regard as embodying the essence of good education. In other words, there is alignment as to the definition and elements of educational quality. Once agreement is reached, the framework is approved by the Minister and published for the institutions. The majority of the various elements are included in sector legislation.

The 2017 assessment framework is made up of five quality areas:
1. Education results: do pupils learn enough?
2. Education process: are pupils taught well?
3. School climate: does school provide a safe environment and what is the atmosphere like?

4. Quality control and ambitions: is there effective quality control; what are the institution's ambitions?
5. Financial management: is there effective financial management?

This is explicitly intended as a broad framework: a broad definition of educational quality and the essential requirements to achieve it.

Within each quality area, standards are described. As an example, the detailed terms of the primary education framework are set out below.

EP	**EDUCATION PROCESS**
EP1	Curriculum
EP2	Development monitoring
EP3	Teaching strategies
EP4	(Extra) Support provided
EP6	Cooperation
EP8	Evaluation and conclusion
SC	**SCHOOL CLIMATE**
SC1	Safety
SC2	Pedagogical climate
ER	**EDUCATION RESULTS**
ER1	Results
ER2	Social and societal competencies
ER3	Subsequent success
QA	**QUALITY CONTROL AND AMBITION**
QA1	Quality control
QA2	Quality culture
QA3	Accountability and dialogue
FM	**FINANCIAL MANAGEMENT**
FM1	Continuity
FM2	Effectiveness
FM3	Legality

Table 5.1 *Quality areas and standards*

The main elements in the assessment framework are described in the WOT. For each of the sectors, each standard is translated into operational guidelines on the basis of the relevant minimum requirements for the sector (basic quality). Some of the elements are self-selected quality aspects that the school and its governing body exhibit or aim to achieve.

Below, one primary education standard – *Curriculum* – is described in detail.

EP1. Curriculum
The curriculum prepares the pupils for subsequent education and society.

Basic quality
The school offers a broad curriculum based on the core objectives that also incorporates the reference levels for language and basic mathematics and that corresponds to the level (or intended level) of all pupils.

The education assumes that pupils grow up in a pluralist society. For this reason, education is aimed at promoting active citizenship and social integration and at knowledge of and introduction to the various backgrounds and cultures of pupils' peers. The curriculum contributes to the basic values of democracy.

The curriculum corresponds to the school entry level of the pupils, is tailored to the educational needs characteristic of the pupil population and prepares them for the curriculum that is offered when they enter further education. In the intervening time, the teachers distribute the content evenly and coherently through the academic years.

The school puts down the educational objectives and curriculum structure in the school plan.

Self-selected quality aspects
What self-selected goals has the school set out in the school plan, is the school achieving these and, if so, how?
Some possible examples:
- [ ] Future-oriented curriculum
- [ ] Curriculum focused on acquisition of learning strategies
- [ ] An attractive, challenging learning environment

Explanation of legal requirements
The school formulates its educational objectives in the school plan (Article 12.2 of the Wet Primair onderwijs (WPO, Primary Education Act)).

Legislation requires that the content of the education shall focus on emotional and intellectual development, on developing creativity and on acquiring the necessary knowledge and social, cultural and physical skills (WPO, Articles 8.2, 9.1 and 9.2). The subject areas and content are laid down in core objectives and reference levels (WPO, Articles 9.1, 9.2, 9.9 and 9.11) and also comprise the broad development and content related to growing up in a pluralist society, the promotion of active citizenship and social integration, and knowledge of and introduction to the various backgrounds and cultures of pupils' peers (WPO, Article 8.3).

The content of the curriculum should be tailored to the different learning needs of pupils and be distributed evenly and coherently through the academic years (WPO, Article 8.1). That also means that education shall be structured such that systematic and identifiable attention is given to combatting shortcomings in all areas including basic mathematics and, in particular, command of the Dutch language (WPO, Article 8.11). The school prepares the pupils for the start of their subsequent education (WPO, Article 2). The requirement for an uninterrupted progression in pupils' development means that the school should offer the content in a logical order/structure, with levels rising in a manner appropriate to the pupil's age.

The school plan should describe in detail how the legislative instructions for the fundamental principles, objectives and content (WPO, Article 12.2(a)) are implemented. This includes the aims of the education and the curriculum structure.

Inspections

Inspectors assess the standards in the framework by carrying out inspections of governing bodies, schools and programmes. Inspectors talk to governors, school management, teachers, pupils and – in some cases – parents. They also attend lessons, assess the progression in pupils' results and examine the school's documents. At the end of the inspection, the inspector reaches a conclusion regarding the standards and produces a report describing the quality of the school. These reports are actively circulated and published on the Inspectorate website.

A school that does not meet the statutory regulations provides education of insufficient quality. This can lead to sanctions and as a last resort to intervention by the Minister. This does not apply to the self-selected quality aspects, as these are the ambitions and objectives that a governing body or school sets for itself. If these elements make a significant contribution to the school's or programme's educational quality (and its continuous and sustainable improvement) the Inspectorate can rate these aspects as 'good'.

Features of Education Supervision

In the supervision carried out by the Dutch Inspectorate of Education, a number of aspects are important:

- Supervision must be proportionate.
- Supervision is primarily risk-based.
- Supervision should also have a motivating effect.
- The governing body is accountable.

Each of these four features will now be discussed.

Carrying Out Proportionate Supervision

An important aspect of supervision by the Inspectorate is *proportionality*. This means that the Inspectorate does not place any burden on the institutions beyond what is necessary to carry out proper supervision. This can be expressed in three ways:

1. the *frequency* of supervision inspection;
2. the *intensity* of supervision inspection;
3. the manner in which the Inspectorate gathers information to carry out its supervision.

This is implemented in the WOT in the requirement that (a) institutions are not placed under any burden beyond what is necessary to carry out supervision with due care and (b) that the intensity of the supervision is dependent on the quality of the education, the safeguards for the professionalism of the institution and the governing body, the observance of legal requirements and the institution's financial situation (WOT, Articles 4.2 and 4.3).

In the early years of the WOT, little emphasis was placed on proportionality, see Smeets and Verkroost (2011). This was partly due to agreements between the Inspectorate and the Dutch parliament, which was, and still is, keen that all schools should be inspected regularly. The result was that frequency as a selective mechanism did not function well. Furthermore, the Inspectorate itself found it difficult to vary the intensity of its supervision, primarily because it was concerned about missing something and believed in the importance of having a complete picture of a school or programme. And as very few schools supply good self-assessments, in the early years the Inspectorate requested from schools the same amount of information as before. In recent years, matters have improved, but carrying out effective proportionate supervision remains a challenge.

Supervision is Risk-Based

Since 2007, supervision has been *risk-based*, which means that the supervision is focusing on schools where quality or finances are at risk. By taking a risk-based approach, the Inspectorate wishes to prevent schools from dropping below a minimum quality standard. Risk-based supervision is aimed at detecting potentially weak and very weak schools quickly and bringing them up to an acceptable quality level. Supervision is also most effective for underperforming schools and programmes. Here too, the greatest gains are to be made. For good schools and programmes, supervision is more likely to be superfluous and may even get in the way of quality improvements.

The general principles of this risk-based supervision can be summarized in the following key points:

*   A risk analysis takes place (annually or more often) on the basis of information already available about the school or institution.
*   Schools and institutions (or departments within institutions) that on the basis of a risk analysis present evidence of risks, are eligible for (further) investigation.
*   Inspections are not more extensive than necessary and no inspections are conducted in no-risk schools (although other investigations may be carried out).

Figure 5.1 shows a diagram of risk-based supervision. Based on a number of input sources (outcomes, annual accounts and signals), an annual risk analysis is carried out for all schools and programmes. If any risk is identified, further investigation is carried out. If necessary, this results in an inspection of the school or programme.

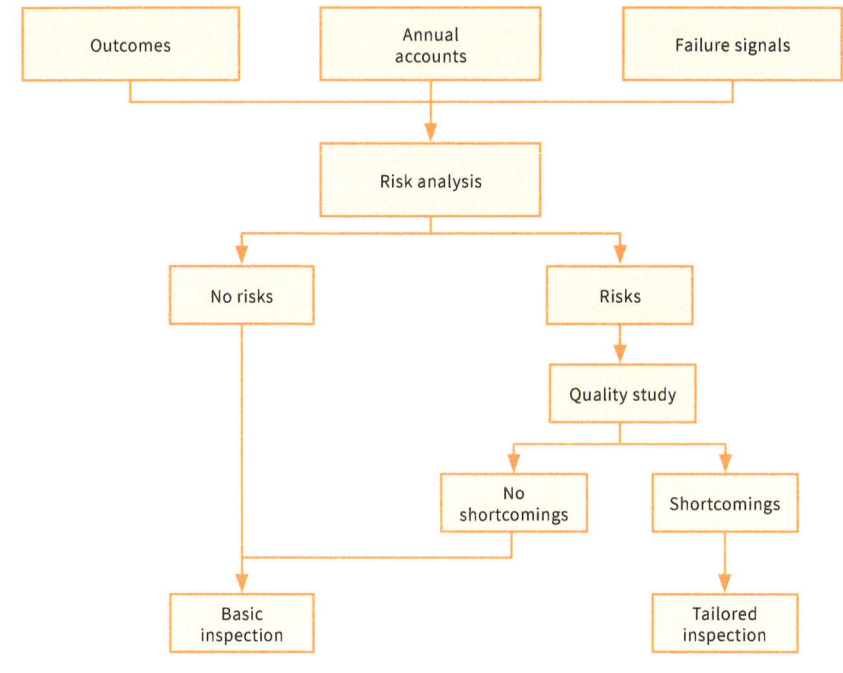

Figure 5.1 *Risk-based supervision (taken from Timmermans, De Wolf, Bosker, Doolaard).*

Potential dangers of risk-based supervision are that the risk model quickly becomes obsolete (also due to strategic behaviour by schools and programmes, see De Wolf & Janssens, 2007) and that inspectors' frames of reference shift when they only, or mainly, visit schools at risk. Partly for these reasons, the Inspectorate always carries out more superficial routine inspections too, alongside risk-based supervision. The Inspectorate uses these routine inspections to ensure it maintains a good overview and to recalibrate the risk model regularly.

The risk-based supervision approach has been evaluated twice (De Wolf and Verkroost, 2011 and Winter, Struiksma and Hollander, 2015). These evaluations revealed that this approach was highly effective in reducing the number of underperforming schools. After a brief increase in this number due to the more focused supervision system, the number dropped in subsequent years to a very low level (between 0.5 and 4 per cent). However, it turned out that this improvement was primarily restricted to the underperforming schools.

Supervision Should Also Have Motivating Effect
Risk-based supervision therefore emerged as very successful in reducing underperforming schools, but did not succeed in motivating the large group of schools performing just above the minimum standard to further improve quality. This closely matches the findings of Matthew and Sammons (2004), who discovered that the effectiveness of Inspectorate supervision was (a)

significant among underperforming schools, (b) largely absent among schools with satisfactory performance and (c) once again significant among schools at the upper end of the spectrum.

This conclusion resulted in 2013 in an initiative to overhaul supervision with the aim of motivating improvement in schools with (just) satisfactory performance. The assessment spectrum for schools, which with the risk-based approach was limited to satisfactory/unsatisfactory[1], was extended at the upper end to include a 'good' rating. Classifying schools as 'good' would stimulate other schools to make improvements and deliver good education. In addition, a number of new motivating elements has been added to the inspection repertoire since 2013. For example, the layout and language used in the reports were substantially revised. And reports are now primarily aimed at school management and teachers. By directing their efforts more explicitly towards teachers, the Inspectorate hopes these reports will play an important role when staff are devising and implementing improvements.

With the more motivating policy, the Inspectorate has also changed its approach of schools. In the risk-based system, an inspector entered a school with the idea that the school might be rated 'unsatisfactory'. In most cases, this expectation was fulfilled. In its inspection and reporting, risk-based supervision focused entirely on the potential presence of shortcomings and, if so, where they could be found. That did not leave much scope for motivating elements. A different tone is used in both oral feedback and reports these days, with explicit scope for positive observations and for more dialogue with the school (for example about the school's own assessment of quality).

The more motivating form of supervision also brings with it a number of inconsistencies and challenges.
1. Is it consistent with the fundamental principles of proportionality? Schools that meet the standards are now being inspected again.
2. Is the Inspectorate the right body to be promoting further quality improvements beyond the legal requirements? And does the Inspectorate have the right methods to achieve this?
3. Shouldn't the Inspectorate restrict itself to determining whether a school or institution meets the legal requirements or not?

As the motivating supervision has only recently been tested in pilot schemes, it is still too early to tell whether it is successful or not. The first evaluations are very favourable and this form of supervision might well be phased in from 1 September 2017.

The Governing Body Is Accountable
A final feature of recent education supervision is a focus on governing bodies instead of on schools. Since 2016, there has been more recognition of the fact that the governing body is

---

[1] With an 'unsatisfactory' rating being further subdivided into two categories: weak and very weak.

accountable for quality. It is also the primary instigator when it comes to taking measures to ensure or improve quality. Nowadays, an assessment of governing bodies and a random sample of its schools is carried out every four years. This assessment focuses on the extent to which this governing body effectively steers on educational quality, how it safeguards improvements of educational quality and how it communicates to the outside world regarding this. In that inspection, the governing body and the schools are jointly investigated and assessed, based on a number of quality aspects.

The quality of management by the governing body of a school/institution determines the way in which the rest of the supervision is carried out. The risk-based component remains, along with the annual risk analysis. But further investigation by the Inspectorate depends largely on the quality of management (or its perception of that quality). A 'good' rating can also be given at school level. This only takes place following an inspection at the request of the governing body and only if the governing body has prepared a proper self-assessment of the school in advance. A 'good' rating is aimed on the one hand at creating a degree of competition between schools and governing bodies, which can result in further improvement of education. On the other hand, it obliges governing bodies to carry out a critical analysis of the situation themselves first, which also sharpens their quality control. Alongside this, all schools are involved in some form of inspection once every four years. It is true that this runs counter to the principle of proportionality, but it reflects the wishes of politicians.

Reflection on system and role of inspectorate

The State of Education in the Netherlands and Activities on Specific Topics
In addition to supervising governing bodies, institutions and schools, the Dutch Inspectorate also has a duty to inform parliament about developments in education. This statutory duty is set out in Article 23 of the Dutch Constitution. The Inspectorate fulfils this duty by publishing the State of Education, an annual report that is sent to parliament (and explained during a discussion with the members of the House of Representatives of the Dutch parliament). The substance of the State of Education is a description of what is going well and what could be improved in schools, in programmes and within the system. The report is independent of schools and policy and is written as far as possible from the pupil's perspective. The State of Education is important to the operation of the Inspectorate because it forces the Inspectorate to keep reflecting on its work. Is it focusing on the right things in its supervision? It protects the Inspectorate against 'capturing' or, as the editor-in-chief of a Dutch newspaper once put it so well: 'so that inspectors describe developments in education, before they become part of it themselves'.

Besides the State of Education in the Netherlands, the Inspectorate of Education also publishes other reports on developments in education. This includes reports on the financial state of education, the national day care assessment, result surveys for primary education, sector overviews for higher education and numerous reports on specific topics. In practice, these reports have significant impact and contribute to improvement of Dutch education and the education system. By describing in detail what inspectors see in practice and supporting this with additional research in key areas, the Inspectorate gives schools, governing bodies, policymakers, politicians and inspectors food for thought and encourages them to improve education.

Cooperation with Academics

The Inspectorate works closely with academics in the field. For example, there is a joint research of inter-rater reliability and quality of supervision. Moreover, the State of Education and a number of reports on specific topics are written in cooperation with academics. One advantage of working with academics is that it ensures objectivity. A supervisory body always has a tendency to develop a particular bias, due to heavy reliance on its supervision tools and activities. Inspectors are more likely to think that there are a lot of deficiencies, as in their work they primarily focus on shortcomings. Inspectors may also tend to think that education quality consists solely of the indicators in the assessment framework and that other aspects of quality are less relevant or irrelevant. Or that the factors in the risk model are actual deficiencies, instead of an indication of a possible issue (including both false positives and false negatives). Academics offer an independent critical eye and quickly expose this unconscious bias. They are also better able to do so partly because they are not stakeholders. They regularly draw inspectors' attention to blind spots (such as bullying, unequal opportunities) and unintended side-effects of supervision. Finally, the close working relationship with academics helps to keep the Inspectorate itself alert and independent; it protects the supervisory body against 'capturing' towards the field of education and the Ministry's policy agenda.

Supervisory Dilemmas

The mode of operation used by the Dutch Inspectorate of Education is described above. This supervisory body has been an important part of the Dutch education system for more than 200 years. Through supervision of schools and programmes and specific topic-related activities, it contributes to improvement of Dutch education and the education system. It is a continuing process to improve supervision and increase its effectiveness. A number of complex dilemmas are at the root of these changes in the Inspectorate's methods. These typify the Dutch education system in general and the Inspectorate of Education in particular.

Dilemma 1: Checking or Motivating

Is it a regulator's primary role to check or to motivate? Every Inspectorate of Education in the world wrestles with this question. The Dutch education system is characterized by a large degree of autonomy for schools and governing bodies. Freedom of education is firmly anchored in Article 23 of the Dutch Constitution and celebrates its centenary this year (see more in Chapter 1). The Netherlands also provides both pupils / students and teachers the freedom to choose a school or institution of their liking. The autonomy and freedom of choice in Dutch education are greatly appreciated and this is one of the most successful aspects of the Dutch education system (see OECD, 2016). It ensures variety within the system and stimulates competition between schools, which often leads to higher-quality education. On top of this, Dutch education does not have a state curriculum; schools are free to organize their own education as long as their pupils meet the key objectives prescribed by law.

What approach can an external regulator best take in such a free education system? Should it focus on checking, to protect pupils in the autonomous education system from underperforming schools and institutions? Or is the proper task of a regulator to motivate and thereby attempt to raise the standard of education at as many schools and programmes as possible? So that all schools bring out the best in their pupils?

Over the decades, the role of the Inspectorate has switched from checking to motivating and vice versa. When the focus was on checking, we saw the regulator primarily checking compliance with legal requirements and taking targeted action to correct shortcomings in education. In the past decade, this mainly took the form of risk-based supervision, which was introduced in 2007 (see above). With risk-based supervision, the focus was on underperforming schools and programmes. When a school or programme was said to be underperforming, the first reaction was generally shock and denial (often enhanced by reports in the press, based on the published lists of very weak schools). After this, teachers and school management got to work to tackle the problem, often supported by their governing bodies, local authorities and in some cases the relevant sector councils. Many of the schools that were rated 'very weak' made significant improvements within a short period of time and became better than the average school. With this risk-based approach, the percentage of weak and very weak schools dropped significantly, from 10 to 15 per cent several years ago to no more than 2 per cent in 2017.

An unintended side-effect of risk-based supervision was a change in the image of the Inspectorate. It came to be regarded as the education police, a bogeyman and an organization that was much too focused on checking easily measurable compliance with legislation and rules. Similar responses are seen in the UK, where Ofsted, the English inspectorate, has always been an inspectorate with a strong focus on checking compliance. And, as we explained above, inspectors also started to behave consistently with this role. They carried out inspections in schools because the risk analysis showed that there were risks. On some occasions, they entered a school with the idea that there must be something going on because 'where there's smoke, there's fire'.

Another effect emerged. With the strict checking approach under risk-based supervision, the percentage of weak and very weak schools did decrease significantly, but at the same time the standard of education as a whole did not rise. Pupils' results did not improve. And on average, the inspectors' ratings also remained unchanged (other than those of the underperforming schools, which did improve). Moreover, there were signs that many schools were quite satisfied if they met the minimum standard set by the Inspectorate. This basic minimum level was regarded as the new standard to aim for, which took away the incentive for schools to improve themselves and achieve good or excellent quality. What turned out to be good supervision for the lower end of the spectrum (focusing on weak schools), did not result in quality improvements in the middle section and at the upper end. And in some cases, it may even have led to a reduction in quality at average or better schools. As a result, the quality of Dutch education remained stable, whereas performance in various other countries improved.

To encourage average and better schools to improve quality, it was decided to focus once again on motivating. This could change perceptions, making supervision more effective again. First, the Ministry created an 'excellent' rating, which rewards very good schools and is intended to motivate average schools to become excellent too. The Inspectorate awards this rating to an increasingly large number of schools each year. Moreover, the Inspectorate also indicates when schools and programmes perform well on *aspects* of the framework and no longer restricts itself to determining when performance is unsatisfactory. The Scottish inspectorate has been doing this for a long time; it has a long tradition of motivating supervision.

Both approaches have advantages and disadvantages. With a checking approach under-performance may be prevented, but there is a risk that non-underperforming institutions are satisfied with their performance and make no extra effort to provide even better education. The supervision also focuses on a limited definition of quality, which is the minimum standard established by law. A motivating approach, on the other hand, works from a broader definition of education quality and motivates schools to improve quality. It does mean that the regulator runs an increased risk of failing to identify underperformers. And of rewarding matters that may turn out unsatisfactory. With its current operation mode, the Inspectorate therefore tries to combine checking and motivating supervision. We will have to wait and see whether this works, but it is already clear that the Inspectorate's image has changed; schools regard it as a critical friend once again (and less as the education police).

Dilemma 2: Public Access and a Transparent Regulator?
Generally, all the Inspectorate of Education's reports and data are publicly accessible. The Inspectorate actively publishes the results of all its inspections and research on the internet, from a report on a primary school to specific topic research into teachers' competencies. The Inspectorate believes that this public access increases confidence both in the regulator and in education. Publication also increases the effectiveness of the Inspectorate's work. It increases

the incentive for school management and governors to bring the quality of their education up to standard or maintain it. And finally, publication improves the quality of the work of the Inspectorate itself. Inspectors and researchers know that their work is publicly accessible, so they make sure it is of good quality. They devote that little bit of extra care to it or check conclusions and findings one more time.

Even before the WOT came into force, there was a move towards public access. This was initiated by a court case brought by a parent, who demanded access to the Inspectorate's conclusions. Her children had attended an underperforming school for years without her knowing. The parent won the court case and since then the inspectors' conclusions and reports about schools have been publicly accessible. This public access was laid down in the WOT. For the Inspectorate, public access is an important element of supervision. For other regulators, publication of findings and conclusions is not a given.

Openness in relation to the Inspectorate's findings and operation mode is intended to contribute to confidence in education and in supervision of it. The level of confidence in education is indeed high. But whether this is actually enhanced by the transparency provided has never been investigated. In her inaugural lecture, De Vries (2016) raises some queries about this. For example, it is possible that openness about incidents gives society the idea that things are not as they should be and danger is everywhere. Moreover, a large degree of openness about the Inspectorate's operation mode could also lead to knowledge of its weak points.

Transparency may also be disadvantageous for the working relationship between school managers/governors and inspectors, which should be based on trust. For a school manager or governor, the threat of publication is always present when speaking to an inspector. Therefore, school managers and governors may be less inclined to share all information openly, hiding any problems from the inspector. They will focus on showing and discussing predominantly positive aspects. Publication can also prevent swift resolution of the problems identified. If a deficiency does become public, a school manager or governor may be more inclined to work on damage control than on resolving the deficiency quickly. Transparency may also result in schools and governing bodies focusing primarily on the aspects made public by the Inspectorate, so not putting their efforts into good education but into optimising the public indicators. This and other types of strategic behaviour are discussed in more detail below.

Dilemma 3: Effects versus Side-Effects

As described above, the effects of supervision are not exclusively positive. There are also unintended and undesirable side-effects. An extensive overview of effects and side-effects of education supervision and accountability in education is provided in De Wolf and Janssens (2007). The main side-effect is window-dressing; teachers, school management and governing bodies generally do their very best to make a good impression. They make sure everything is in (excellent) order for the Inspectorate. This is a human response. The question is at which point this goes too far and becomes undesired strategic behaviour. For example, this would be the case if teachers help their pupils during tests and exams or replace their answers with the correct ones afterwards. This sounds extreme, but it happens in Dutch education too. Or what if a teacher advises a pupil to stay home during a test or exam, with the argument that it's too difficult and they feel sorry for the pupil. This also happens regularly. What message does this send to this pupil? We call this 'reshaping the test pool', keeping low-scoring pupils away from tests and exams. Other ways of reshaping the test pool include having high numbers of weak pupils repeat the pre-exam year (so they can practise for an extra year) or referring relatively high numbers of weak pupils to different types of education or schools. There is also evidence of schools discouraging potentially weak pupils from applying, to improve their 'score'.

Another significant side-effect is a fixation on indicators and a shift in objectives. This occurs when schools and governing bodies primarily focus on the Inspectorate's indicators and these become objectives in themselves. Examples are all indicators relating to pupils' results. These indicators can become objectives for schools. This then leads to strategic behaviour (such as getting large numbers of pupils to repeat a year). Another example is the standard that dealt with the number of education hours. Secondary schools kept students at school for extra hours without engaging them in any educational activity. This quickly became known as 'lock-up hours'. The standard for education hours was aimed at ensuring that students get sufficient hours of good education, but this way it resulted in hours spent pointlessly in order to satisfy the requirement.

Focusing on indicators and standards can also lead to teaching to the test. This occurs when schools primarily focus on matters that the Inspectorate points out to schools (or 'marks them down for', as some schools see it). For example, if the Inspectorate primarily focuses on primary school pupils' results in basic mathematics, schools will be inclined to invest more in maths teaching. They can increase the hours they spend on this, purchase new instruction methods and give the best maths teachers the most critical classes. If this actually improves pupils' performance in basic maths, then there is nothing wrong with it. But this focus on maths may also lead to less attention for other subjects, such as world orientation or culture. If it results in a reduced curriculum, it is often undesirable.

It is important that regulators are aware of these types of strategic behaviour, for which they are partly responsible. For this reason, the Dutch Inspectorate conducts regular research into any side-effects of its supervision. And it revises its assessment framework if there are indications of undesirable types of strategic behaviour. In this context, the Inspectorate does have the tendency to counteract strategic behaviour relating to indicators with new indicators. For example, in secondary education we saw schools giving students increasingly high marks for their non-national school examinations to produce a positive effect on success rates. The Inspectorate responded to this by adopting a new indicator, involving the difference between the school examination and the national examination. This quickly degenerates into a cat-and-mouse game between the Inspectorate and schools. It is questionable whether this results in pupils getting a better education.

In this article we have described education supervision in the Netherlands and outlined some recent developments and dilemmas. It is an ongoing challenge to navigate these dilemmas and maintain the right course. With the ultimate goal to maintain and improve the quality of Dutch education and the education system.

Key Questions
- To what extent does the operation mode used for supervision (the framework, the governing body-based approach and the proportionality) contribute to better education for all pupils?
- To what extent can supervision encourage variety in Dutch education but at the same time protect pupils from excessive differences in quality between schools?
- Governing bodies are accountable for the quality of the education in schools. Do they now face dilemmas regarding checking (what is the quality of the school?) and motivating to improve? Does their requirement for accountability of schools get in the way of quality improvement in schools?

About the authors

Prof. dr. Inge de Wolf is a coordinating inspector at the Inspectorate of Education and endowed professor specializing in the education system at the University of Maastricht. She is responsible for the Dutch Inspectorate's State of Education publication and works on improving supervision. Her academic research covers the quality of schools, the education system and the effects (and side-effects) of supervision. She also participates in projects for the OECD and the World Bank.

Contact: i.dewolf@owinsp.nl.

Dr. Jos Verkroost is a coordinating inspector. He assisted in establishing risk-based supervision and in the development and set-up of governing body-based supervision. He also designed the Inspectorate's enforcement policy and works on the integration of financial and quality supervision. In 2016, he completed a doctorate in these subjects at the Erasmus University in Rotterdam.

Contact: j.verkroost@owinsp.nl.

Drs. Herman Franssen is a primary education inspector. One of his roles is coordinator of international cooperation with other European education inspectorates. In recent years, he has been involved in the training of new inspectors and increasing professionalism among inspectors with respect to Dutch language teaching.

Contact: h.franssen@owinsp.nl.

References

De Vries, F. (2016) Leidt transparantie tot meer vertrouwen in de toezichthouder? (Does transparancy results in higher trust in inspectorates?) Inaugural lecture, Groningen University.

De Wolf, I.F., & Janssens, F.J.G. (2007). Effects and side effects of inspections and accountability in education: an overview of empirical studies. *Oxford Review of Education, 33*(3), 379-396.

De Wolf, I.F., & Verkroost, J.J.H. (2011). Evaluatie van de theorie en praktijk van het nieuwe onderwijstoezicht. [Evaluation of the theory and practice of the new style of education supervision.] *Tijdschrift voor Toezicht, 2*(2), 7-24.

Ehren (2006). Toezicht en schoolverbetering. (Supervision and school improvement.) Dissertation University of Twente.

Inspectie van het onderwijs (Dutch Inspectorate of Education) (2016). *Onderzoekkader 2017 voor het toezicht op voorschoolse educatie en primair onderwijs.* [Research framework 2017 for supervision of pre-school education and primary education.] Utrecht: Inspectie van het Onderwijs.

Matthews, P., & Sammons, P. (2004). *Improvement through inspection. An evaluation of the impact of Ofsted's work.* London: HMI.

Scheerens, J., Seidel, T., Witziers, B., Hendriks, M. & Doornekamp, G. (2005). Positioning and Validating the Supervision Framework. Enschede: University of Twente.

Smeets, G., & Verkroost, J.J.H. (2011). *Selectief en slagvaardig. Werken met de WOT (2000-2010).* [Selective and efficient. Working with the Act on the Inspectorate of Education (2000-2010).] Utrecht: Inspectie van het Onderwijs.

Timmermans, A.C., De Wolf, I.F., Bosker, R.J., & Doolaard, S. (2015). Risk-based educational accountability in Dutch primary education. *Educational Assessment, Evaluation and Accountability, 27*(4), 323-346.

Winter, H., Struiksma, N., & Hollander, M. (2015). *De selectiviteit, efficiency en effectiviteit van het risicogerichte toezicht op grond van de WOT.* [The selectiveness, efficiency and effectiveness of risk-based supervision under the Act on the Inspectorate of Education.] Groningen: Rijksuniversiteit Groningen.

NYNKE
VAN DER SLUIS
PARENT

'I DON'T THINK PRIMARY SCHOOLS CAN MANAGE WITHOUT PARENTS THESE DAYS'

Mother to Fardau (aged 9) and Sven (aged 7), Nynke van der Sluis is a firm believer in the importance of getting parents and pupils actively involved in the education process. This is the reason she became chairman of the parent/teacher participation council at her children's school. But Nynke also believes that many more parties should be involved in shaping Dutch education.

'Education in the Netherlands has changed a great deal over the past year. It seems to me that the pace of change is accelerating. Particularly when it comes to the teacher's role. There are no longer hard and fast rules about how to teach or about the form lessons should take. Of course, teachers still have to work within the framework set out by the government, but they are also given the scope to create their own identities. The same applies to schools and to the pupils who attend them.'

CHILDREN CAN BE THEMSELVES

'I'm very proud that my children go to a school where they're allowed to be themselves. They are really challenged to look at the world in an open and inquiring way. They are asked what they want to learn instead of told what they have to learn. This means every child can develop in its own way and I think that's a really good thing.'

"I'm very proud that my children are allowed to be themselves at school."

PARENTAL INVOLVEMENT

'Where 5 years ago the school board would have told us exactly how everything worked, these days we parents are being asked for more involvement. I don't even think primary schools can manage without parents any longer. At my children's school we are asked to take an active part in shaping the policy of the school. And you see this happening in more and more schools. Through participation councils, parent panels and pupil councils.

It's not just happening regionally, at my children's school. At national level too, there are increasing numbers of parent organizations representing the interests of parents and

"More and more is being required of our children, requiring teachers to be flexible too."

children. Although schools have different identities, they are working together – where possible – and finding ways to empower each other by combining forces, expertise and funds. This can take all kinds of forms, from joint sports days for schools in small villages to a complete regional child welfare team.'

CONTINUALLY CHALLENGING ONE ANOTHER

'I think we need to keep challenging each other. In my view, Dutch education in the future should be aimed at training our children to be enterprising, creative, inquiring and innovative professionals. More and more knowledge and skills are being required of them, so that they can adapt to all kinds of situations. This requires teachers to be flexible too. Education will always keep evolving and be subject to political and technological developments such as digitization and robotization. A huge challenge that requires a good cooperation of all parties involved. That's the only way to ensure my children can go on learning throughout their lives.' ‹

Chapter 6

Excellence in Emancipation, a Century-Long Search for Balance

Prof. dr. Marc Vermeulen & Prof. dr. Sietske Waslander,
TIAS Tilburg University

ntroduction

During the last century, education was without a doubt one of the great equalizing forces in Dutch society. Due to unique historic circumstances, the Dutch education system has some very specific characteristics. These features have contributed in important ways to the emancipation of women, children from lower socio-economic backgrounds, and religious groups, particularly Catholics. The emancipatory role of education has in that sense been exemplary. However, educational opportunities are by no means distributed equally today. For example: students from ethnic minority groups in the Netherlands do relatively worse when compared to other European countries. Also, inequality of educational opportunities by socio-economic background is increasing. With the turn of the century, characteristics that for so long contributed to excellence in education, have come under increasing pressure. This poses new challenges to The Dutch Way.

A Turning Point

In Dutch politics, 1917 was a remarkable year. After very contentious elections in 1913, no coalition government could be established in the highly divided political landscape. An extra-parliamentary government of many non-politicians took office. Under pressure of the First World War – in which the Netherlands did not take part and kept its neutrality – this unusual government did remarkable things. By revising the constitution, the so called Pacification settled several issues that had almost torn the country apart. Two revisions were particularly important for emancipation. Firstly, the process of achieving gender equality in political representation was started. Secondly, equal funding rights for schools were secured in the constitution. Publicly and privately run (religion-based) schools gained the right of equal funding, while upholding the freedom of education. This meant that all religious groups were free to start their own schools, which were all eligible for public funding (See more in Chapter 1).

Obviously 1917 was a special year, one of the darkest years in Europe. The industrial massacres of the First World War defied every imagination and the Russian Revolution brought communism into power. Those threatening conditions opened a political window of opportunity in Dutch politics that made groundbreaking emancipations possible.

At the beginning of the 20th century, the Netherlands was struggling with a combination of three major emancipatory issues, all related to industrialization and modernization:
* the so-called *social question*: how could capitalism be balanced with social demands of laborers, reasonable payments and fair and safe working conditions;
* *gender equality*: social, political and economic male dominance was challenged by women;
* *religious emancipation*, particularly of Catholics. In the 19th century, state and church were separated by law, but since Protestants (e.g. the royalty) dominated the political system, the

position of Catholics in society was far from equal. When religious groups were given the right to start their own schools with equal public funding and minimal curricular guidance, both Catholic and Protestant (and to a lesser extent Jewish) education became an important tool for the emancipation of religious groups.

For over a century, the Dutch educational system has undeniably played a crucial role in the emancipation of women, people from lower social economic backgrounds, and people with various religious backgrounds.

This chapter of *The Dutch Way* investigates how the education system – which was so successful for emancipation in the past – holds up when looking to the future. A hundred years after 1917, emancipation issues have not vanished. We will focus on three issues: gender, social background and ethnicity. Although women have entered the educational system on a large scale, remaining gender differences in education are persistent, and gender inequality in the labor market is still substantial. Despite the fact that social economic background has become less important for school success, the latest figures point to growing inequality. The emancipation of migrants in the Netherlands, specifically those with a Muslim background, remains a big issue.

Education Matters

Education may be seen as one of the few positive or optimistic institutions in the modern welfare state. While other institutions deal with problems and threats (poverty, illness, insecurity, etc.), education is by definition hopeful. It is geared towards a better future, is concerned with developing talent and opportunities, and helps youngsters to find their way in society.

Education plays an important role in the distribution of wealth and happiness in society. To give just two examples: the chances of being unemployed are four times higher for people with a low level of education than for people with a high level of education (Vrooman et al., 2014). Obviously, unemployment risks follow the business cycle. But the lower educated are more vulnerable to these cycles than the higher educated. For the last thirty years, the difference in unemployment risk between educational levels is increasing rather than decreasing. If we look at health differences between people with different levels of education, we find a similar pattern. On average, people with a degree in higher education live five to six years longer than people with low educational credentials. Even more significantly, not only mortality differs. Higher-educated people have a much healthier life than lower-educated people. Higher-educated people report up to twenty years more *living in good health* than people with only lower education (Vrooman op.cit.).

We could extend this list with data on divorce, crime, housing conditions, political and religious extremism, and so forth, and show similar patterns over and over again. Such indicators are of course interconnected, and to a large extent reflect competencies to survive in modern societies. In a way, the impact of education in all those fields is good news. The meritocratic ideal holds that chances in life should be based on individual merit, talent and achievement, instead of on ascribed characteristics such as gender, social background or ethnicity. Modern societies are willing to put considerable amounts of money and political and legal pressure into fulfilling this meritocratic ideal.

Meritocracy and Modernization: Idea and Critics

In pre-modern societies, social positions were inherited. The famous Dutch artist Louis Davids had a brilliant song in the early thirties of the last century: 'You will never become a quarter when you are born a dime', meaning that if you are born poor, you will remain so all your life. Social background determined your social position no matter your capacities or motivations. The idea of modern societies is that social positions (and thus social inequality e.g. in income or influence) should be distributed according to capacity lines. The most talented may have the most influence, no matter their social background. Merit determines position, thus the word meritocracy. Education was the place to discover and develop talents and thus became a key in modernization.

As early as 1958, the famous British sociologist Sir Michael Young drew –in his book *The Rise of Meritocracy* – a grim picture of a perfect meritocratic society, if all social positions were to be distributed on the basis of talents and degrees. Degrees are the results of talents (IQ) and effort. But what happens if you do not have the talents to be competitive? Your position will be at the lower end of the social ladder and the system cannot be blamed for it.

Interestingly enough, Young had a hard time getting his ideas published. He redid his work in the form of a satiric novel, stepping in the tradition of Aldous Huxley's *Brave New World*, a dystopian novel published in 1932. Meritocracy sounds as a good idea and probably is, but it has a number of dark sides to it. The first one would be a too narrow focus on talents and efforts and a neglect of other personal characteristics giving rise to new forms of unjustified inequality (Rawls, 1972). Dahrendorf (2005) elaborates on this by drawing attention to the question who is to blame if you are not in a good position. Before meritocracy, this could be attributed to external factors (parents, family background, gender) but now it is only attributable to yourself (lack of talent and/or effort). Guinier (2015) criticizes the *tyranny of meritocracy* because of the rat race it produces for positions in higher education and the dehumanization of curricula as consequence of this.

> For the Netherlands, Elshout et al. (2016) follow up on this by looking at self-esteem of people at the bottom of the meritocracy. Bovens and Wille (2015) ask our attention for the lack of political power, frustration and the increase of extremist political views by those who are outside the degree democracy as they call it.

However, the fact that a society has turned into a meritocracy does not imply that social background or other inherited characteristics are no longer important. Rather, their impact on one's social position has changed from direct to indirect. While social positions were once directly inherited from one generation to the next, nowadays educational credentials are key. Because these characteristics continue to influence educational credentials, they continue to impact one's social position, but indirectly. More importantly, educational credentials are not only indicators of better schooling and higher productivity which are converted into higher earnings in the labor market and more advantageous social positions in society. Education is also – in economic terms – a positional good. That is to say, the value of one's educational credentials is not absolute, but depends on the educational credentials of others. In many social processes, it is the relative position in an imaginary queue which is most important (Hirsch, 1977). Being ahead of others is what matters most. As education becomes more important in the distribution of social positions in society, the other side of the coin is that education increasingly turns into a rat race.

Expansion in Education

As in many other Western countries, educational participation has increased enormously in the Netherlands. Roughly one out of four inhabitants in the Netherlands is in one way or another in education. The teaching sector is a very large sector, with over half a million employees. The growth of education can be illustrated by looking at different age groups. In 1960, of all 18-year-olds only one out of five was in education. In 2016, this is completely reversed: now four out of five are in education. Of 22-year-olds, in 1960 only a few percent was in education whereas in 2016, almost half of this age group is in some form of education. From an international perspective, educational participation is rather high in the Netherlands. As far as educational enrolment for people aged 20-29 in Europe is concerned, NL is in the top 5 (32%, Finland 45%). This is above average (28%). France, for instance, only has a 21% enrolment in this age group.

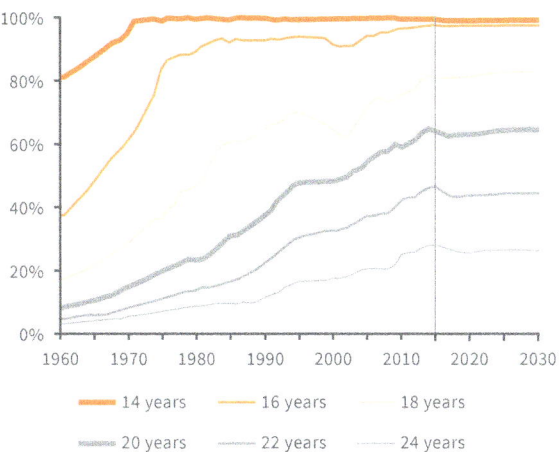

Figure 6.1   *Full-time education enrolment in the Netherlands per age. Source: Ministry of Education, Culture and Science (2016).*

Educational participation has definitely enhanced the educational levels in the labor force. In the sixties of the last century, only one out of ten employees had higher education, now it is over 40%. This in itself is a necessary precondition for high-level economic development (knowledge economy) and is stimulated for this reason. However, there is some overproduction. The educational level of the population increases more rapidly than the labor market can absorb. According to Salverda (2016), almost one quarter of all employees has a higher degree than necessary for their job. For higher-educated employees this is 40%, and this has not changed between 1990-2010.

Women have caught up on their backlog in educational level. In the first year enrolment in higher education, female students are a small majority (52%). Interestingly, this is not evenly distributed over the various sectors, as men and women still tend to have rather traditional patterns in their choice for specific disciplines and sectors in education (Volman, 2016).

Differences in educational attainments between religious groups have disappeared, with the important exception of migrants (Muslims). Migrants are still at a distance in educational attainment from non-migrants, but they are catching up. The percentage of migrant students entering higher education has increased more than this percentage for non-migrants. Interestingly enough, it is specifically the group of female migrants that seems to catch up rapidly (see Chapter 7).

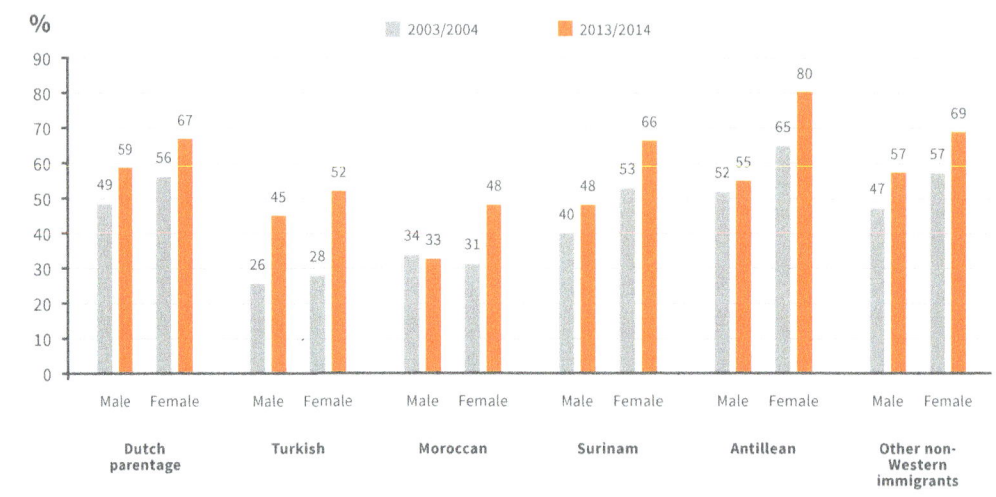

Figure 6.2 *Trends influx higher education. Source: Nederlands Jeugdinstituut ([Netherlands Youth Institute], 2015).*

Social Inequality in Educational Attainment

Differences in educational attainment are still related to differences in social background of families. Three interconnected mechanisms are at play here. First, even at a very young age, children come to school with different competencies related to their social background. This is partly due to inherited characteristics and partly to differences in childrearing practices, particularly with regard to early language acquisition. As research shows, due to the plasticity of the brain, inherited and acquired differences cannot be distinguished (Leseman, 2005). Secondly, once in school not only the extent to which, but more importantly the way in which parents stimulate children to perform, is related to social conditions of the family (Deforges & Abouchaar, 2003; Bakker et al., 2014). Apart from direct parental support, higher-educated parents support their children more often by 'buying' additional support in the form of tutors and test training. Higher-educated parents also tend to have stronger social networks which are advantageous for children and help them in schools. The third mechanism points to processes in schools. Teachers have different expectations of pupils related to their gender, social background and ethnicity. A clear and very recent example of this lies in the fact that pupils with different backgrounds but similar test scores at the end of primary education, are referred to different educational tracks in secondary education (Dutch Inspectorate of Education, 2016).

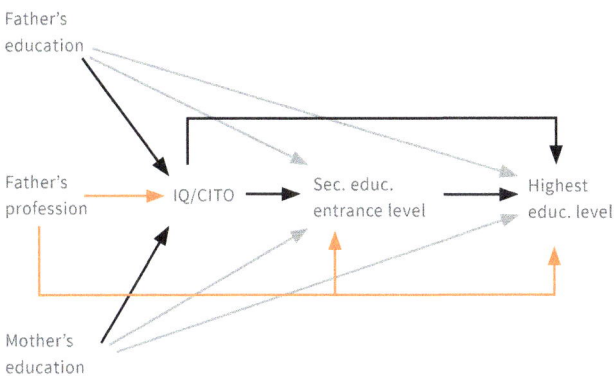

Note: Black arrows consistent with meritocracy; orange arrows
inconsistent with meritocracy; grey arrows indicate uncertainty

Figure 6.3   Education career model.

Dronkers and Van de Werfhorst (2016) present the model above to explain how parental characteristics may influence educational attainment of children in different stages of the education career. Their conclusion is that parental influence is still strong on primary school results (as measured by a general aptitude test CITO). These test scores at the end of primary education have an important impact on choices in secondary education. As the most recent data shows, the educational level of parents continues to have an effect for the whole education career and even into the labor market (Dutch Inspectorate of Education, 2016). All these small influences at any one moment add up over time, so that there is a distinct effect of parental educational level when children reach the end of their education career. Interestingly, the impact of the *education* of parents has become more important, whereas the impact of occupational status (and thus income) has decreased. The social impact on educational performance of children appears to be more cultural than material in nature. This is confirmed by Buis (2015), who used large cohort data to analyze how the impact of fathers' occupational status influences the educational attainments of sons and daughters. He was able to reconstruct this impact for persons born between 1910 and 1990. For those, both the parental occupational status (father) and their own highest level of completed education are known. Comparing birth cohorts over time, he found that for men the parental effect in the oldest cohorts was lower but increased until after the Second World War. After the war, this effect started to decrease again. For the youngest cohorts – those born after 1970 – the effect of parental education is still decreasing, but only slowly. For women, the pattern is slightly different. The impact of the occupational status of fathers on their daughters' educational level decreased continuously over time. Furthermore, this relation seems to continue to decrease for the youngest cohorts, rather than slowing down as it does for men.

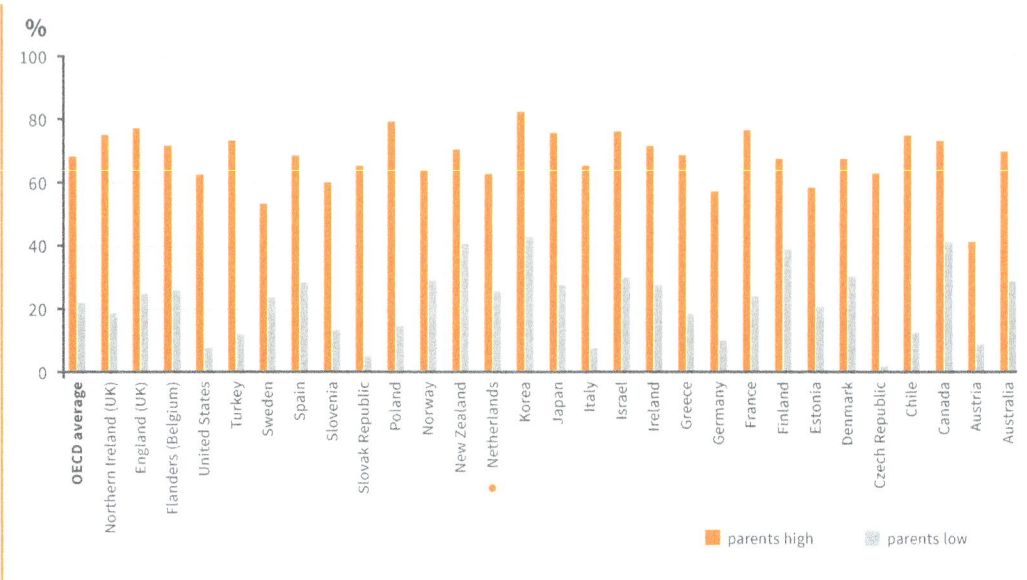

Figure 6.4 *Children in tertiary education by parental educational background.*

The Organization for Economic Co-operation and Development (OECD, 2016, Education at a Glance, table A4.3) provides interesting insights regarding international variation in the extent to which social background influences educational performance. Within the OECD countries, on average 22% of the children from parents with less than upper secondary education, completed higher education. Of the children from families with parents having higher education, 68% complete higher education themselves. For the Netherlands, this is 26% and 63%, so a slightly smaller gap. The smallest gaps between higher- and lower-educated families bringing their children to higher education are in Finland and New Zealand. Extreme large gaps are found in former communist countries such as the Czech Republic, but for instance also in Germany. Based on the same data, we can compare migrant and non-migrant families. In the Netherlands, the chance of migrant and non-migrant parents with a low level of education bringing their children to higher education, is 29% for migrant families and 18% for non-migrants. For the OECD as a whole, these difference are much smaller. This is to a large extent the effect of traditional migrant countries such as Australia and New Zealand, where migrants have the better options compared to non-migrants. More or less the same can be seen in the UK.

The End of the Meritocracy?

The large expansion of education also implies that the emancipatory role of the Dutch education system may slowly but surely grind to a halt. Many people attain more or less the highest level of education available within the current system. Education was a motor for emancipation and for a long time, parents' ideal was for their children to reach for a higher level of education than they had attained themselves. However, when parents complete the highest level of education, by sheer logic their children cannot reach higher. Therefore, chances of downward education mobility – when children complete lower levels of education than their parents – increase. Thijssen and Wolbers (2015) show some first indication of this development. The percentage of men with a *lower*-level education than their parents increases over time. For women this is not (yet) the case.

Although increasing rates of downward education mobility is by no means a specific Dutch phenomenon (OECD, 2015a), these trends do pose particular challenges. The Dutch education system has specific features which have contributed to its successful emancipatory role in the last century. Precisely these features are currently under increasing pressure. Three typically Dutch features stand out.

This chapter started with the constitutional freedom of education and rights of *equal public funding* for schools. These rights are deeply ingrained in the whole education system and in education policy. The autonomy of school boards is almost unsurpassed in the world (OECD, 2015b). The Netherlands has no national curriculum, nor are there any formal requirements for education professionals other than teachers (e.g. principals, board members). The right of public funding enabled a wide variety of schools within the public system itself. The private sector has therefore long been almost non-existent. Nowadays, this sector is still small by international comparison, but growing very rapidly. For example: the main private provider of secondary education – Luzac – saw its student numbers increase with more than 1000% between 2006 and 2015 (Luzac, 2015). A growing private sector poses new challenges to the emancipatory role of the education system as a whole.

A second feature can be found in the combination of selection at the age of twelve, and a highly tracked system of secondary education. Formally, there are seven different tracks, informally there are at least eight. According to the law, the highest track is VWO, or preparatory university education. In lieu of formal recognition, the gymnasia – that offer a classic education with Latin and Greek – have survived as independent schools catering mostly for the elite. For long, the potentially negative impact of early selection was offset by a mandatory standardized test at the end of primary school. Placement in different tracks was mainly based on these test scores. Recently, the market for tests at the end of primary education was opened up, which has resulted in a growing number of test providers. These tests differ not only in nature, but also in difficulty. More importantly, test scores have become less important for track placement in favor of advice given by teachers. These changes make track placement more vulnerable to influences of social background, which is exactly what has been shown lately (Dutch Inspectorate of Education, 2015). At the same time, the number of independent gymnasia has increased as did the number of students attending gymnasia. Because the government does not distinguish these schools in its registrations, full data are not available. Another indication for 'differentiation at the top' is a rising number of schools with selective profiles and sometimes completely separate tracks in the area of science, culture or foreign languages (see also Weenink, 2009). Current data and registrations, including national standardized examinations, are unsusceptible for these 'differentiations at the top'. That is not to say that these differences do not matter when it comes to access to higher education, or finding a job.

The third typical feature of Dutch education is the large sector of vocational education, catering for roughly half of all pupils (Karsten, 2016). While the choice for vocational education is in many countries associated with hampered educational opportunities, in the Netherlands the vocational sector has served a very important emancipatory role (see more in Chapter 8). A strong feature of the Dutch education system is that all tracks of vocational education give access to higher levels of vocational education, all the way to bachelor, and more recently also master, degrees. Students who are placed in vocational tracks at the age of twelve, can therefore still attain higher education. This feature is now under increased pressure as the number of students utilizing these opportunities is decreasing. This is particularly the case for students finishing vocational education at the medium level who could continue in higher education. Following the major expansion of higher education, in combination with hardly increasing budgets over the last twenty years, institutions for higher education are looking for ways to cope (see more in Chapter 7). A growing number of programs in higher education is selective, blocking and/or discouraging chances for these students to gain access (Fettelaar et al., 2013). Also, a system of student grants was recently abolished in favor of student loans. This may also discourage students, particularly those from lower socio-economic and ethnic backgrounds.

Synthesis, a Mixed Challenge for Education

Although a strong emancipation has taken place in Dutch society over the last century and education played a major role in this, not all chances are distributed fairly in our society today. Dutch society can be divided in three different social categories, all creating their own specific challenges for education. In Figure 6.5 we tried to schematize this.

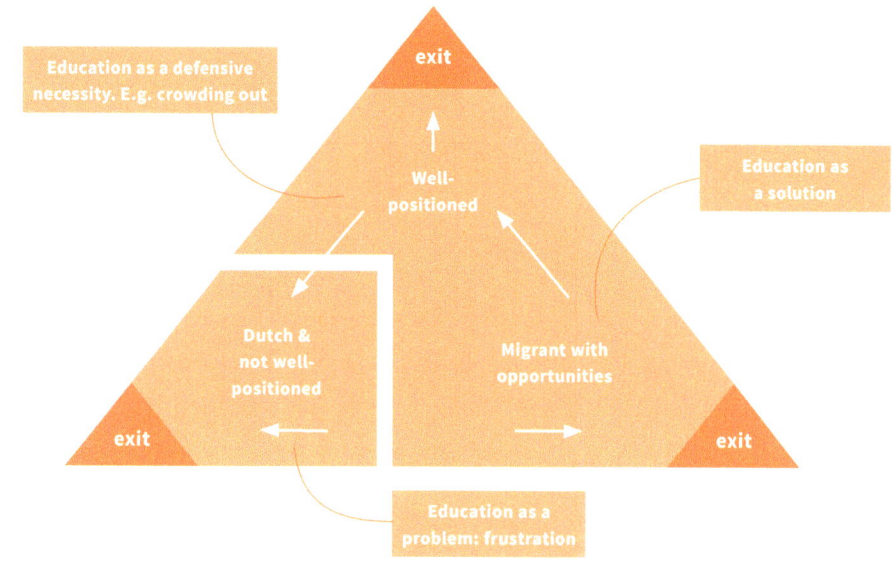

Figure 6.5 *Tension in the role education plays.*

In the upper part of the pyramid are the *haves* of our society, the people that have strong social and economic positions. (Upper) middle class people have good incomes, own their houses, work in steady and rewarding jobs, etc. Education backed up their position, brought them where they are, professionals and thus well to do. The main challenge here is to prevent downward education mobility, so that their children have equal chances in society.

In the lower right corner, we represented a group of not-yet-establishment, most of them having migrant backgrounds. They do have talents and capacities, but education has not served them *yet* because of a lack of social and cultural capital. For this group, more and better education continues to hold the promise of emancipation.

In the lower left corner of the triangle, the promise of emancipation through education has come to nothing. Here we find people who were unable to succeed in education because of a lack of personal skills and talents. They may have had good opportunities, but failed to cash in on them. Negative selection and crowding out may be the cause of their position. More education doesn't help them because of a lack of capacities. In a society that is increasingly meritocratic, lack of success is considered a personal failure. Most notably, also by people themselves (e.g. Mijs, 2016). Here we find the victims of the meritocracy.

In all three corners of the triangle we might find extreme positions. In the top corner, this will be abundant hedonist behavior, tax avoidance etc. There is no positive contribution to society at large. In the lower right side, frustration over social exclusion may take forms of extremism, violence etc. that we might witness e.g. in criminal behavior, support for IS, etc. This group may include young migrants who are not willing to profit from education because they failed earlier or faced discrimination. In the lower left side, we also see forms of extremism and violence, e.g. in motor gangs, drug networks etc. Institution in the Dutch society has failed to find a room for this group and there are no prospects that their positions will improve. Rightwing political extremism may be stirred by this position (Bovens & Wille, 2011).

For all three positions, educational efforts are quite different. Starting with the group in the lower right corner, education will provide solutions and thus optimism. If young migrants get better qualifications, the road to the (migrant) middle class is still open (Crul, 2016). Upward social mobility is a positive prospect and education will be the means to that. Schools can play their role as opportunity builders and teachers will have a positive impact and an agenda helping young people to a better future.

For the establishment, education is more of a defensive necessity (a term already coined in 1973 by Daniel Bell). It may not bring you very many extras but you will lose your position in the establishment if you do not get the right credentials. Another part of the same game is that regular higher education is not enough anymore, you need to have some add-ons in order to stand out in the competitive elite. MBAs at business schools, smaller university colleges, traineeships abroad and extra-curricular activities will provide extra profile to your resume. Schools catering for this group need to be exclusive, they must provide extra status. Creating a new inner circle is probably not so much a cognitive and instrumental matter, but more a social and cultural issue. Teachers should be able to provide this chic and elite type of role models. Within the public system, the pressure to expand into extra education has a risk of becoming ineffective. Overinvestment in higher education, serving only the elite to preserve their positions, may not be a good public option. The market will catch up in this segment by all forms of private initiatives but that in itself may erode a public investment in emancipation and mobility. Will private mobility crowd out public emancipation?

On the lower left side, education may play a grim role, not being able to provide emancipation and new horizons. More of the same education does not work for this group, because it is where they failed the first time. In a way, extra education puts this group even more at a distance from the other two positions, educational defensive barriers make it harder and harder to compete with the establishment and the success of migrants in education may provide an extra threat to their position. However, education does play a role in the following ways:
1. It has to be able to select on a fair basis, excluding social impacts as much as possible.
2. It may provide –in close cooperation with other social organizations – new socialization and qualification mechanisms empowering low-ability people to some form of sustainable position in society.
3. Non-scholarly but emancipatory interventions by social services will be useful for people in major life events (birth of children, health issues etc.).

4. Recognition of prior and informal learning may also play a role in providing opportunities for people in this group.

Finally, all three positions have their own form of extremism and for all three positions education may play a role in keeping people from going into a social exit. Personal attention for frustrating experiences, active social inclusion and citizenship are at stake for all three positions.

The Way Forward

The above may be too schematized and polarized, but the underlying dynamics are already very visible in Dutch society and in Dutch schools. In our view, it may be uncomfortable but realistic to face the flip sight of educational expansion and meritocracy.

Concluding that education dug its own grave by expanding so much, could be considered tragic, but this would be too pessimistic. A new realism, looking for new ways of providing social positions and emancipations might be more fruitful. Going back one hundred years, four mechanisms provided a basis for emancipation in the Netherlands:

- *Congruence*: an alignment between values of schools and the larger social group they worked for. This brought a strong sense of ownership in society for education.
- *Competition*: a peaceful competition between religious groups – organized in their own pillars – provided a mechanism to deal with possible toxic social differences. Each group could show its quality and compete with others.
- *Compensation*: the differentiated system provided some forms of targeted compensation: not all schools were treated in the same way, not only on a financial level, but also in terms of political support, etc.
- *Coordination*: although school systems were pillarized, in the top of the system all forms of coordination took place, both formal (national educational policies) and informal (elites looking for forms of mutual understanding).

In a way, those mechanisms have lost their strength in the Dutch educational system. Coordination became elitist and bureaucratic, competition between schools sometimes brought a waste of energy and budgets. Parents hardly feel strongly committed to schools of *their* pillar (with an exception for Muslim schools). Specific compensation has lost its rationale and became a bureaucratic burden.

The challenges education face are complex and dynamic, may even be framed as wicked problems. Such problems call for new forms of organizing education, social innovations and out-of-the-box solutions. It may be seen as a call for coordinated anarchy, where many different types of schools may grow, but within a larger institutional frame. Flexibility and balance is what we are looking for. The distributed system we still have, may -with some re-invention – provide a good basis to answer current challenges. If we, for instance, would define *new pillars*, this might induce new forms of commitment and give new energy to coordination. A distributed system also provides better opportunities for specific and situational extra compensation both in terms of budgets and in terms of moral support, networks etc. And lastly, smart competition may help to bring out quality again and may open options for new initiatives, challenging old institutions.

Key Questions

- How a differentiated system, with an early choice at the age of 12, may provide new tailor-made solutions to promote emancipation? Differentiation can cause lock-ins but can also provide opportunities to specifically address needs and issues of targeted groups. Can planned and mild forms of exclusion be at the base of strong forms of inclusion?
- Social innovation may bring a new configuration of schooling, labor and social networks. What would be the role of these innovations, induced and/or supported by new technologies, for groups that have lost their prospects on mobility within regular education? Social entrepreneurship may be a way of carving out new job opportunities and new social positions for people who seem to get the worst of social positions at this moment.
- How could some forms of coordination be introduced in a system where schools are very autonomous, without losing the strength of autonomy. The independence of schools and the lack of a strong national regulation seem to have worked well. However, a number of social issues, such as inclusion and the prevention of exits, call for some form of collaborative action. What would be the spark for collaboration? Regions, networks, pop-ups?
We see a fascinating scene ahead of us: old and new emancipation issues projected on an educational system that proved to be able to provide effective pathways one hundred years ago and is challenged to provide such pathways once again.

About the authors

Prof. dr. Marc Vermeulen is a professor of strategy, innovation and governance for non-profits at TIAS, School for Business and Society and a professor of sociology of education at Tilburg University and at the Dutch Open University. He specializes in strategic analyses of public organizations as a researcher, a teacher and a consultant. Effective social inclusion and public value management are at the core of his work.

Contact: m.vermeulen@tias.edu.

Prof. dr. Sietske Waslander is professor of sociology at TIAS, School for Business and Society. She is also a member of the Education Council. She has an active interest in all aspects of educational sociology; she has published work on subjects ranging from market forces and tailored education to mass-customisation, educational innovation, the curriculum and leadership. She has also carried out several analyses of the public and political debate about education. Her research and teaching is aimed at connecting research, policy and practice.

Contact: s.waslander@tias.edu.

References

Andarabi-van Klaveren, D. (2015). *Uitgaven voor onderwijs 2013. Trends en ontwikkelingen.* [Educational expenses 2013. Trends and developments.] The Hague: CBS.

Bakker, J., Denessen, E., Denissen, M., & Oolbekking-Marchand, H. (2014). *Leraren en ouderbetrokkenheid. Een reviewstudie naar de effectiviteit van ouderbetrokkenheid en de rol die leraren daarbij kunnen vervullen.* [Teachers and parental involvement. A review study of the effectiveness of parental involvement and the role that teachers may play.] Nijmegen: Radboud Universiteit Nijmegen.

Bovens, M., & Wille, A. (2011). Diplomademocratie. *Over de spanning tussen meritocratie en democratie.* [Diploma democracy. On the tensions between meritocracy and democracy.] Amsterdam: Bert Bakker.

Buis, M. (2015). Langetermijntrends in onderwijsuitkomsten in Nederland. [Long-term trends in educational results in the Netherlands.] In H. v.d. Werfhorst (Red.). *Een kloof van alle tijden.* [A gap of all times.] Amsterdam: Amsterdam University Press.

Crul, M. (2016). Super-diversity vs. assimilation: how complex diversity in majority–minority cities challenges the assumptions of assimilation. *Journal of Ethnic and Migration Studies, 42*(1), 54-68.

Dahrendorf, R. (2005). *The rise and fall of meritocracy.* Retrieved from https://www. project-syndicate.org/commentary/the-rise-and-fall-of-meritocracy?barrier =accessreg#Dg4gMP3qTl8Dbjof.99.

Deforges, C., & Abouchaar, A. (2003). *The impact of parental involvement, parental support and family education on pupil achievement and adjustment: a literature review.* Nottingham: Department for Education and skills, Queen's Printer.

Dronkers, J., & Van de Werfhorst, H. (2016). Meritocratisering in schoolloopbanen in Nederland. [Meritocratization in school careers in the Netherlands.] In P. de Beer & M. van Pinxteren. *Meritocratie. Op weg naar een nieuwe klassensamenleving?* [Meritocracy. On the road to a new class society?] Amsterdam: Amsterdam University Press.

Elshout, J., Tonkens, E., & Swierstra, T. (2016). Meritocratie als aanslag op het zelfrespect van 'verliezers'. [Meritocracy as an attack on the selfrespect of 'losers'.] In P. de Beer & M. van Pinxteren. *Meritocratie. Op weg naar een nieuwe klassensamenleving?* [Meritocracy. On the road to a new class society?] Amsterdam: Amsterdam University Press.

Fettelaar, D., Leest, B., Van Eck, E., Verbeek, F., Van der Vegt, A.L., & Jongeneed, M. (2013). *Selectiemechanismen in het onderwijs.* [Selection mechanisms in education.] Nijmegen: Radboud Universiteit.

Guinier, L. (2015) *The tyranny of the meritocracy.* Boston: Beacon Press.

Hirsch, F. (1977). *Social limits to growth.* London: Routledge & Kegan Paul.

Inspectorate of Education (2016). Technisch rapport Deel I: Onderwijskansen. [Technical report part 1: educational opportunities.] Bijlage bij: *De staat van het onderwijs 2014/2015.* [Appendix to: The state of education in the Netherlands 2014/2015.] De Meern: Inspectie van het Onderwijs.

Karsten, S. (2016). *Hoofdstroom in de Nederlandse onderwijsdelta.* [The main current in the Dutch education delta.] Antwerpen/Apeldoorn: Garant.

Leseman, P. (2005). Genetische onbepaaldheid en culturele variatie: is het meritocratische ideaal houdbaar? [Genetic indeterminacy and cultural variety: can the meritocratic ideal be sustained?] In: S. Karsten & P. Sleegers (Red.) *Onderwijs en ongelijkheid: grenzen aan de maakbaarheid?* [Education and inequality: limits to manipulability?] Antwerpen/ Apeldoorn: Garant.

Luzac (2015). www.luzac.nl. Information retrieved on December 12, 2015.

Ministry of Education, Culture and Science (2016). *Referentieramingen 2016.* [Reference forecast.] Retrieved from: https://www.rijksoverheid.nl/documenten/rapporten/2016/09/20/ referentieraming-2016.

Mijs, J.B. (2016). Stratified failure: educational stratification and students' attributions of their mathematics performance in 24 countries. *Sociology of Education*, *89*(2), 137-153.

Nederlands Jeugdinstituut (Netherlands Youth Institute, 2015). *Cijfers over Jeugd en Opvoeding: Onderwijsprestaties.* [Figures on Youth and Upbringing: Educational Performance.] Retrieved from: http://www.nji.nl/nl/Databank/Cijfers-over-Jeugd-en-Opvoeding/Cijfers- per-onderwerp/Onderwijsprestaties.

OECD (2015a). *Education at a glance*. Paris: OECD.

OECD (2015b), *PISA 2015 Database*, Table II.4.5.

OECD (2016). *Foundations for the Future.* In the series *Reviews of National Policies of Education: Netherlands 2016.* Paris: OECD.

Rawls, J. (1972). *A Theory of Justice.* Oxford: Clarendon Press.

Salverda, W. (2016). Merit en werk 1960-2010. [Merit and work 1960-2010.] In H. van der Werfhorst (Red.). *Een kloof van alle tijden*. [A gap of all times.] Amsterdam: Amsterdam University Press.

Volman, M. (2016). Sekseverschillen in het onderwijs: meisjessucces en jongensprobleem? [Gender differences in education: girls' success and boys' problem?] In B. Eidhof, M. van Houtte, & M. Vermeulen (Red.) *Sociologen over onderwijs.* [Sociologists on education.] Antwerpen/Apeldoorn: Garant.

Vrooman, C., Gijsberts, M., & Boelhouwer, J. (2014). *Verschil in Nederland. Sociaal en Cultureel Rapport 2014.* [Difference in the Netherlands. Social and cultural report 2014.] The Hague: SCP.

Weenink, D. (2009). Creating a niche in the education market: the rise of internationalised secondary education in the Netherlands. *Journal of Education Policy*, *24*(4), 495-511.

ISABELLA BINEY
STUDENT

'STUDENTS SHOULD ALSO HAVE AN ACTIVE ROLE IN EDUCATION'

In the Netherlands, increasing numbers of schools require pupils to show initiative. Pre-university secondary school student Isabella Biney is living proof of this: she helps junior students with their English and is a member of her school's participation council. 'I believe it's not just teachers who should have an active role in education, but students too!'

'The first word that springs to mind when I think of the Dutch education system is 'opportunities'. As a pupil you get to choose what kind of school you go to and you also get the opportunity to move on to different levels within that school. For example, I started at the lowest level of secondary general education but will soon finish at the highest, pre-university level. That would never have been possible if the Dutch education system didn't offer everyone the same opportunities.'

"Stimulating personal talent is just as important as teaching school subjects."

ROOM FOR PERSONAL DEVELOPMENT

'When you work hard and are highly motivated, all doors are open to you. You're not stuck at any level and I believe that's really important. This ensures that as a student you can find or create your own place during your school career. Of course there's always room for improvement. For example, personally I would like to see even more focus on talent development in the school's policy.

The fact is that education is now primarily aimed at teaching you things like mathematics and biology. But a school is also the place where students spend the highest number of hours every week. So it's just as important for it to stimulate personal development. For example, I enjoy learning how to speak in public, and how to convince my audience. Fortunately, my school offered extra lessons in rhetoric. I was able to take these in my free time to expand my talents in this area. I think that should be possible in every school!'

THE IDEAL PICTURE OF THE FUTURE

'I would like to see more cooperation between student and teacher, and between students. Every student should have the opportunity to be heard in the classroom. So I think it would be great if we could work more flexibly, instead of adhering to a traditional timetable based on subjects and subject clusters. Because if you're interested in for instance history and chemistry, then surely you should be able to choose both? Personal attention is an important part of this too. In classes of 25 students, it hardly exists. When I was in a class of 10 pupils preparing for my examinations, I noticed that there was much more personal attention and that as a

"Every pupil should have the opportunity to be heard in the classroom."

result I was paying much more attention than in my usual lessons!' ‹

Chapter 7

Super-Diversity:
an Opportunity for
Schools and Higher
Education

Dr. Rick Wolff,
Risbo, Erasmus University Rotterdam

ntroduction

Dutch education has undergone a real metamorphosis in recent decades. Classes have become more and more colourful, first as a result of the arrival of various groups of migrants and their children from Dutch colonies (and former colonies), later due to migrant workers coming from Southern Europe, North Africa (in particular, Morocco) and Turkey. The children of the various refugee communities have added to the mix. These developments have strongly manifested themselves in the *Randstad*, the densely populated region in the west of the country, which includes the four main cities of Amsterdam, Rotterdam, The Hague and Utrecht. By way of illustration, Amsterdam entered the 21st century with almost half the population of secondary schools consisting of pupils of non-Western origin[1] (O+S, 2002). In Amsterdam, pupils with Dutch 'roots' are a minority.

Higher education in the Netherlands has also become more colourful[2]. Figures published by the Centraal Bureau Statistiek (CBS, Statistics Netherlands) show that the percentage of students of non-Western origin in the total first year student population at research universities and universities of applied sciences have risen from eight per cent in the 1990s to around fifteen per cent in 2015. This is a national average. It is in the *Randstad* that these developments are most apparent, both in higher professional education and in academic education. As an example, Figure 7.1 shows that in the 2015/16 academic year more than 20 per cent of the student populations of Erasmus University Rotterdam and Vrije Universiteit Amsterdam was of non-Western origin, whereas at many other research universities this figure is less than 10 per cent. Within institutions, these figures may differ as well. For example, there are higher professional education programmes in the Randstad (such as Law and Public Administration) where half the first-year admissions are non-Western[3].

---

[1] I have adopted the definition of non-Western used by the CBS (Statistics Netherlands): a person with at least one parent born in one of the countries in Africa, Latin America and Asia (excluding Indonesia and Japan) or in Turkey.

[2] Dutch higher education follows a binary system: academic education is provided by research universities and higher professional education by universities of applied sciences. Academic education is more selective. Students eligible for a research university are also able to attend programmes at universities of applied sciences. The vast majority of students commencing at a university of applied sciences, however, are not eligible to study at a research university.

[3] Source: Vereniging van Hogescholen (Netherlands Association of Universities of Applied Sciences): http://www. vereniginghogescholen.nl/kennisbank/feiten-en-cijfers/artikelen/studentenaantallen

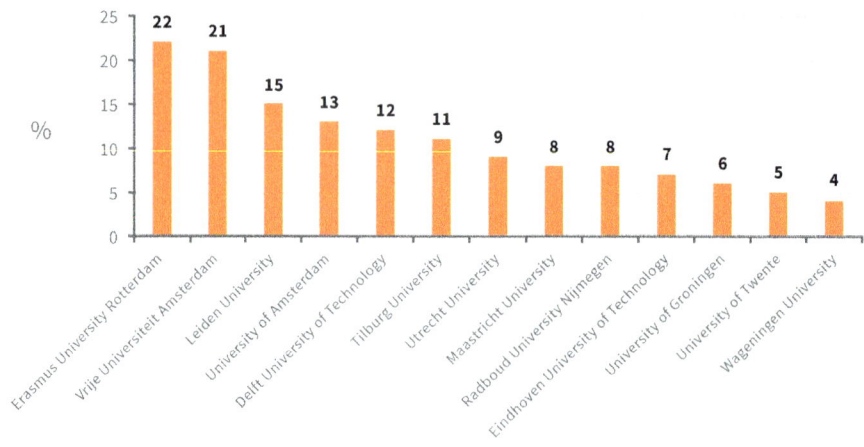

Figure 7.1 *Source: University of Amsterdam Diversity Commission (2016a, p. 32), adapted by Rick Wolff.*

As a result of the changes to the student loan system in 2015[4], there is a concern that access to higher education will become more difficult for young people from less affluent backgrounds, a group that includes most students with a non-Western migration background. However, at present this group still forms a significant proportion of the Dutch student population.

Super-Diversity[5] Due to a Relatively Open System

The phenomenon of super-diversity is found at every level of education. Diversity refers to a situation with one ethnic majority group and various ethnic minority groups. The pupil and student populations of a number of primary, secondary and higher education institutions in large cities consist of various ethnic groups, none of which makes up a significant majority, a situation known as super-diversity. This is a positive sign. It shows that in principle all levels of education and the various types of education provided at each level are accessible to all young people. Dutch higher education is largely state-funded. In contrast to the situation in other countries, completing the right secondary education or senior secondary vocational education programme is sufficient to gain access to higher education. There is no requirement to sit an entrance examination, as for example in Spain. Institutions may differ in quality – for certain programmes, one university of applied sciences may be better than another, for certain studies, one research university may be more highly regarded than another. These differences, however, are much less

---

[4] Prior to 2015, a proportion of the money students borrowed from the government was converted into a gift (if they graduated within 10 years). Since 2015, students have to repay the full amount they borrow.

[5] Diversity in education manifests itself in many ways, including diversity in terms of ethnic background, social class, gender, disability and previous education. This chapter focuses on ethnic diversity. Processes appropriate to this type of diversity can also provide examples of processes for use with other types of diversity.

significant than in the United States, for example, where top universities like Princeton, Yale and Harvard are largely private institutions, only accessible to students with enough money and/ or exceptional talent. These pronounced differences in status between universities also exist in other countries; consider, for example, universities like Oxford and Cambridge in the United Kingdom and the grandes écoles in France. In the Netherlands, some universities of applied sciences and research universities are more ethnically diverse than others. However, this has little to do with one institution being more selective or prestigious than another, but is determined by geographical location. It is safe to say that in the Netherlands, once a prospective student has obtained a 'ticket' to higher education, selection is based on their previous education. In general, students who have completed an education programme giving access to higher professional education, are eligible to commence studies at *all* universities of applied sciences. If they have completed an education programme giving access to academic education, they will generally be able to commence studies at all research universities and universities of applied sciences. The qualification that this is generally the case is due to the fact that some courses have specific admission requirements. Examples are study programmes with a limited number of places or academies for music or dance, which only admit students with sufficient talent for music or dance.

Diversity in Higher Education, but Reached via a Detour

There are significant differences between young people without a migration background and those with a non-Western migration background in the ways in which they reach higher education. Figure 7.2 shows that in the second year of secondary education, almost half of the students without a migration background are on course for direct entry to higher education. For students of Antillean, Turkish or Moroccan origin, this is true for only a quarter of them.

It appears that a separation occurs at the end of primary education. The pre-higher education route is primarily populated by pupils with no migration background. Pupils with a non-Western background primarily go to vocational secondary education. An explanation for this can be sought in the education system (see also Chapter 6). Ground-breaking international comparative studies in this field have been led by Crul (Crul, Schneider & Lelie, 2013; Crul, Pasztor, Lelie, Mijs & Schnell, 2009). These studies show that in the Netherlands, second-generation[6] Turkish young people with poorly educated parents progress much less often to pre-university education than those in Sweden and France. This is partly because migrant children in France go to school at the age of two or three. In the Netherlands, they go to school at the age of four. So migrant children in France learn French at an earlier stage than migrant children in the Netherlands learn Dutch. Moreover, in the Netherlands, selection for the different secondary education programmes takes

---

[6]   Second-generation migrant children are born in the country of residence with at least one parent born in another country.

place at an earlier stage (at the age of 12), which means that pupils have less time to develop the talents necessary for pre-higher education routes than in France or Sweden.

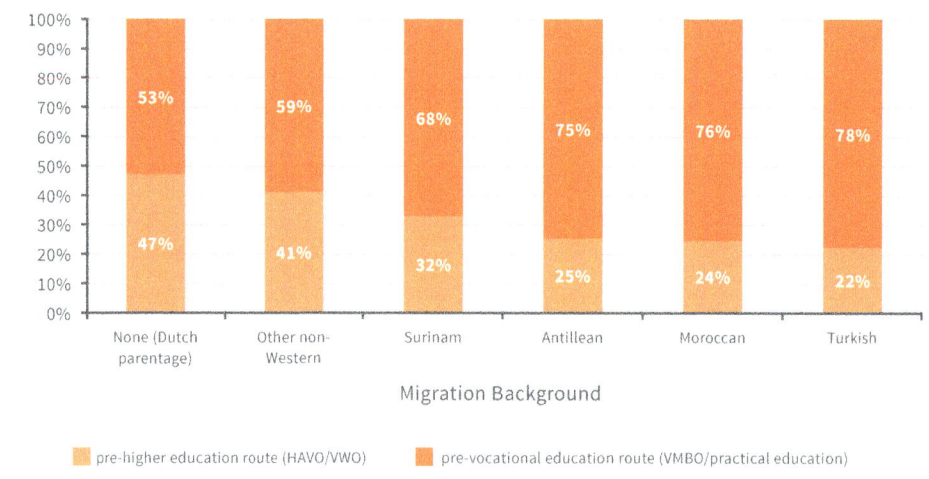

Figure 7.2   *Pupils in the third year of secondary education classified by education programme level and migration background, 2014/15 (in percentages). Source: CBS (Statistics Netherlands)/StatLine, adapted by Rick Wolff.*

However, the gap in secondary education between the various groups appears to be narrowing. The Sociaal-Cultureel Planbureau (SCP, Netherlands Institute of Social Research, 2016) finds that pupils of non-Western origin 'are gradually participating more in the higher levels of secondary education' (p. 57), with the result that they are catching up with their peers who have Dutch parentage. Another positive fact is that pupils of non-Western origin relatively frequently 'stack' diplomas to reach a higher level of secondary education, for example by continuing from lower secondary vocational education (VMBO) to the pre-higher professional education (HAVO) or to senior secondary vocational education (MBO), both of which give access to higher professional education (SCP, 2016). The CBS (Statistics Netherlands, 2016) has calculated that five years after successful completion of VMBO education, pupils of non-Western origin are more likely to be attending higher professional education than pupils without a migration background (see also Dutch Inspectorate of Education, 2016).

Apparently, the differences in the Dutch education system between pupils with and without a migration background on the transition from primary to secondary education, are partially 'repaired' within secondary education: the education system is set up in such a way that several routes lead to higher education. But for pupils of non-Western origin this often comes at a cost. In many cases they follow routes to higher education that take more time (up to three years extra even without delays) and therefore require more effort and motivation compared with the direct route from primary education to pre-higher education. This detour is 'a route that requires a great deal of perseverance and ambition' (Crul et al, 2013, p. 49).

Inequality in Study Success as a Given

Higher education is an interesting test case. It is the jewel in the crown of the Dutch education system: it supplies the employment market with the most highly qualified candidates. From the perspective of ethnic minority groups, higher education is also relevant for the emancipation of migrant communities. Young people from these communities who complete higher education are the pride of their families and can develop to be role models and standard bearers for their community, moving on to occupy prominent positions in areas of key significance in society. Together with all the other higher education graduates, they bear responsibility for the society of the future.

Many students of non-Western origin enter higher education with backgrounds that differ from most students without a migration history. A high proportion of them have gained access to higher education via alternative routes. Often they come from underprivileged (often inner city) neighbourhoods and from population groups whose educational level, position in the employment market and income compare unfavourably with the Dutch average (SCP, 2012; SCP, 2016). For many of them, even those born in the Netherlands, Dutch higher education is initially 'foreign' to them in many ways. Are universities of applied sciences and research universities in a position to provide these students with the same opportunities to succeed in their studies as students without a migration background?

This does not appear to be the case. Statistics concerning graduation rates 5 years after entering higher education indicate that young people from non-Western migrant groups are less successful in their studies than students without a migration background. At both universities of applied sciences and research universities, all non-Western student groups show lower graduation efficiency than the group of students of Dutch parentage. The following figure shows graduation efficiency of research university students after five years of study (Figure 7.3). Students from the 'Other non-Western immigrants' group come closest to the graduation efficiency of students from Dutch parentage (the difference being six to nine percentage points). The other groups trail behind (in some cases, far behind). Although differences between the Dutch parentage group and the various non-Western groups seem to be decreasing over time, they remain clearly identifiable.

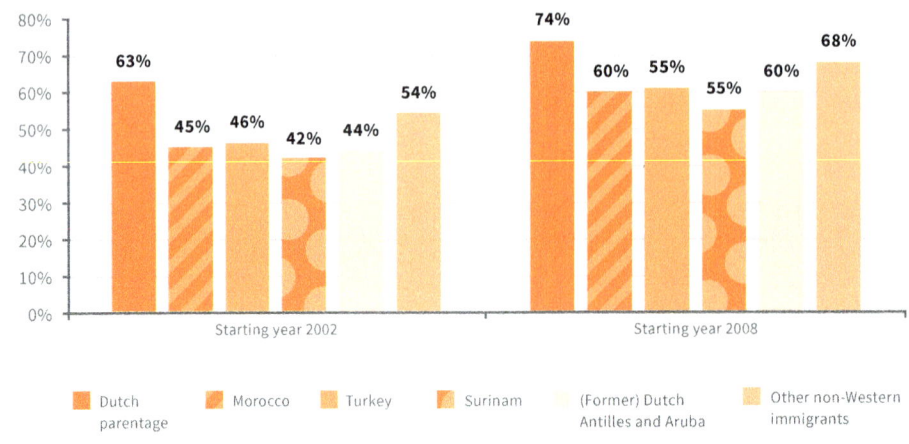

Figure 7.3 *Graduation efficiency after 5 years (nominal duration is 3 years), full-time research university bachelor degree students by ethnic origin group (starting years 2002 and 2008). Source: CBS (Statistics Netherlands)/StatLine, adapted by Rick Wolff.*

In higher professional education, differences between the Dutch parentage group and the various non-Western groups are even greater (differences of 15 percentage points are commonplace) and these differences are increasing[7].

The SCP (Netherlands Institute for Social Research) therefore concludes that in higher education the study paths of students of non-Western origin 'progress less favourably' than those of students of Dutch parentage (SCP, 2016, p. 58). This is not a recent development: as early as the mid-1990s students with a non-Western migration background dropped out more often and achieved significantly lower graduation efficiency than students of Dutch parentage (Wolff, 2013). So significant differences in efficiency between ethnic groups already existed before many of the current first year students were even born.

This leads us to two key questions:
1. Why are students of non-Western origin less successful in their studies than students without a migration background?
2. What changes are needed to give students with and without a migration background equal opportunities for study success?

[7]   Source: CBS (Statistics Netherlands) website/StatLine

A Closer Look at Differences in Study Success

Explanations for differences in study success between students with a non-Western migration background and 'white' students can be considered from various perspectives. One can focus on student characteristics, such as differences in learning styles (Boogaard, 1997; Severiens & Joukes, 2001; Herfs, 2009), language proficiency (Boogaard, 1997; Herfs, 2009) and the choice of study: students of non-Western origin, particularly students whose parents are less educated, allow their choice to be determined more by the image and status of an occupation (focusing on courses in business, law or medicine) than by intrinsic motivators (Wolff & Severiens, 2011). The fact that higher education is 'foreign' to them has already been mentioned. In their research into the educational careers of Turkish and Moroccan lawyers, Groenendijk and Hahn (2006) report that in studying law these students were confronted with a 'migration to a new environment' in both socioeconomic and ethnocultural terms. The limited success of students of non-Western origin can also be partially attributed to general factors: this group contains a relatively large proportion of students with a high drop-out risk, such as students who have taken longer to complete the studies needed to reach higher education and students who switch to new studies (Wolff, 2013).

Another aspect to be considered could be the characteristics of the various studies: to what extent do learning environments in higher education cause differences in study success? In this context, the University of Amsterdam Diversity Commission wrote in its final report: 'People who are seen as belonging to ethnic minorities not only suffer from exclusion in everyday interactions, but are also disadvantaged more systematically. On average, study results of students with ethnic minority backgrounds are lower.' (2016b, p. 3). The importance of the learning environment is also reflected in the conclusion by Meeuwisse (2012) that good formal (i.e. study-related) contacts with lecturers and fellow students are particularly important for students of non-Western origin to enable them to feel at home in their chosen studies. Precisely these interactions are crucial 'for the retention of non-Western immigrant students within higher education' (p. 148). However, these contacts do not always run smoothly, as is shown by De Jong (2012) in her study of identity development in Moroccan-Dutch higher professional education students. Many of the students she spoke, felt that in contacts with lecturers and fellow students they were reduced to 'Moroccan' or 'Muslim', with all the negative connotations associated with that word' (p. 192). Students of non-Western origin interviewed in a study by Wolff (2013) also state that their ethnic origins play a role in interactions: they are regularly made to feel 'different' in their contacts with fellow students, lecturers and student supervisors (many of whom are of Dutch parentage). Some of them feel they are not taken seriously and their migration background rarely leads to a positive attitude. In some cases, students feel that they are excluded by fellow students who are of Dutch parentage, or not treated equally by lecturers.

As well as student experiences, we need to consider the lecturer perspective on diversity. Based on a study of 25 teams of higher professional education lecturers, Van Middelkoop and Meerman (2014) distinguish three categories of lecturer: lecturers who do not see diversity, lecturers who recognize diversity and lecturers who understand the significance of diversity and want to exploit its potential. They conclude that the majority regard diversity as problematic because they do not *want* to take account of diversity ('I treat everyone in the same manner') or because they are not *able* to do so (lecturers recognize diversity, but do not know how to deal with it). With regard to 'not being able', De Jong (2014) observes that lecturers are regularly confronted with awkward situations that result in uncertainty as to how to act, or reluctance to act. Examples of these are student behaviour such as rude remarks or racially-tinged 'jokes' and/or situations touching on sensitive subjects such as refugee policy, crime, homosexuality, fundamentalism (including religious fundamentalism), radicalisation, discrimination and racism.

The Integration and Capital Approaches as Theoretical Interpretations

From the education perspective, it is interesting to consider in more detail the role of learning communities in achieving study success. What insights are offered by the theory in this area? The dual concepts of academic integration (interactions relating to the learning process) and social integration (the process of interacting socially and making friends), originating from the interactional drop-out model in Tinto (1993), are a good starting point. Tinto claims that the better the contact between students and their fellow students, lecturers and student supervisors, both in formal learning situations and elsewhere, the better they integrate within the social and academic systems in their learning environment and the greater their chances of study success. Tinto's theory is appealing and sounds plausible. But it is generic in nature and needs to be further expanded to enable understanding of differences in academic and social integration processes between groups. A good starting point can be found in the work of Nora (2004), who states that the closer the match between a student's system of values and the dominant culture in the educational programme (the better the 'fit'), the more he/she feels at home and valued and the more study success will be achieved. Why then do some student groups fit better in a learning environment than others? An answer to that question can be found in the capital approach, in which cultural and social capital are important components.

Cultural capital, as explained in the work of Bourdieu (1997), can be understood as knowledge about standards, styles, conventions and 'taste' valued in higher (more educated) circles, which puts someone in a position to move in these circles and be successful (see Massey, Charles, Lundy & Fischer, 2002, p. 6). Cultural capital is built and passed on through a process of social reproduction. Students from higher social classes have an advantage because they acquire the (generally unwritten) rules of higher education, consciously or unconsciously, as part of their upbringing. This puts them in a better position than students from less educated backgrounds to know what to expect in their new learning environment and how they need to act to be successful. Bourdieu and Wacquant (1992) use the 'fish' metaphor for this: students with parents who have attended higher education often feel like 'fish in water' in higher education. Students from less educated backgrounds start out unfamiliar with the university of applied sciences or research university environment and have to make much more effort to find their way. They are 'fish out of water' (Thomas & Quinn, 2007).

Social capital, according to Putnam (2000) and Coleman (1988), refers in this case to contacts, connections and networks that are relevant for achieving study success. Establishing that A and B know each other, does not say anything about the substance or quality of their relationship. Social contacts, connections and networks only acquire significance due to the *value* that those involved attach to them (Putnam, 2000, p. 18/19). This value can be regarded as social capital. With respect to higher education, social capital can be said to apply if the network provides knowledge about how to study successfully, as in planning work, reading and writing documents, preparing presentations and knowing what is important for a test or assessment. More social capital relating to study success will be present in groups with more higher education experience (highly educated circles) than in groups with less higher education experience.

Tinto's interactional model suggests reciprocity. The analysis of capital above primarily focuses on students but it can also be applied to lecturers, student supervisors and management. These professionals operate within the learning environment of their study programme and the concept of 'habitus' is relevant here. Habitus has to do with the way in which an individual relates to his or her environment, and it can be understood as a system, ensuing from the sum of a person's experiences and background, that serves as a kind of compass for a person's perceptions, preferences and actions. Habitus makes people perceive, interpret and act in the world in such a natural way that they are scarcely aware of this. According to Bourdieu (1971), people with matching cultural capital share a common habitus. They have similar lifestyles and world views. Thomas (2002) extends this to higher education: a learning environment can be said to have an 'institutional habitus'. She was inspired by the work of Reay, David and Ball (2001), who describe 'institutional habitus' as '*the impact of a cultural group or social class on an individual's behaviour as it is mediated through an organisation*' (see Thomas 2002: p. 430). In other words, an organisation (study programme, institution) consists of a group of people (lecturers, student supervisors, management) who agree on what is considered 'good' and thereby influence the behaviour of individuals (students).

The reference to 'cultural group or social class' is important. In higher education, this consists of a team of highly educated professionals. In Thomas' vision, lecturers will more readily recognize and value the cultural capital of students with highly educated parents (because it fits within the 'institutional habitus') than that which students with less educated parents have to offer. As a result, the bond between lecturers and their students from less educated backgrounds will be less close, less social capital will be passed on and academic and social integration processes will be less smooth, with less chance of study success (see also Gay, 2010). This is further reinforced when these students have limited financial resources (economic capital) and have to dedicate some of their time, which they would otherwise be able to spend studying, to generating income. For Bourdieu, social class plays the principal role in the processes described above. However, they could equally apply to ethnic origin. In that case, the assumption is that lecturers and student supervisors (predominantly of Dutch parentage) more easily identify with students of Dutch parentage (and vice versa) than with non-Western immigrant students. This has consequences for interactions in the study programme, the availability of social resources, social and academic integration processes and ultimately, the degree of study success.

Equal Opportunities for Study Success: Social Capital Investment as an Inviting Prospect

Now that we have sought explanations for the differences in the study success of ethnic student groups, we come to the second key question: what is needed to offer students with and without a migration background equal opportunities for study success?

Based on earlier studies (Severiens, Wolff & Rezai, 2006; Severiens, Wolff, Meeuwisse, Rezai & De Vos, 2008; Severiens & Wolff, 2008), Wolff (2013) examined the correlation between learning environment characteristics and differences in study progress between various ethnic student groups at a number of higher professional and academic education programmes in the *Randstad*. A total of three academic and six higher professional education programmes were studied through interviews with students, lecturers, student supervisors and management and by examining the set-up of year 1 (and for teacher education universities year 2 as well). On six of these study programmes, students of non-Western origin performed less well than students of Dutch parentage. However, three programmes – an economics programme at a research university, a social work programme at a university of applied sciences and a teacher education programme – showed surprising results: students from both groups performed equally well. How do these programmes succeed in levelling out differences in study progress between ethnic groups? The programmes all turned out to be similar in the following three elements:

- A strong focus on *student supervision*, for instance by staff dividing students into groups, by rapid rotation of group composition and by compulsory attendance for many subjects.
- Lecturers and student supervisors who *approach students personally and show commitment,* for example through intensive study counselling and interest in students' backgrounds from both social and didactic perspectives.
- A *small-scale approach* applied at all levels, such as working in small groups, block teaching, clear correlation between subjects, and inter-collegial meetings of lecturers.

The strength of these learning environments lies primarily in *the combination of the three elements*. The absence of one of these elements can upset the balance and increase differences in study success between groups. For example, one study programme in which students of non-Western origin were less successful than students without a migration background did have a small-scale set-up and the team was made up of committed lecturers and student supervisors, but supervision was lacking. The students of non-Western origin felt that they were left to their fates and probably partly due to this, differences in study success arose. This outcome suggests that students with a non-Western migration background are more dependent on learning environment for their study success than students without a migration background (see also Severiens, Wolff & Rezai (2006) and Meeuwisse & Severiens (2012)).

Learning environments combining the three elements mentioned, appear to be set up in such a way that home backgrounds have little impact on study success. Study programmes with this type of learning environment facilitate *all* students in acquiring and utilising social capital, for example through committed lecturers and student supervisors and staff division of students into groups, which compensates for any shortage of cultural capital (see also Thomas (2002) and Mountford-Zimdars, Sabri, Moore, Sanders, Jones & Higham (2015)). This is a significant finding in view of the earlier observation that many young people of non-Western origin, even those born in the Netherlands as second-generation immigrants, start higher education from a totally different context than most young people without a migration background. In a learning environment in which study success is equally obtainable for students with a non-Western migration background and for those without a migration background, the acquisition and utilisation of social capital relevant for study success has little or no relation to ethnic origin, with the result that different groups are able to make equal progress in social and academic integration processes and the achievement of study success.

The elements identified are of a general nature. Strict supervision at the start and consistent implementation of small-scale education are measures aimed at all students. The personal approach and commitment of lecturers/student supervisors to students' development can be regarded as a general attitude towards all students. In other words, these are general measures that have a positive effect on specific groups, such as students of non-Western origin. Implementation of these general measures with systematic attention and care based on the idea of the individual student as the central focus, may create a climate in which diversity (including ethnic diversity) is regarded as adding value to the learning process.

Diversity as an Opportunity, Super-Diversity as a Super-Opportunity

Focusing on diversity is generally associated with delayed development and overcoming deficiencies. We are talking about all kinds of shortcomings students may have, such as not having the appropriate arsenal of study and academic skills, having the wrong attitude to study, lacking motivation, being unable to conform to the accepted customs of the programme and insufficient language proficiency. Measures relating to diversity are generally employed to rectify shortcomings in students and in general policy.

Internationalization, on the other hand, is something educational institutions welcome and even regard as a necessity (Gaalen, Roodenburg, Hobbes, Huberts & Gielesen, 2014). It is considered interesting to, for example, get to know students, professionals, habits and customs from other countries, share experiences, expand horizons and work on international and intercultural competencies. And rightly so. The advantages of internationalization seem obvious. But why are initiatives promoting internationalization trumpeted whereas the added of value of diversity still needs to be recognized, as witnessed by the systematic gap in graduation efficiency between students of non-Western origin and their 'white' fellow students? Both internationalization and diversity are about difference, recognizing and learning to understand the 'other' and, as a result, yourself as well. Is it a matter of framing? Do we regard internationalization as glamorous, while diversity makes us sigh and think about falling standards? Let's experiment and try looking at diversity with the same enthusiastic approach we normally reserve for internationalization.

Let's assume that students and lecturers with a non-Western migrant background are an asset to learning communities in higher education. Many of them have reached universities of applied science or research universities via a detour and in doing so have shown they have the perseverance and motivation to make it to higher education. By complementing students of non-Western origin with this, instead of constantly confronting them with what they aren't able to do, they will probably increase their efforts to excel. These students come to university to learn, but they also bring valuable experiences that both fellow students and lecturers can learn from. For example, they are continually switching between contexts that differ widely, such as their home situation, the situation in their circle of friends and the situation at university. So they know what it's like to be flexible. An important skill in a world that is constantly and ever rapidly changing. How do they do that? And what are the advantages and disadvantages of being able to switch between contexts? On top of this, many of them come from groups in society that are vulnerable in areas such as education, work and income, healthcare, housing, quality of life and safety. Their experiences, and those of their relatives and friends, can make a significant contribution to better insight into social issues and appropriate interventions to deal with these social challenges. And a diverse student population offers all students opportunities to develop skills in areas such as intercultural sensitivity and communication, and cooperation in teams with members from different backgrounds. Skills whose value for their subsequent professional lives should not be underestimated. The findings of Milem (2003) can be viewed in this context. He summarizes the proven benefits of diversity for higher education. He mentions, for example, that the interaction between students with different ethnic backgrounds stimulates students' capacity for critical thought and an active approach to their studies, and increases their ability to empathize and readiness to scrutinize different perspectives, which can in the long term lead to achieving higher levels of creativity and innovation. Interaction with students from other ethnic groups also results in greater satisfaction with their study programmes and increases students' perseverance to complete their studies successfully. Moreover, diversity can lead to positive developments at programme level: educational processes become more student-centred.

Thus it seems that diversity, like internationalization, offers distinct advantages to learning communities. However, this requires a learning environment which gives diversity the space to grow. This is possible in environments such as those outlined above, where all students are offered the opportunity to acquire and utilize social capital. Which also begins to formulate an answer to the questions raised earlier about why students of non-Western origin are less successful in their studies than students without a migration background, and what is needed to offer these student groups equal opportunities to succeed. A context with 'free movement of social capital' creates the possibility of dialogue between students and between students and lecturers that has added value for their mutual learning processes. And if diversity offers opportunities in this way, then super-diversity offers super-opportunities.

Key Questions
- How can we ensure that *teams* of lecturers in higher education acquire a stronger sense of ownership of the topic of diversity?
- How can a learning environment be created in which students and lecturers feel secure enough to be able to exchange views freely on sensitive issues such as crime, homosexuality, fundamentalism (including religious fundamentalism), radicalisation, discrimination and racism when these topics arise?
- What does it say about Dutch higher education that, as a group, students of Dutch parentage *systematically* achieve more study success than students from non-Western migrant groups?

About the author

Dr. Rick Wolff (1965) is a senior researcher at Risbo*/Erasmus University Rotterdam. His research is focused on study success in higher education, in particular the study success of students of non-Western origin. On this topic he completed his doctoral research in November 2013. He is a member of the EUR Working Group on Educational Interventions for Diversity and the Taskforce 'The Future is Diversity', a collaboration between various universities including the Erasmus University Rotterdam. Wolff is also involved in evaluation and monitoring of educational innovations in higher professional and academic education.

Contact: wolff@risbo.eur.nl.

---

* Risbo is an independent institution for research, training and advice, linked to the Faculty of Social Sciences of Erasmus University Rotterdam.

References

Boogaard, M. (1997). *Van buiten, geleerd. Allochtone en buitenlandse studenten in het Nederlandse hoger onderwijs.* [From outside, learned. Immigrant and foreign students in Dutch higher education.] Amsterdam: Het Spinhuis.

Bourdieu, P. (1971). Systems of education and systems of thought. In: M.K.D. Young (Ed.). *Knowledge and control: New directions for the sociology of education (pp. 189-207).* London: Collier Macmillan.

Bourdieu, P. (1997). The Forms of Capital. In: A.H. Halsey, H. Lauder, Ph. Brown & A. Stuart Wells (Eds.). *Education: Culture, Economy, and Society (pp. 46-58).* Oxford: Oxford University Press.

Bourdieu, P., & Wacquant, L. (1992). *An Invitation to Reflexive Sociology*, Chicago: Chicago University Press.

CBS (Statistics Netherlands) (2016), Jaarrapport 2016 Landelijke Jeugdmonitor. [Annual Report 2016 National Youth Monitor.] The Hague/Heerlen/Bonaire: CBS.

Coleman, J.S. (1988). Social capital in the creation of human capital. *American Journal of Sociology, 94*(suppl), S95-S120.

Crul, M., Pasztor, A., Lelie, F., Mijs, J., & Schnell, P. (2009). *Valkuilen en springplanken in het onderwijs.* [Pitfalls and springboards in education.] The Hague: NICIS Institute.

Crul, M., Schneider, J., & Lelie, F. (2013). *Superdiversiteit.* [Super-Diversity.] Amsterdam: VU University Press.

De Jong, M. (2012). *Ik ben die Marokkaan niet! Onderzoek naar identiteitsvorming van Marokkaans-Nederlandse hbo-studenten.* [I'm not that Moroccan! Research into the formation of identity in Moroccan-Dutch higher professional education students.] Amsterdam: VU University Press.

De Jong, M. (2014). *Over allochtoon en autochtoon. Diversiteit in het hoger onderwijs.* [On immigrants and non-immigrants. Diversity in higher education.] Groningen: Noordhoff.

Dutch Inspectorate of Education (2016). *De Staat van het Onderwijs. Onderwijsverslag 2014/2015.* [The State of Education. Education Report 2014/2015.] Utrecht: Inspectorate of Education.

Gay, G. (2010). Classroom practices for teaching diversity: an example from Washington State (United States). In: OECD. *Educating Teachers for Diversity. Meeting the challenge.* Paris: OECD/Centre for Educational Research and Innovation.

Groenendijk, K., & Hahn, A. (2006). *Met recht geslaagd. Nederlandse juristen van Marokkaanse en Turkse afkomst.* [Rightful success in law. Dutch lawyers of Moroccan and Turkish origin.] The Hague: Sdu Publishing.

Herfs, P. (2009). *Buitenlandse artsen in Nederland.* [Foreign doctors in the Netherlands.] Utrecht: Utrecht University.

Massey, D.S., Charles, C.Z., Lundy, G.F., & Fischer, M.J. (2002). *The source of the river.* Princeton: Princeton University Press.

Meeuwisse, M. (2012). *Being smart is not enough. The role of psychosocial factors in study success of ethnic minority and ethnic majority students.* Rotterdam: EUR/Risbo.

Meeuwisse, M., & Severiens, S.E. (2012). Studiesucces en leeromgeving. Een studie naar thuisvoelen, inzet en tijdbesteding. [Study success and learning environment. A study into feeling at home, effort and allocation of time.] *HO Management, 4*(1), 18-20.

Milem, J.F. (2003). The educational benefits of diversity: evidence from multiple sectors. In: M.J. Chang, D. Witt, J. Jones, K. Hakuta (Eds.). *Compelling interest. Examining the evidence on racial dynamics in colleges and universities (pp. 126-169)*. Stanford: Stanford University Press.

Mountford-Zimdars, A., Sabri, D., Moore, J., Sanders, J., Jones, S., & Higham, L. (2015). *Causes of differences in student outcomes.* Bristol: HEFCE.

Netherlands Institute for Social Research (2012). *Jaarrapport Integratie 2011.* [Annual Report on Integration 2011.] The Hague: Netherlands Institute for Social Research.

Netherlands Institute for Social Research (2016). *Integratie in zicht? De integratie van migranten in Nederland op acht terreinen nader bekeken.* [Integration in sight? A closer look at eight aspects of the integration of migrants in the Netherlands.] The Hague: Netherlands Institute for Social Research.

Nora, A. (2004). The role of habitus and cultural capital in choosing a college, transitioning from high school to higher education, and persisting in college among minority and nonminority Students. *Journal of Hispanic Higher Education, 3*(2), 180-208.

O+S (2002). *Amsterdam in Cijfers, Jaarboek 2002.* [Amsterdam in figures, Annual issue 2002.] Amsterdam: Amsterdam Department for Research and Statistics.

Putnam, R.D. (2000). *Bowling alone. The collapse and revival of American community.* New York, Simon & Schuster.

Reay, D., David, M., & Ball, S. (2001). Making a difference? Institutional habituses and familial habituses and higher education choice. *Sociological Research Online, 5*(4), 519-529.

Severiens, S., & Joukes, G. (2001). *Studenten in het hoger technisch onderwijs. Verschillen in leerstrategieën, motivatie en positie.* [Students in higher technical education. Differences in learning strategies, motivation and position.] Delft: Stichting Axis.

Severiens, S., Wolff, R., & Rezai, S. (2006). *Diversiteit in leergemeenschappen: Een onderzoek naar stimulerende factoren in de leeromgeving voor allochtone studenten in het hoger onderwijs.* [Diversity in learning communities: A study of stimulating factors in the learning environment for immigrant students in higher education.] Utrecht: ECHO.

Severiens, S., Wolff, R., Meeuwisse, M., Rezai, S., & De Vos, W. (2008). *Waarom stoppen zoveel allochtone studenten met de pabo? Samenvatting van vijf studies.* [Why do so many immigrant students drop out of primary school teacher training? A summary of five studies.] The Hague: SBO.

Severiens, S., & Wolff, R. (2008). A comparison of ethnic minority and majority students: Social and academic integration, and quality of learning. *Studies in Higher Education, 33*(3), 253-266.

Thomas, L. (2002). Student retention in higher education: the role of institutional habitus. *Journal of Education Policy, 17*(4), 423-442.

Thomas, L., & Quinn, J. (2007). *First generation entry into higher education. An international study.* Maidenhaid Berkshire: Open University Press.

Tinto, V. (1993). *Leaving college, rethinking the causes and cures of student attrition* (2nd edition). Chicago/London: The University of Chicago Press.

University of Amsterdam Diversity Commission (2016a). *Diversiteit is een werkwoord. / Let's do diversity.* Amsterdam: University of Amsterdam.

University of Amsterdam Diversity Commission (2016b). *Diversiteit is een werkwoord. Samenvatting rapport.* [Let's do diversity. Report summary.] Amsterdam: University of Amsterdam.

Van Gaalen, A., Roodenburg, S., Hobbes, H.J., Huberts, D., & Gielesen, R. (2014). *Studenten internationaliseren in eigen land – deel II. De praktijk.* [Students internationalising in their own country – part II. In Practice.] The Hague: Nuffic.

Van Middelkoop, D., & Meerman, M. (2014), *Studiesucces en diversiteit. En wat hbo-docenten daarmee te maken hebben.* [Study Success and diversity. And how it affects higher professional education lecturers.] Amsterdam: CAREM/Differentiated HRM Research Group/Amsterdam University of Applied Sciences.

Wolff, R. (2013). *Presteren op vreemde bodem. Een onderzoek naar sociale hulpbronnen en de leeromgeving als studiesuccesfactoren voor niet-westerse allochtone studenten in het Nederlandse hoger onderwijs (1997-2010).* [Performing in a foreign environment. A study of social resources and the learning environment as study success factors for non-Western immigrant students in Dutch higher education (1997-2010).] Amsterdam: University of Amsterdam.

Wolff, R., & Severiens, S. (2011). De weg naar een keuze, een afslag naar succes? [The road to a choice, an exit to success?] *THEMA, 2,* 16-21.

VÉRONIQUE DAMOISEAUX
LECTURER

'I WOULD THROW AWAY ALL WORKBOOKS AND COMBINE SUBJECTS'

As a Dutch language lecturer at the KPZ Teacher Education University in Zwolle, Véronique Damoiseaux teaches her students more than just her subject. Even if we can't look far ahead, training the teacher of the future requires more than just didactic knowledge. It's about making informed decisions, critical self-reflection and continuous self-development.

'Dealing with a changing society means thinking about the choices you have as a teacher. As a specialist Dutch language teacher, naturally I teach my students how to teach pupils to read, write, speak and listen. I let them see and experience that language plays a role throughout the day, in everything you do in class. If it were up to me, I would throw away all workbooks and combine subjects. For example in history you form a picture of time, learn to understand interesting texts and write a historical text based on all the knowledge you have acquired. A teacher therefore needs to know exactly what he wants to teach the children and how he can do this.'

"Learning doesn't stop after teacher training."

ACTING AS A ROLE MODEL

'In class, I try to promote my vision by being a role model for students. For example, I could simply tell them how to improve young children's vocabulary and discuss the theory. But I can also take a practical approach using a picture book and let them experience it themselves. The actions imprint into their bodies, with the result that they retain the theory better too. And that's the whole point.

Fortunately, teachers have a lot of freedom in Dutch education. Of course there is a framework but there is also a great deal of

"I try to be a role model for students and teachers."

autonomy in designing education. In teacher education universities, we work together with all levels within the profession. I believe this is very important because it ensures a constant exchange of knowledge, experience and developments between the study programme and the profession. We learn with and from one another and that is important, both for primary school children and for our students. After all, together we are training future teachers.'

LIFELONG LEARNING

'Learning doesn't stop once you have completed teacher training. I sometimes say that the study programme should last six years: four years at school, two years in practice, and then back to school again for two years. It keeps new teachers on their toes: are they still doing what they have learned, what issues is the school facing and how do they seek and find answers? We need reflective, critical and creative schools that are able to see past the current issues and work on the education of the future. This task confronts higher professional education too. It's important to do so based on the necessary knowledge and sound reasoning: in education you never stop learning.' ‹

Chapter 8

Vocational Education in the Netherlands

Prof. dr. Marc van der Meer,
Tilburg University

ntroduction

Dutch vocational education has been developed alongside general education with relatively little interconnection. It is made up of three more or less autonomous domains, each with their own rules, facilities and administrative considerations: preparatory vocational secondary education (VMBO), upper or senior secondary vocational education and training (MBO) and higher professional education (HBO). Yet international research indicates that this collective system of skill formation attainment has resulted in an innovative, high-quality professional population, as it has in German-speaking and Scandinavian countries. Vocational education and training is constantly developing, creating new balances partly in response to upcoming changes in the field of labour. This chapter focuses primarily on MBO, but also explains its relationship with the student-supplying VMBO schools and the HBO schools where these students may continue their school careers.

The Three Levels of Dutch Vocational Education

Pre-vocational Education (VMBO)
VMBO is the result of a merger in 1999 between what was known as junior vocational education (LBO) and junior general secondary education (MAVO). Of all pupils aged 12 to 16, about 60% attend VMBO, which makes it the largest form of secondary education in the Netherlands. VMBO is often part of a comprehensive school community, although there are also independent schools for preparatory practical or theoretical education. In August 2016, the number of subject clusters was reduced from 35 to 10. Pupils are also able to take elective courses. Recent years have seen an upward pressure in VMBO: the practically oriented learning pathways attract fewer students and theoretical learning pathways are becoming more popular. Due to these developments, the progression to general and vocational education is currently under revision.

Senior Secondary Vocational Education (MBO)
The present MBO dates from the 1990s. It is an extended form of education, with great significance for the Dutch labour market. It provides education and training to the backbone of the Dutch workforce: construction sector workers, professional drivers, ICT workers, media specialists, metal sector operators, police officers, care-givers, general nurses and so on. The 482,000 MBO students generally come from pre-vocational education (VMBO) or senior general secondary education (HAVO). MBO provides them with a starting qualification to enter the labour market, which helps them to find a job or continue their studies elsewhere. Students follow one of two equivalent, parallel learning pathways: the school-based route (BOL) with 20-60% practical instruction, or the dual or work-based route, that consists of apprenticeships with 20-40% theoretical explanation (BBL). In MBO, the national umbrella associations representing employers and employees still have significant responsibility, on the one hand

for the establishment of the qualification structure and on the other hand for providing a high-quality network of companies offering practical on-the-job training.

Higher Professional Education (HBO)
The current form of HBO dates from the 1980s and is aimed at students who have completed senior general secondary education (HAVO), pre-university secondary education (VWO) or upper secondary vocational education (MBO). Unlike in MBO, there is no systematic cooperation with trade and industry; internships are more dependent on market forces than on arrangements made at institution level. In recent years, HBO has been reshaped, following the Veerman Committee's recommendations for clearer differentiation, internationalization and more selective admissions in higher education (2010). Education is increasingly tailored as closely as possible to society's profiles for the future of e.g. work, energy, health care and technology.

History and Development of MBO

Under the Dutch Constitution, educational institutions are free to decide their educational set-up. This means that the government determines the *educational objectives* that are set and the schools decide how to achieve these objectives. In designing their education programmes, educational institutions therefore have significant freedom; they are at liberty to make choices about educational and teaching forms on the basis of the institution's fundamental principles and educational vision (see Chapter 1). This separation of responsibilities offers teaching professionals and management significant scope to decide how to organize the education they provide. Students are then able to choose the type of education that suits them.

A legal basis for MBO was first created in 1921 by the commencement of the Nijverheidswet (the Industrial, Technical and Domestic Education Act), four years after the establishment of the Ministry of Education in 1917. The current MBO institutions were created twenty years ago on the introduction of the Wet Educatie en Beroepsonderwijs (WEB, Adult and Vocational Education Act) in 1996. Until then, vocational education was divided into two systems, day schools and apprenticeship training, which were accordingly combined. One of the aims of this Act was to enhance the opportunities for institutions to develop and to enhance educational innovation. All types of upper secondary vocational education were brought under one roof of so-called VET-colleges, resulting in an increase in scale, new forms of management, and competition between institutions. At present, there are 44 regional training centres or colleges that offer all types of vocational education with a threefold ambition: qualification for the labour market, socialization and preparation for further learning. Education is organized by sector (administration, construction, economics, health care, logistics, technology, welfare, and so on), by level (entry level, MBO 2, MBO 3, MBO 4), by pathway (BOL and BBL) and by study year (1, 2, 3, 4). There are also 12 specialist institutions (specialist VET-colleges, *vakscholen*) specializing in a single area (such as creative craftsmanship, IT & media, furniture, technology etc.) and 12 agricultural VET colleges focused on agriculture, horticulture and other 'green' sector areas.

In 2011, the government published its 'Focus on craftsmanship' Action Programme, expressing its ambition to make MBO more attractive and challenging (De Bruijn et al, 2017; Chin-a-Fat et al., 2016). Study programmes were made more intensive and shorter (three years instead of four), the qualification structure was extensively revised and a new operational model with strong performance incentives was implemented. With the introduction of national examinations for some subjects (Dutch, basic mathematics and English), the curriculum became more general. At the same time, the government initiated a different approach to industrial policy with the introduction of a 'top sector policy' (strengthening the high value added sectors of production) and by creating market conditions for the allocation of innovation grants.[1] All these initiatives have led to increased quality awareness among the various regional training centres, working together in networks to take measures to ensure they are 'in control' (Douma et al., 2012).

According to the most recent 'State of Education' report (Dutch Inspectorate of Education, 2016), the education climate in MBO is steadily improving: graduation rates are rising, drop-out rates are further reduced and MBO graduates are attaining higher success rates in higher-level education. The number of students obtaining a diploma at MBO 4 level is increasing. There are a few programmes that are not up to standard and according to the Inspectorate, examination quality is not yet at the expected level but improvements can be seen in these areas too. The Inspectorate also rightly expresses its concerns about the issue of (un)equal opportunities, especially between higher and lower qualified persons, though it is often commented in international literature that youth unemployment levels and the number of young people in the NEET category (*Not in employment, education or training*) in the Netherlands compare very favourably with those in most European countries, at least once they have obtained a basic qualification.

Figure 8.1 sketches the position of vocational education within the larger education structure in the Netherlands, with primary education at the basis and doctorate degree in the top. VMBO is pictured at the bottom-right, MBO in the right-upper corner and HBO at the left.

[1]   See PBT (2016), Van der Meer et al. (2017).

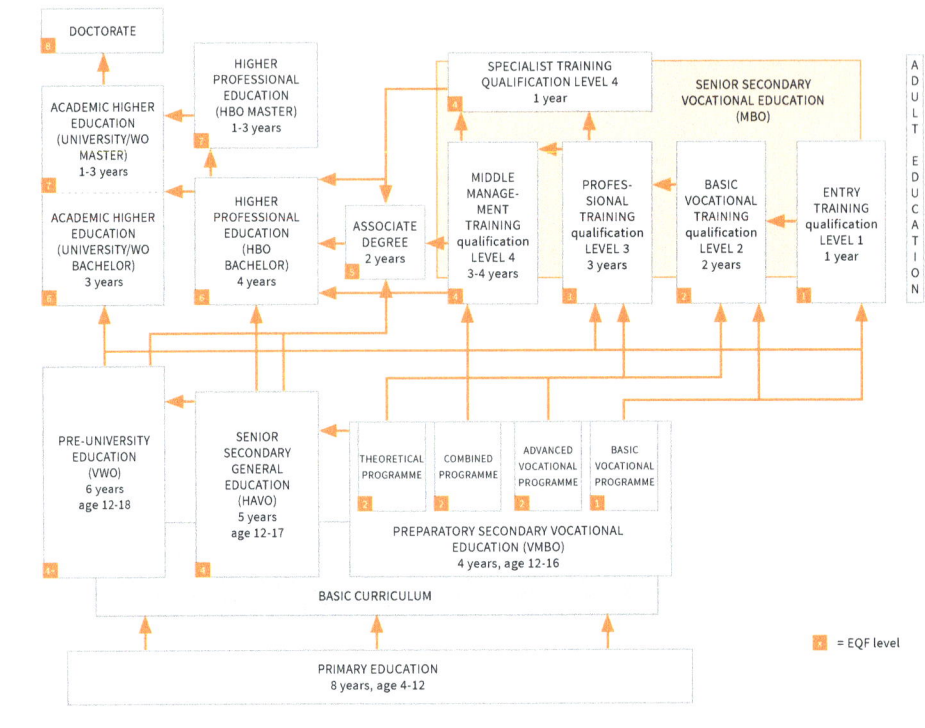

Figure 8.1 *Overview Dutch educational system. Source: SBB (2017).*

Dutch vocational education comprises both publicly-funded and a well-developed system of privately-funded institutions. In 'Skills beyond school' (2014) the Organisation for Economic Co-operation and Development (OECD) comments positively on this inclusive Dutch system. They state that a hybrid form has been created with a role for the various organizations in society (educational institutions, business and employee representatives), which operates to reduce the risks posed by government failures (excessive government intervention) and market failures (an inadequately trained labour force) as much as possible. The report does advise the Netherlands that VMBO-MBO alignment, and that of MBO with associate degrees, higher professional education (HBO) and university, needs to be improved significantly and that much more emphasis needs to be placed on lifelong learning. Naturally, this puts demands on teaching staff (OECD, 2014).

At the same time, it is difficult to establish whether the education provided is a success in terms of its crafts-based, vocational character. After obtaining a basic qualification, students are certainly not in a bad position in the labour market, but the general impression is that the results in terms of practical vocational training leave room for improvement, certainly given the fact that general subjects have received more attention in the curriculum. As we shall see, the challenge for the future is to further improve learning results through cooperation and boundary-crossing between vocational education and local businesses.

In the remainder of this chapter, we will outline the challenges MBO is facing. First we discuss the quantitative and qualitative dimensions of the teachers' agenda, then we focus on student pathways through the system, shifts in the economic structure, the qualification structure, innovation policy, and life-long learning. The final section concludes with three key questions for the future.

Internal and External Challenges

Teachers' Agenda

In recent years the issue of the role of teachers has gained priority in the national policy agenda. Following advice from many commissions, the Ministry of Education, Culture and Science (2013) published the 'Lerarenagenda 2013-2020' ('Teachers' Agenda 2013-2020) and negotiated with the social partners in education the Nationaal Onderwijsakkoord 'De route naar geweldig onderwijs' (National Education Agreement 'The road to great education') (Ministry of Education, Culture and Science and Foundation of Education, 2013), referring to the fundamental principle that good education can only be provided by teachers who understand their job. To achieve this, it is considered necessary to raise professional standards, to improve teacher training and induction, and to ensure teachers facilities and time to meet the required standards. For vocational education (both VMBO and MBO), these ambitions present extra challenges as the impact of specific aspects are not always taken into account, such as workplace learning in authentic work environments, lateral entry to the teaching profession and the role of workplace trainers and supervisors. Moreover, the teaching staff in VET has to deal with a heavy administrative burden and more or less permanent political intervention in education.[2] This gives rise to various quantitative and qualitative issues.

Based on quantitative extrapolations, clear trends in education participation can be identified. The Netherlands is experiencing population shrinkage in outlying areas and growth in large cities, where the population today is super-diverse (Crul e.a., 2012, see also Chapter 7). Significant shifts are occurring within the various sections of education: the number of VMBO pupils is decreasing, in particular the volume of those taking the two most practical learning routes; at the same time, an upward pressure towards senior general secondary education (HAVO) can be noted (Westerhuis & De Bruijn, 2015). The consequence of this educational race is that in time, the proportion of students attending MBO will also decrease. Indexed to participation in 1995 (= 100), a peak occurred in 2010 (= 116) which will gradually decrease to 92 in 2030. Participation in higher professional education (HBO) and university education, on the other hand, will continue to rise in the next few years. The index figure for higher education is currently 165 (1995 = 100). It will rise to 169 in 2020 and then gradually decrease.[3]

---

[2]   On the shortcomings in the teachers' agenda and the need for quality-improvement in VET, see Van der Meer (2014)
[3]   Source: Ministry of Education, Culture and Science. Referentieraming 2015 (Reference forecast 2015).

The demographic shifts in student orientation therefore also have consequences for teacher requirements in quantitative terms, even more so given the significantly ageing teaching population. Twenty years ago, too few students studied technical subjects; now – a generation later – not enough of them have gone into teaching. The continuity of technical education in VMBO and MBO schools is under serious threat due to the reduction in teachers and facilities. According to an exploratory study commissioned by the MBO Raad (Ockam/IPS, 2015), the shortage of technology teachers may rise to 1500 teachers and 900 education assistants in the next five years. As the baby boom generation retires, the profession will need more new entrants, current teachers will have to work longer (retirement age has already gone up to 67) or the number of students per class must increase (which would increase productivity in quantitative terms).

In qualitative terms, there are more uncertainties, given that teacher training programmes are often insufficiently tailored to V(MBO). The Ministry of Education, Culture and Science's recent establishment of specializations and minors in vocational education in teacher training is a first positive step. Other adjustment mechanisms also play a role in the quality of teaching staff. How attractive is teaching as a profession? What prior education level is required? And how is the work remunerated and valued? A persistent problem is that approximately half of all new teachers leave the education sector within five years. Apparently, the profession is not sufficiently attractive to them, wage are relatively moderate and working conditions are challenging, whereas many starting teachers simply do not survive in the demanding educational (V)MBO environment.

Prospects

Traditionally, vocational education has made significant use of lateral entrants to the teaching profession. To empower this group, even different solutions are needed. In line with the recent proposal by the Platform Bèta Techniek (National Platform Science & Technology) regarding 'circular careers' (2016), dual appointments with both an educational institution and a company could become possible. Such hybrid combinations are currently in the experimental phase. The development of a common pedagogical and educational repertoire makes new forms of team teaching possible. Later on, VMBO-MBO teacher exchanges could be introduced, with mutual supervision and coaching. This would immediately lead to a modernization of employment relationships in educational establishments and in business.

Another significant challenge for MBO institutions is improving the *effects* of the educational teams and giving them a more external, labour market-focused orientation. In accordance with the applicable Professional Statute (2009), and unlike the situation in other educational sectors, the educational teams in MBO are the main actors in the internal educational system. Each team has a team leader, and this also establishes the line of authority. The regulations stipulate that all members of the team should engage in professional development. The challenging task the team leader faces is to combine the professionalization of team members and the provision of meaningfulness to them with the attainment of good education results (see Chapter 4). Diverse competencies, task variation and focus points come together in a team (for example, teachers in their role as pedagogues, didacticians or mentors). In the *basic profile* for teachers, having sufficient theoretical as well as practical knowledge and creating a good climate for learning are all relevant. In recent years, more attention has been given to differentiation of roles, such as actively shaping curriculum development (subject clusters and elective subjects) and carrying out independent research in class.

Much is expected of teachers' investigative capacity. The road is long but it is worth persevering, given the defective knowledge infrastructure in MBO.[4] The first generation of teachers is now receiving in-service training to attain a master-degree; if they can take the lead in educational innovation in regional training centres then a great deal can be achieved. Recently many VET-centres are initiating small centres for expertise and inquiry under the label 'practoraten', to strengthen practical investigation and reflexive capacities. Available tools such as *Learning analytics* can also contribute to student capabilities analysis and provide infrastructural support for tailor-made programmes (using individual portfolios).

If in the coming period even more differentiation arises in the educational pathways of the already diverse student population, this will also require more flexibility from teachers with respect to assessing, evaluating and supervising cognitive and practical differences between students, difference that often represent strong sociocultural orientations. Alongside teaching and examining, a number of indirect functions play an important role in vocational education: such as career counselling and supervision during the work-based learning period (Meijers et al., 2014).

Another relevant development is the growing availability of information technology, making the interpretation of online information and social media increasingly important (cf. Kennisnet, a public organization for Education & ICT, 2016). This places a great responsibility on educational teams, and not just in the context of civic education, which is a compulsory part of the MBO curriculum. In the practice-oriented (V)MBO education, aspects such as reading and reproducing, but also combining, analysing, recognizing patterns and structures, discussing, philosophizing and listening, converge uniquely within the context of the educational institution, as social aspects of the learning process. In addition, we can expect that new teaching methods and learning tools will increasingly become available online and that e-learning (focused on very specific skills and actions) will more easily be developed in business companies. Apparently, ICT will likely act as information carrier and network structure rather than as a form of education replacing the educational institution.

---

[4]   See Van der Meer and Verheijen (publication in progress).

Easier Pathways to the Next Level of Education

The purpose of VMBO is to offer pupils a sufficient basis for further learning including a practical orientation to work processes, that of MBO is to give them qualifications enabling them to start a career. Yet in management and organizational terms, VMBO and MBO are two quite different worlds. This is evidenced by the fact that in recent years they have revised their curricula completely independently of one another, even though 85% of pupils completing VMBO continues its education in MBO. These students often struggle to adapt to the different learning context in MBO, which involves stronger autonomy and self-responsibility with more demanding requirements.

It appears that students are particularly vulnerable at this pivotal point and these changeover times form the bottleneck for progression from one level of education to the next (Klatter, 2014; Elffers, 2011). For this reason, the topic of career orientation and supervision has been included in the new curriculum for VMBO. This requires a new, quite different approach from teaching staff, who need to take a more reflective attitude when discussing the pupils' educational choices and career opportunities. Student need to 'come into the world', as Pols (2015) puts it.

This is also important in MBO, which needs to better consider the intake and entry of students from the levels of education that precede it. And, of course, the progression and transfer of students to higher professional education (HBO) also contains significant alignment issues, particularly in view of the high drop-out rate among MBO graduates during the early years of HBO programmes.

Prospects

These topics are now on the government's agenda, as it aims to promote seamless progression from one level of education to the next (see Ministry of Education, Culture and Science, 2017). Educational institutions are also seeking bottom-up solutions to this problem. Within the 'Consortium Beroepsonderwijs' (Vocational Education Consortium), an association of secondary education and MBO institutions, a continuous learning line from VMBO to MBO has been developed entitled 'The Metal Pivot'. There are now connected curricula in 'Production, Installation, Energy' (PIE) and 'Nursing, Health, Welfare and Social Care', which are also recognized and utilized by the relevant sectors themselves (Klatter, 2014). The government has also taken a number of initiatives to create programmes supporting progression to the next level of education. Initially, it experimented with progression programmes from VMBO up to MBO 2. More recently, new specialised 'craftsmanship' and 'technology routes' have been developed linking VMBO with MBO that aim at a better alignment based on content. Where VMBO and MBO are housed in the same building, this improves coordination. It also helps if there is local pressure. For example, in areas where the population is shrinking, such as the provinces of Groningen, Limburg and Zeeland, efforts are now being made to create an integrated curriculum. This for example has resulted in Arcus College and Leeuwenborgh Regional Training Centre developing programmes for mechanical operators at MBO 2 level. Based on analysis by car company Nedcar-VDL of core tasks and work processes, new practical assignments are being developed, which form the basis of a new curriculum.

Shifts in the Economic Structure

In the Netherlands, qualifications are important; they have significant signalling value as indicators of proficiency, certainly for people entering the labour market. More than in other education sectors, MBO works from a direct connection between education and the field of employment. For this reason, the Dutch system is sometimes regarded as the best of both worlds, having a full-time version (the school-based route or BOL) as in Belgium and Scandinavia, and a dual version (the work-based route or BBL) as in Germany, which gives the system the flexibility to respond to the economic climate. Through this, vocational education can enhance the competitiveness and degree of innovation of businesses and institutions (De Bruijn, e.a. 2017; Busemeijer & Trampusch, 2012; Busemeijer, 2016).

At the same time, the international economic crisis following the collapse of Lehman Brothers in 2008 has affected the labour market much more profoundly than was generally expected. Due to technological developments, more jobs are at risk than initially predicted.[5] MBO institutions have noticed the effects of these events on the number of students taking each of the MBO learning pathways: during the crisis, the number of students opting for the school-based pathway rose to 381,000 but the number choosing the work-based pathway declined from 167,000 (2008-9) to 95,000 (2015-16), with a particularly sharp drop in the number of adults enrolling. Now that the economic climate is improving, BBL- enrolments have gradually increased again to 101,000 students (see Table 8.1).

---

[5] In 2008, the Bakker Committee still predicted significant employment market shortages due to the ageing labour force. Then the financial crisis occurred and the retirement age was raised, which forces people to work longer.

Year of study	Dual pathway (BBL)	School-based pathway (BOL)	Total
2009/2010	167,091	348,457	515,548
2010/2011	164,894	354,623	519,517
2011/2012	154,404	354,457	508,861
2012/2013	143,062	357,262	500,324
2013/2014	120,718	368,175	488,893
2014/2015	100,434	375,676	476,110
2015/2016	95,772	376,111	471,883
2016/2017	100,946	380,950	481,896

Table 8.1   *Study routes in Dutch MBO. Source: DUO/SBB.*

This pattern is reinforced by the influence of new technologies in production processes, which is likely to result in many routine jobs disappearing. The mid-segments of the economy appears to be under particular pressure, although interpretations of the significance of international (primarily Anglo-Saxon) research outcomes for the Netherlands vary. Some consultancy companies blindly predict the erosion of the mid-section of the labour market and the disappearance of two to three million jobs (Deloitte, 2016). Based on research into wage-data and working tasks by the Centraal Planbureau (Economic Policy Analysis, CPB, 2015), learning and working (Social and Cultural Planning Office, SCP, 2016) and allocation of students (Bol & Van de Werfhorst, 2016), it is also concluded that the labour market is becoming polarized, though data differ significantly for the various sectors. It should be added that a feature of Dutch vocational training is that (in the Rhineland tradition) MBO institutions give students a 'broad' training, not just for the performance of an isolated, single task (as in Anglo-Saxon countries) but to qualify them for a broader job territory (with an added focus on socialization and lifelong learning), so that they also have better career opportunities. The Researchcentrum voor Onderwijs en Arbeidsmarkt (ROA, Research Centre for Education and the Labour Market) is much more cautious in its predictions on the future of jobs and occupations. It points at the significant ageing of the work force and thus needs for replacements in the labour market and the fact that more is being required of workers (ROA, 2016). In summary, the best approach is therefore to point out the underlying trend of upgrading and flexibilization of occupations and jobs, which naturally has a variety of characteristics.

Prospects

In the agricultural sector, diversification and internationalisation of production processes occurs, with the emergence of new forms of sustainable energy production and technology-based food enhancement, leading to a need for further training in jobs. Industrial companies, on their turn, have largely become integrated into international production chains. Due to robotization and automation, traditional production work has diminished in scale. Dutch branch offices are often specialized in research and design, marketing and sales. This means that employment opportunities with many industrial firms have become more tertiary in nature. At the same time, there are vacancies for craftsmen in the mid-segments of the labour market, such as construction workers, installation engineers, ICT specialists and logistics workers, due to insufficient investment in training for these workers during the crisis years. In financial and economic services, there is significant pressure on jobs due to automation. In related industries such as the healthcare and welfare sector, significant rationalization and separation of tasks in production processes is notable. In local growth sectors such as the creative industry, hospitality and tourism, specific organizational processes are being developed with their own particular methods of standardizing and increasing flexibility of work processes. In the hospitality sector, for instance, long-term permanent contracts occur but also a great deal of short-term cyclical employment.

The general expectation is that in the 'flat world' (Friedman, 2005) of the open, global economy, local occupations, such as hairdressers, chefs, mechanics and other service providers, will continue to exist, but these can also be carried out in informal employment relationships. In addition, as a result of ICT applications, there is a trend towards more generalist occupations (insurance, application management) because employees have access to more information (expert systems et cetera). There is also an emerging entertainment industry in the broadest sense of the word, which is to some extent creating its own demand. This leads to significant interaction between industries and sectors (for example, 3D printing, electronic cars and new logistic requirements).

The position of work for youngsters is becoming more flexible in all dimensions: numerical, qualitative and functional. The substantial fluctuations in consumer demand have added to this. Besides this, we see both simplification and upgrading of the demands placed on workers, depending on the sector or field of work. Work is generally becoming more complex. While the optometrist may be disappearing, the optician's profession will become broader in scope.

The increasing flexibility of the labour market means that people can have several jobs at the same time. Young people will want to build up a portfolio of relevant learning experiences in certain occupational fields, in which changing job opportunities and new career paths arise depending on the competencies and expertise they have developed. Moreover, self-employment and independent work forms are on the rise, which requires more focus on entrepreneurial skills in education. The looser collaborative associations that professionals (and partnerships) are adopting, offer opportunities for shared workspaces and new forms of organization. In all this, it is not yet clear how the increasing flexibility of employment contracts, on entry and on exit, will be compensated with facilities for retraining and in-service training as new forms of social security. At the same time, the decentralization and de-collectivization of social security policies from the central government in The Hague to local municipal level, are raising new issues for the development of on-the-job training arrangements for unemployed target groups.

Significance of the Qualification Structure

In the light of these external changes, the social partners have repeatedly revised the qualification structure in MBO, although this never resulted in full dualization of vocational education. As of 2008, a transition was made from education focused on final attainment targets to 'competency based' education, formally referred to since 2012 as 'occupation-focused education'. During the most recent revision since 2011, the qualification structure has been simplified and 700 elective options are currently being introduced. To start with, advice on this is being provided by the eight sector chambers of the newly-established national Samenwerkingsorganisatie Beroepsonderwijs Bedrijfsleven (SBB, Cooperation Organization for Vocational Education, Training and the Labour Market). In technical terms, the profiles and elective options that are now being introduced in MBO, offer significant opportunities for educational innovation at a local level. Institutions are not required to offer all the elective options, they can be selective in this, both for organizational and logistic reasons and in response to regional needs.

Unlike VMBO and HBO, MBO has a close-knit network of relationships with local SME businesses. Expressed in figures, this amounts to more than 230,000 work placement companies, with relationships varying in intensity. SMEs constitute the principal market for MBO students and, looked at from the opposite angle, MBO is the main supplier of entry-level professionals (novices) for SMEs. The main challenge is tailoring the national qualification structure to regional variations in employment even more closely, so that sufficient young people obtain the right qualifications. Alongside all these issues, the topic of macro-efficiency has also been placed on the agenda. The intention is that regional training colleges serve their own region, rather than (as was previously the case) compete with one another for students. For this, SBB is providing improved information files and developing new tools with labour market information (*Opportunities for work; opportunities for traineeships*), to stimulate students to choose MBO programmes that offer them better access to work. The future will tell whether this will be successful and responsibility for success cannot be exclusively left to the regional organizations, for the simple reason that changes to healthcare or technology branches are not confined to a single region but occur throughout the country. Moreover, the national government has a duty to protect the validity and recognition of qualifications ('civiel effect') to guarantee access to work.

Prospects

MBO therefore needs to adapt to this new reality. To equip students for the labour market (Van der Veer et al., 2014), it is important to have not only outstanding general and vocational education ('stock'), but also the institutional mechanisms for the transition ('flow') from school to school, school to work, work to further learning and work to work and a suitable combination with the care for family members. Such 'transition routes' are key intervention points from the perspective of socioeconomic policy. Finally, there needs to be customized reintegration ('buffer') to find solutions for drop-outs (young people not switching studies but dropping out of studying entirely and recorded as NEETs). At a local level, refugees and asylum seekers add to the problems, because it is often at regional training centres that they can try to build up their lives again.

In this context, the MBO-2 certificate is an important benchmark in Dutch education policy, constituting the threshold for a long-term future in the labour market. The MBO-2 programmes are currently broadened, as aspects such as communication, working together, entrepreneurship and networking skills become important in working environments, but these are also learned on the job. At the same time, the value attached to this MBO-2 certificate is shifting. As a general rule, the higher the level of education completed, the more senior the position a student can expect to obtain in a firm. The opportunities in the labour market to workers with MBO-1 and -2 certificates and those available to MBO-3 and -4 and HBO graduates differ significantly. In other words, the 'threshold' is shifting from MBO-2 to MBO-3.

Innovation Policy

In the Netherlands, there has been a significant reassessment of the idea of 'embedded capitalism' in recent years. Cooperation in the 'multiple helix' between companies, government bodies and knowledge organizations (R&D-institutes and schools) is regarded as essential in achieving an innovative employment market climate. Regional production chains are embedded in local and regional networks in which supplying and purchasing companies cooperate with authorities and educational and research institutions. The awareness that regional development can be reinforced by cooperation between government and local businesses has been strongly 'promoted' in the last ten years; first in Limburg, Amsterdam, Rotterdam-Rijnmond-Drecht Cities, Brainport Eindhoven and Twente, later joined by North-Holland-North, Flevoland, Groningen-Eemsdelta and the Gelderland Valley with its leading agricultural university in Wageningen, which operates in a worldwide network.

Prospects

So what is the result of these innovations? Unlike HBO, which was awarded lectureships in 2000 to support the professionalization of its teaching staff and forge links with universities,

MBO institutions were not strengthened by any alliance between their staff and academic or research institutions. From 2003-2004 onwards, the content development of MBO institutions was supported by an innovation programme, '*Het Platform Beroepsonderwijs*' (The Vocational Education Platform or HPBO), that was launched by the national Stichting van de Arbeid (Labour Foundation, representing employers and employees). This programme involved innovation at the basis, and in the width and depth of MBO in its totality. It laid the foundations for regional co-makership programmes in MBO, for effective learning and innovation within the institution, for learning in the workplace and for professionalization. Evaluations of these programmes reveal that innovation management within the institutions was often lacking or poorly organized, with the result that innovative projects sometimes produced little or no result. The breakthrough projects launched in that period aimed to improve areas such workplace learning, onward progression of students and effective organization. By placing these projects on the agenda at various education institutions at the same time, the participating institutions had to learn to work together and take a common approach. According to those involved, this created the basis for co-makership and hybrid working environments in their current form.[6] In Figure 8.2 is portrayed how VET and companies can join their educational and organizational resources to initiate a new learning environment, that accordingly can be placed within the school or in a company location.

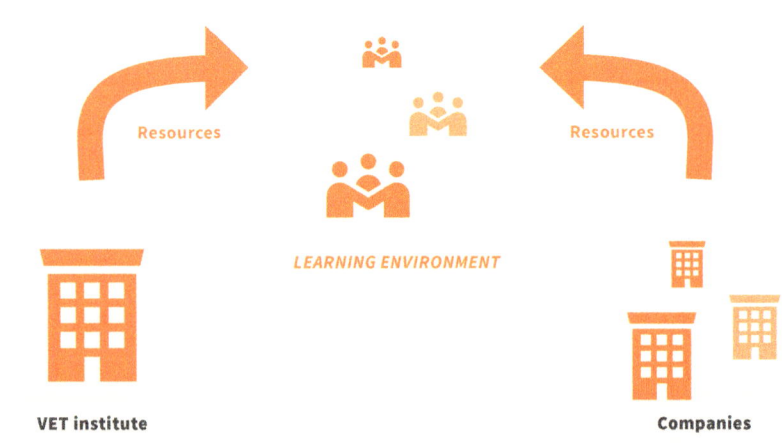

Figure 8.2   *A new entity. Linking education and business. (Source: Smulders e.a. 2012)*

---

[6]   See for example the final publication 'Innovisier' by HPBO (2016). For other overviews, see Smulders et al. (2012), Van der Meer (2014) and Bakker et al. (2016).

In 2010, the government, pressed by several captains of industry, initiated a different course in industrial policy by supporting the 'Top Sectors policy' (in several leading economic sectors in the Netherlands such as agrifood, chemicals, creative sector and ICT, water management). This led to a different use of innovation funds in vocational education, which became allocated via the Ministry of Economic Affairs. Since then, more than 100 Centres for Innovative Craftsmanship have been set up in MBO and Centres of Expertise in HBO. These are partnerships between educational institutions and companies aimed at improving technological and educational innovation. In recent years, the Ministry of Education, Culture and Science added a Regional Investment Fund, so that other sectors can also profit from these resources. A Healthcare Pact was also created for regional innovation between educational institutions and health and welfare organizations.

The philosophy is not merely working together but placing vocational education at the heart of the regional ecosystem, according to Platform Bèta Techniek (PBT) (National Platform Science & Technology) as 'producer' and 'accelerator' and not just as a 'system supplier' (PBT, 2016). The substantial investments in these forms of co-makership have a powerful effect in agenda-setting, all the more so given that funds are available in these programmes for targeted exploratory studies into the future. The evaluations available to date primarily discuss the quantitative growth of the number of participants in these programmes and the sustainability of the many new forms of cooperation in the Centres for Innovative Craftsmanship and Centres of Expertise, but do not (yet) provide systematic analysis in a qualitative sense of the requirements for specific educational improvements to vocational programmes. Moreover, a lot more attention should be given in coming years to knowledge dissemination about the added value of regional economic cooperation.

Post-Initial Education

With the creation of regional training centres, adult education was also placed under the auspices of vocational education. The 1996 act had the explicit aim of 'creating more cohesion in the field of adult education', though ever since a striking number of statutory and consequently organizational shifts have occurred. In recent years, the field of (adult) education has been subject to strong market forces, whereas, on the other hand, the second-chance general secondary education for adults (VAVO, Voortgezet Algemeen Volwassenen Onderwijs) has been brought back to the regional training centres.

In addition to the publicly-financed MBO institutions, there is also an extensive market of private, i.e. not state-funded institutions for vocational education. These institutions generally serve a different target group which tends to be older and require training tailored to a specific job. In some cases, they also develop programmes jointly with publicly financed MBO institutions, such as the VAPRO programme in the processing industry, which exists for sixty years. Generally it can be said that private education has a significant market share in providing courses for life-long learning (approximately 85% for private education as compared to 15% for MBO, higher professional education and universities; see Buisman & Van Wijk, 2012).

Prospects

The public VET-schools value their commercial activities, as they allow them to innovate their curriculums, teaching methods and equipment and enter into new organizational ties with companies. That is no simple matter for educational institutions. Tailor-made programmes, targeted at lifelong learning by employees in regional businesses, are not always compatible with the organization of full-time initial VET-programmes, since innovation is not based on student numbers and individual competency objectives. Investments in and knowledge exchange between networks of private and public parties are needed to achieve this, even if the outcome is by no means certain.

The Future

Internationally, Dutch vocational education has a good reputation. One aspect of this success comes from the double supply of learning routes (school-based and work-based), which increasingly develop in combinations. Youth unemployment is also relatively low by European standards and significant opportunities are available in the labour market for young people who complete a vocational training programme. At the same time, considerable challenges exist in view of the technological and organizational changes in the labour market and shifts in student population. In view of these potentially far-reaching changes, collaboration in innovative arrangements combining school-based learning and workplace learning ('forming a connective learning architecture') provides the model for the future. This presupposes that vocational education and firms are able to articulate their interests and develop a joint vocabulary at local level. Educational institutions need to bring their students' future work field within their walls, as it were, whilst trade and industry might benefit from the educational institutions' pedagogical, didactical and educational knowledge. From an administrative point of view, that also requires cooperation between secondary education (pre-vocational education (VMBO) and senior general secondary education (HAVO), MBO and higher professional education, in order to better use the regional infrastructure and equipment of schools and companies.

To achieve this, it is not necessary to change everything at the same time; in recent years repeated policy reforms have been enacted. Instead, a period of relative stability and stepwise improvement is needed: the issue is the 'speed of change'. Due to all policy changes in recent years education teams have underestimated the importance of a good pedagogical and didactic basis for vocational education for too long. Teams should be given, and make use of, the scope to develop their own vision on education, to better understand one another while applying new activating didactical methods attuned to developments in real work processes. What then constitutes good and effective vocational education undisputedly remains a normative issue. Therefore it should be asked: effective for whom, and effective for what? In 'The Craftsman', the sociologist Richard Sennett (2009) rightly argues that competencies are not a kind of 'tricks': *21st century skills* do not deliver a recipe for flexible, omnipotent employees. Therefore, school management must express 'conscious trust' in the professionalism of teaching teams to create – for an increasingly diverse student population – the right balance in the curriculum between general skills, occupation-specific skills and personal skills of students that have unique value in the labour market.

It would be incorrect to conclude in this context that a national policy is no longer required. The development of tasks and positions in the labour market, the changes in occupations and the new variety in career paths should not be left up to the market alone, but requires social investments in a capacitation approach directed to training and lifelong learning, good facilities for the transition from school to work and specific tailor-made reintegration for vulnerable groups. At least, this asks for a meticulous national evaluation and policy feedback, uniform quality standards, markedly valid qualification files for the labour market, and coordinated agenda of research and development to facilitate youngsters proper progression within professions. We should be aiming to further expand the social significance, the 'outcome', of vocational education. This requires cooperation at local level between educational institutions and companies, supported by knowledge centres and teacher training programmes (both HBO and universities). Since many of the challenges ahead are 'wicked policy issues', relatively intensive content supervision is required, and targeted local experiments to achieve innovation and development.

For the near future, it is therefore relevant to ask how political parties define the task assigned to vocational education. The MBO institution as a leading regional knowledge centre with a significant research and development role focussing on developing the regional economy, aligned with VMBO and HBO and supported by strategic partnership with companies, provides a different organizational model from the MBO institution as an organizer of simple education services. For the target group of young people aged 16 to 23, the linked triple of qualification, socialization and preparation for further training, has significant added value for their personal development into young adults and the creation of a professional identity.

It remains to be seen how lifelong learning programmes will be given further impulse in the coming years. It is conceivable that the government will invest – more than is presently the case – in employees' skills, with help of individual learning vouchers and thus expanding the role of public MBO. It is also conceivable that public vocational education will join forces with regional businesses to fulfil certain key tasks, with other areas being developed within general education or by private parties (topics such as project leadership and entrepreneurship, for which the infrastructure investments are limited). Following this reasoning, core skills such as the Dutch language and basic mathematics could be taught by a different type of teacher, certainly when it comes to 'catch-up facilities', given the problems that schools experience in meeting the national standards in line with all that pupils are required to learn in primary and secondary education.

In general terms, we can expect that – in an overall shrinking student market – institutions will wish to distinct themselves and that the relationship between vocational education and general education will grow stronger, certainly at education programme level. In recent years, a growing variety of educational institutions have developed – the networking school, specialist VET-schools, the neighbourhood school, the associate degree-colleges – though not all have met with success. Finally, we see the significant rise of the private sector in vocational education and the growth of company schools. If the business world believes in the importance of a strong public vocational education sector in the long term, then it will need to be prepared to invest in high-quality public education programmes too.

Key Questions
- How should regional arrangements between vocational education, related school providers, national and local government and local industry be designed in order to enhance regional VET-colleges to develop into recognized and leading knowledge centres in their region?
- What factors determine the pedagogical and didactical repertoire of teaching, strengthening the learning processes of students and employees in a context of a flexible and upgrading labour market?
- Under what financial and organizational conditions can the new generation of recently trained teachers induce a coherent climate of inquiry and stepwise improvement of learning within the regional VET-centres?

About the author

Prof. dr. Marc van der Meer is endowed professor for the labour market in the education sector, associated with Reflect/Tilburg Law School and CAOP in The Hague since 2013. He is also an independent academic advisor to the Samenwerkingsorganisatie Beroepsonderwijs Bedrijfsleven (SBB, Cooperation Organization for Vocational Education, Training and the Labour Market). Recently he has contributed to various exploratory studies including *Skills beyond school in the Netherlands* (OECD, 2014); *MBO naar 2025* (2015); *Leren en opleiden in de ambachtseconomie 2020* [Learning and training in the craft economy 2020] (2016); and a series of position papers on the future of MBO, commissioned by the Ministry of OCW (2017), on which this chapter is based.

Contact: marc.vandermeer@uvt.nl.

References

Bakker, A., Zitter, I., Beaudaert, S., & De Bruijn, E. (2016). *Tussen opleiding en beroep – het perspectief van boundary crossing.* [Between education and work – the prospect of boundary crossing.] Assen: Van Gorcum.

Bol, T., & Van de Werfhorst, H. (2016). *De link tussen school en werk in een polariserende arbeidsmarkt.* [The link between school and work in an increasingly polarized employment market.] Amsterdam: UvA.

Bruijn, E., S. Billet, J.Onstenk, (2017), *Enhancing Teaching and Learning in the Dutch Vocational Education System – Reforms Enacted.* Berlijn: Springer Verlag.

Buisman, M. & B. Van Wijk,(2012). *Een leven lang leren.* [Lifelong learning.] 's-Hertogenbosch: ecbo.

Busemeijer, M. (2016). *Skills and inequality. Partisan politics and the political economy of education reforms in Western welfare states.* Cambridge: Cambridge University Press.

Busemeijer, M., & Trampusch, C. (2012). *The political economy of skill formation*, Oxford: Oxford University Press.

Chin-a-Fat, N., M.van der Steen, I. de Jong (2016). *Bewegende verhoudingen- een discoursanalyse van overheidssturing in het MBO*, [Shifting relations- a discourse analysis of government steering in VET-education], Den Haag: NSOB.

Centraal Planbureau (2015), *Baanpolarisatie in Nederland*; [Job polarization in the Netherlands), CPB Policy Brief 2015/13.

Crul, M, J. Schneider & F. Lelie (2013) *Super-diversity. A new perspective on Integration.* Amsterdam: VU University Press.

CVAE (Centre for the Crafts Economy) (2016). *Leren en werken in de ambachtseconomie 2020.* [Learning and working in the crafts economy 2020.] Zoetermeer: CVAE.

Deloitte (2016); De impact van robotisering op het Nederlandse onderwijs; [The impact of robotization on Dutch education], Deloitte.

Dutch Inspectorate of Education (2016). *Staat van het Onderwijs 2014/2015.* [State of Education 2014/2015] The Hague: Ministry of Education, Culture and Science.

Friedman T. (2005). *The world is flat – a brief history of the 21st century.* New York: Picador.

Kennisnet (2016). *Technologiekompas voor het onderwijs. Trendrapport 2016-2017.* [Technology compass for education. Trend report 2016-2017.] Zoetermeer: Kennisnet.

Klatter, E., & Van der Meer, M. (2017). *Een lerende instelling. Inquiry naar het professioneel kapitaal in het mbo.* [A learning orientation. Inquiry into the professional capital in MBO.] Position paper for Ministry of Education, Culture and Science / Netherlands Initiative for Education Research.

Klatter, E. (2014). *Visiedocument: Opleiden, leren en exmineren in het beroepsonderwijs.* [Vision document: Training, learning and examining in vocational education.] Edition VII. Amersfoort: Stichting Consortium Beroepsonderwijs.

MBO Raad (2015). *MBO 2025.* Woerden: MBO Raad.

MBO Raad (2016), Onderzoek naar mogelijke tekorten onderwijsgevenden in de technische sectoren in het MBO. (Study on the potential shortage of teachers in technical sectors in VET]. Woerden/Utrecht, MBO Raad/Ockham IPS.

Meijers, F., Kuijpers, M., Mittendorff, K., Wijers, G. (2014). *Het onzekere voor het zekere* [Uncertainty over certainty]. Garant, Antwerpen/Apeldoorn.

Ministry of Education, Culture and Science (2011). *Focus op Vakmanschap.* [Focus on Craftsmanship.] The Hague: Ministry of Education, Culture and Science.

Ministry of Education, Culture and Science (2013). *Lerarenagenda* 2013-2010: de leraar maakt het verschil. [Teachers Agenda 2013-2020: the teacher makes the difference.] The Hague: Ministry of Education, Culture and Science.

Ministry of Education, Culture and Science (2016). *Derde voortgangsevaluatie lerarenagenda.* [Third progress assessment of teachers' agenda.] The Hague: Ministry of Education, Culture and Science.

Ministry of Education, Culture and Science (2017). *Brief versterking beroepsonderwijs.* [Letter on consolidation of vocational education.] The Hague: Ministry of Education, Culture and Science.

Ministry of Education, Culture and Science and Foundation of Education (2013). Nationaal Onderwijsakkoord 'De route naar geweldig onderwijs'. [National Education Agreement 'The road to great education'.] The Hague: Ministry of Education, Culture and Science.

Ockham/IPS (2015), Onderzoek naar mogelijke tekorten onderwijsgevenden in de technische sectoren in het MBO. [Study on the potential shortage of teachers in technical sectors in VET]. Woerden/ Utrecht: MBO Raad/ Ockham IPS.

OECD (2014). *Skills beyond school – the case of the Netherlands.* Paris: OECD.

Onderwijsraad [Education Council of the Netherlands] (2013a). *Kiezen voor kwalitatief sterke leraren.* [Choosing high-quality teachers.] The Hague: Onderwijsraad.

Onderwijsraad [Education Council of the Netherlands] (2013b). *De stand van educatief Nederland 2013. Een smalle kijk op onderwijskwaliteit.* [The state of education in the Netherlands in 2013. A narrow assessment of education quality.] The Hague: Onderwijsraad.

Platform Bèta Techniek (2016). *Forum beroepsonderwijs: verbindende vooruitzichten beroepsonderwijs.* [National Platform Science & Technology: Vocational education forum: connecting prospects in vocational education.] The Hague: Platform Bèta Techniek.

Pols, W. (2015). *In de wereld komen. Een studie naar de pedagogische betekenissen van opvoeding, onderwijs en het leraarschap.* [Coming into the world. A study of the pedagogical significance of upbringing, education and teaching.] Doctoral thesis. Apeldoorn: Garant Publishers.

Research Centre for Education and the Labour Market (2016). *Arbeidsmarkt naar functies en beroepen.* [The labour market subdivided into functions and occupations.] Maastricht: Research Centre for Education and the Labour Market.

SBB (2017). *The Dutch educational system*. Available at: https://www.s-bb.nl/en/education/dutch-educational-system.

Sennet, R. (2009), *The craftsman*, Penguin Books.

Smulders, H., Hoeve, A. & Van der Meer, M. (2012). *Krachten bundelen voor vakmanschap: over co-makership tussen onderwijs en bedrijfsleven.* [Joining forces for craftmanship: on co-makership between education and business.] 's-Hertogenbosch: ecbo.

SCP [Social and Cultural Planning Office] (2016), *De toekomst tegemoet. Sociaal en Cultureel Rapport 2016.* [Facing the future. Social and cultural report 2016], The Hague: SCP.

Van der Meer, M. (2014). *Vakmensen en bewust vertrouwen: een institutionele beschouwing over de arbeidsmarkt in het middelbaar beroepsonderwijs.* [Professionals and conscious trust: an institutional reflection on the labour market in MBO.] Inaugural lecture, Tilburg University.

Van der Meer, M. en E.Verheijen (2016), *De blik van buiten- enkele lessen over de kennisinfrastructuur in het beroepsonderwijs, een analyse van vier sectoren.* [An outside-in perspective: some lessons about the knowledge infrastructure in vocational education. An analysis of four sectors]. 's-Hertogenbosch: ecbo.

Van der Meer, M., & Nieuwenhuis, L. (2017). *Regionaal beleid en het mbo.* [Regional policy and MBO.] Position paper for Ministry of Education, Culture and Science / Netherlands Initiative for Education Research.

Van der Meer, M., Van den Toren, J.P., & Lie, T. (2017). 'Transforming Vocational Education: Encouraging Innovation via Public Private Partnerships.' In: E. de Bruijn, S. Billett, J. Onstenk (Eds.). *Enhancing Teaching and Learning in the Dutch Vocational Education System – Reforms Enacted.* Berlijn: Springer Verlag. Publication in progress.

Van der Veer, J., Van der Meer, M., & Hemerijck, A. (2014). *De toerusting over de levensloop: een beschouwing over institutionele herijking in het beroepsonderwijs.* [Capacitation over the life-course: a reflection on institutional reconversion in vocational education.] 's-Hertogenbosch: ecbo.

Veerman-Committee (2010), Differentiëren in drievoud : omwille van de kwaliteit en verscheidenheid in het hoger onderwijs [Threefold differentiation: regarding quality and diversity in higher education]. The Hague: Ministry of Education, Culture and Science.

Westerhuis, A., & De Bruijn, E. (2015). *De educatieve wedloop.* [The educational race.] Preparatory study for the Education Council of the Netherlands, The Hague.

HELMA VAN DER HOORN

CHAIRMAN

'NEW-STYLE EDUCATION STILL NEEDS TO BE INVENTED'

One of her most powerful motivations is to make Dutch education focus on the future. Helma van der Hoorn, chairman of the governing board of primary school foundation SaKS, is convinced that the education system is due for a transformation. And if you ask her, we're in the middle of it right now.

'The future of education is all about globalization, technological advances and changing economies. This places very different demands on today's children and future children. In the old days, you became a farmer or a doctor and you trained to do this. These days, we don't know exactly what kind of professions we are training children for. Because most of the future professions aren't known to us yet.'

INVENTING NEW-STYLE EDUCATION

'Education needs to be personalized and focused on the 21st century. We shouldn't just be teaching basic mathematics and Dutch, we need to give lessons in critical thought, cooperation and ICT literacy. We need to get children to discover who they are and stimulate their talents so that they can develop them in the best possible way. That way, they will have the resources to hold their own later in the new, unknown world. And this is a very different proposition from the current education system, in which we are primarily concerned with results rather than strengthening talents.

"We don't know exactly what we are training our children for. Their future profession probably doesn't exist yet."

I think Dutch education is ideally suited to turn my vision into reality. It has its foundation in the autonomy of the school governing body. And I notice that many school governors share my belief that change is needed. Despite this, we are all still searching for the right way. Normally, you mark out a specific objective for the future and follow a plan to achieve it, but this situation is

"A child benefits from optimum development of a wide range of talents so that it can hold its own in the new world."

different. The objective's form and location are still unknown. New-style education still needs to be invented. By teachers, working together with pupils. It develops organically and should only be adjusted where necessary. That requires a whole new management philosophy.'

AUTONOMY AT ALL LEVELS

'We need to create autonomy at all levels, in which we all take responsibility for our own particular roles. This is asking a lot of people. As a school governing body, we help by giving teachers enough space and focusing on personal development. For example, we no longer have assessment interviews; instead we conduct motivation interviews and development interviews, asking 'Where does your passion lie?' and 'What do you still want to learn?'

As governors, we can optimize educational gains by focusing on development rather than output. Each pupil will be in charge of his own learning process, the teacher will give him the resources and guidance to develop his talents and school management will provide the space and freedom to do this. This will lead to intrinsic motivation at all levels, which is an essential requirement for learning and development. This approach founded on trust will undoubtedly contribute to optimum total development of the child, making it the best possible preparation for the unknown future of our country. And it is my view that we can't go far enough in achieving this.' ‹

Chapter 9

Get a Dutch Innovation Mindset[1]

Prof. dr. ir. Caroline Hummels,
Eindhoven University of Technology

This chapter uses parts of Designing disruptive innovative systems, products and services: RTD process (Hummels and Frens, 2011) as well as Eindhoven designs: developing the competence of designing intelligent systems (Hummels and Vinke, 2009).

ntroduction

Within a department of Industrial Design, my natural working habitat, innovation is like the floor we walk on or the air we breathe. Designers are generally driven to create new meaningful propositions that, one way or another, break with the status quo, be it on a social, cultural, technological, business, personal or other level. Designers aim at localizing (making matter concrete), questioning (reflecting on its quality) and opening up (expanding its sense); the three abilities that Sennett (2008) sees as the basis of craftsmanship, and which I consider closely interwoven with design and innovation.

At our department, this innovation-oriented attitude is not only applicable to the things we design and our way of designing, but has also been the basis for our educational approach as of the department's foundation in 2000. In this chapter, I would like to show you what a Dutch innovative mindset could entail and how my journey at Industrial Design might inspire you to explore and implement your own educational innovations.

I will first describe some major shifts in societal and educational paradigms, which form the basis of our work. Then, I'll describe our own position and approach towards education. I elucidate our stance with four concrete examples of innovative ways of learning: self-directed life-long learning; city-situated learning; embodied ways of learning; and tools to support 21st century skills of children. I'll conclude this chapter with three questions stimulating you to explore the Dutch innovation mindset even further from the perspective offered in this contribution.

One of the real challenges is to innovate fundamentally in education. Innovation is hard because it means doing something that people don't find very easy, for the most part. It means challenging what we take for granted, things that we think are obvious.

Ken Robinson, Bring on the learning revolution! (2010a)

Societal and Educational Paradigm Shifts

Our society is changing continuously, and when we look back, say three decades ago, our lives were rather different due to the absence for most people of e.g. personal computers, mobile phones, post-it notes, low-cost airlines, a 24/7 economy and blurring boundaries between work and leisure time. When looking more closely, one can detect several underlying paradigms and types of societies over the last 40-50 years, such as the industrial society (Williams, 2002), experience economy (Pine and Gilmore, 1998), network society (Van Dijk, 1991; Castells, 1996), information society (Crawford, 1983), service economy (Shelp, 1982), circular economy (Pearce and Turner, 1989), the performance economy (Stahel, 2006) and the transformation society (Pine and Gilmore, 1998; Brand and Rocchi, 2011). These economies/societies are mostly different with respect to shared beliefs, values, models and exemplars to guide a community of practitioners and theorists, which Kuhn (1970) defines as different paradigms. Although some of these concepts are fairly close and might relate to a similar paradigm.

Over decades, shifts have taken place in for instance our economic drivers (from mass production towards value networks), business goals (from profit to growth to development and even transformation), perspective (from local to global to contextual to systemic nowadays), the relationship between institutes and citizens/consumers/clients/users, etcetera (from linear top-down to networked) and the value propositions that are pursued (from commodities to targeted experiences to enabling self-development and to ethical value exchange) (Brand & Rocchi, 2011).

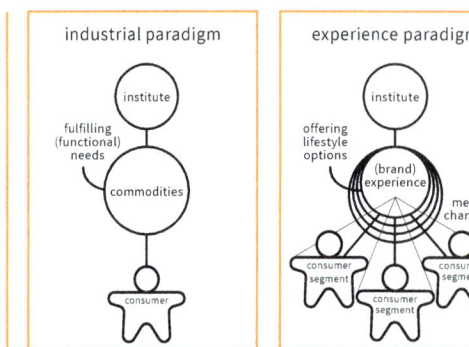 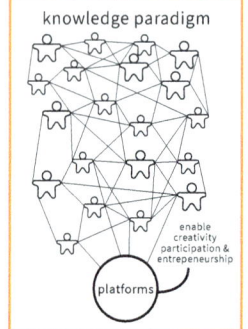 

Figure 9.1   *Different paradigms that have different presence and implications over the years. (Hummels, 2012, after Brand & Rocchi, 2011).*

Given these changes over the last half century, it seems somewhat strange that the overall educational paradigm for primary, secondary and higher education seems not that sensitive too change, or at least changes very slowly in comparison to other fields. In many cases, our educational systems still seem to fit the industrial paradigm or if lucky, the experience paradigm. Ken Robinson advocates for more than a decade now, that the underlying paradigm of our current form of education is outdated and should change:

> *I believe we have a system of education that is modelled on the interests of industrialism and in the image of it. I'll give you a couple of examples. Schools are still pretty much organized on factory lines; ringing bells, separate facilities, specialized into separate subjects. We still educate children by batches; we put them through the system by age group .... I believe we've got to go in the exact opposite direction. That's what I mean about changing the paradigm (Robinson, 2010b).*

Also the poet, filmmaker and speaker Prince Ea makes through his movie *The people vs the school system* (2016) a strong appealing public plea for changing the current educational paradigm by acknowledging aspects such as diversity, individuality, creativity, growth and collaboration; aspects that are more related to the knowledge and transformation paradigms:

> *Do we prepare students for the future or the past? … Today, we don't need to make robot zombies. The world has progressed. And now we need people who think creatively, innovatively, critically, independently with the ability to connect. … This educational malpractice, where one teacher stands in front of 20 kids, each one having different strengths, different needs, different gifts and different dreams, and you teach the same thing the same way? That is horrific. … If we can customize healthcare, cars and Facebook pages, then it is our duty to do the same for education, to upgrade and change…* (Prince Ae, 2016).

Changing the classical educational paradigm means changing the definition of learning, the role of the learner and the teacher, and disrupting the general desire for certainty, truth, simplicity and objective knowledge, as is often aimed for in 'classical' research (Fleener, 2005), and in 'classical' education (Doll, 1986).

Towards Self-Directed, Competency-Centred, Life-Long Situated Learning

In a classical educational approach, it seems that education is centred around the teacher who takes a 'God's-eye' view. Teachers determine what the student should know, operationalized in uniform curricula, and measured with tests that are considered objective and predictive. A new educational paradigm, however, asks for an approach centred around the student as Ken Robinson and Prince Ae promote. There is a desire and need for transformative curricula that emphasize and support a variety of approaches, procedures and interpretations, depending on the individual student (Doll, 1986). This also asks for new perspectives and learning theories that focus on the student in his lifeworld. In this new paradigm, students learn to learn (what, how and why) and teachers facilitate their learning. Moreover, teachers are becoming learners again. Or as Ken Robinson (2010b) is saying:

> *I think we have to change metaphors. We have to go from what is essentially an industrial model of education, a manufacturing model, which is based on linearity and conformity and batching people. We have to move to a model that is based more on principles of agriculture. We have to recognise that human flourishing is not a mechanical process; it's an organic process. And you cannot predict the outcome of human development. All you can do, like a farmer, is create the conditions under which they will begin to flourish.*

I'm happy to see that learning theories such as constructivism, that are tightly coupled to this new paradigm, seem to gain interest. Constructivism stresses the notion of activity: it is the learner who creates meaning, affected by and reflecting his socio-cultural environment. The way this is done depends on the type of constructivism. The individual or cognitive variants of constructivism assume the locus of knowledge construction to be in the individual learner; the social or situative variants assume this locus to be in socially organized networks (Birenbaum, 2003).

This new paradigm is about learning and performing through practical application, while simultaneously acquiring theoretical skills and building knowledge. Instead of separating theory and practice, it unites them, thus giving a crucial role to experience (Dewey, 1938; Hillen, 2017). That is not quite the image one gets nowadays when walking into a school building, where theoretical skill seems to be more valued. This new paradigm, however, starts from the traits and characteristics of the individual person, who learns through doing and from experiences, and thus develops knowledge, skills and attitudes in a specific context. It is through reflection in, on and for action that a student gains an understanding arising from experience (Schön, 1983). When integrating these learning experiences, the student develops competencies which he can demonstrate when applying them. Such competency-centred learning is experiential (learn by doing), exemplary (learn from specific situations), context-related (learn within a variety of contexts), reflective (in, on and for action) and it is self-directed, because it is the learner who creates meaning, which can lead to competency development (Vinke & Hummels, 2010).

I believe that students need to trust their intuition, use their common sense, and dare to make mistakes. It is important for students to develop the ability to reflect in and on action as well as reflect for action, to stimulate learning and direct development. Especially in a learner-centred paradigm, students need to become able to direct their learning (with help if needed), thus becoming autonomous and lifelong learners in a social context.

A recent study done by our Industrial Design graduate master student Yasemin Arslan (2017), shows that a feeling of urgency for the new educational paradigm is very present in society, at least in the Eindhoven context, both for people with an education-related profession, and for other stakeholders from e.g. city governance, cultural organizations and business.

Our Position and Approach: 10 Parameters

When looking at the field of design, the advances in science and technology follow each other so quickly that large amounts of knowledge and information get outdated rapidly. Functioning effectively as a designer (but also for other professionals), in such a rapidly changing society requires the ability to learn continuously. When I look at my own design education (between 1985 and 1993) in comparison to the current design field, there has been an enormous change in focus (more on systems and service), tools (the introduction of computers) and techniques (from sketching versus interactive 3D prototyping). So with a society that changes rapidly, the need to become self-directed lifelong learners is becoming even more important. Consequently, a major pillar of our educational system is learning how to learn.

To substantiate our preferences regarding a new educational paradigm, we are also researching and designing for it, e.g. by developing frameworks, processes, methods and tools. This design research is based on embodied (being-in-the world) theories such as phenomenology, which has close links with constructivism. These theories state that meaning is created in the interaction between the human being and the world. We perceive the world in terms of what we can do with it, and by physically interacting in a social context we access and express this meaning (Merleau-Ponty, 1962). The perspective we take based on these theories, aims at overcoming two 'Cartesian' splits. Firstly, to bridge the separation between 'immaterial' and 'material' (c.f. the mind-body problem in philosophy) and secondly, to bridge the distinction between the (inner) person and the (outside) world (c.f. phenomenology's critique of the subject-object distinction in science) (Van Dijk & Hummels, 2017). Therefore, we stress the unity of theory and practice and the use of reflection in and on action as a mechanism to learn and grow. And we question and explore the context of learning regarding e.g. time, place, social network and driving force.

We discern 10 parameters, which we consider important in explaining the differences between our approach and the classical educational approach. Moreover, they help us to pinpoint the direction of the frameworks, processes, methods, tools and platforms we develop. First, I will briefly explain the 10 parameters, then I will show examples of our approach, our designs.
I label every parameter based on two (or three) opposites, but it is not always a matter of one or the other; it can also be a strive for a combination of both, as you can see in the discussion above about the unity of theory and practice. In general, we are aiming at combinations of different parameters to create and explore new educational approaches.

Self-Directed Versus Directed Learning
Within a self-directed learning approach, it is the learner who is responsible for his development and who is in control of his learning activities. It requires behaviourally, meta-cognitively and motivationally active learning. This is in contrast with the classical approach in which the teacher has the lead, determines what needs to be learned, and assesses if the students live up to the pre-determined expectations. We take as much as possible a self-directed approach.

Competency-Centred Versus Knowledge-Oriented Learning
Competency-centred learning offers students the opportunity to give equal weight to knowledge, skills and attitudes, and stimulates them to learn by doing. We define a competency as an individual's ability to select, acquire, and use the knowledge, skills, and attitudes that are required for effective behaviour in a specific professional, social or learning context (Hummels & Vinke, 2009). Especially in the higher grades of primary schools as well as in secondary schools,

knowledge orientation seems to be key, thus offering and valuing especially courses that contribute to this knowledge and often devaluing courses that are more practical like music or sports. We take a competency-centred approach.

Perceiving and Doing Versus Making Versus Thinking

Dewey (1938) gives a crucial role to experience, stressing the importance of the unity of knowledge and skills. Knowledge can be obtained through e.g. the analytical skills of the student (e.g. reading a book), the perceptual-motor skills (e.g. sensing the physical qualities of materials) as well as through the synthetic skills (e.g. building physical models), thus automatically relating knowledge and skills. By using different ways of obtaining and generating information, we aim at connecting the abstract to the sensorial, the intuitive to the analytical, imagination to reason, and making (synthesize and concretize) to thinking (analyse and abstract) (Hummels & Levy, 2013). Given our embodied starting point, we often begin the design process from a hands-on, experiential perspective before moving to analysis and abstraction. Also for communication for make use of the wide spectrum of skills.

Formal Versus Informal Learning

In the Netherlands, as in many other countries, the education landscape is predominantly based on formal education given by authorized and accredited institutes. Diplomas are very important for one's career, although there are always exceptional self-made (wo)men. New media have given a boost to more informal ways of learning, such as the Khan Academy or YouTube channels. Although the university is a formal educational institute, we are exploring the edges, e.g. by offering time for informal learning activities, including informal activities into the formal grading procedure and developing platforms that operate at the edges and support also informal learning.

Learning at an Institute Versus in Society

Related to formal versus informal learning is the place of learning. It seems common to learn at a school or campus, in dedicated rooms, often equipped with tables and chairs that 'tell' students to sit still and learn. Occasionally, there are other types of rooms, depending on learning topic and activity. One can see initiatives where society is brought into the school context, e.g. by bringing in experts for dedicated lectures or classes. It is not that common yet to leave the school building and learn in a societal or practical setting, apart from special activities such as internships. Yet, this way of learning is very different and can work extremely well for competency-centred learning. Especially for courses that focus on societal challenges, I move part of my educational activities into the societal context in the centre of the city, in order to add meaning to the more classical (and often more practical) setting, with respect to environment, situation and people involved.

Learning during Dedicated Time Slots Versus 24/7 Learning

Questioning the directed, formal learning approach at school or a university campus, and exploring new terrain, automatically leads to questioning the nine-to-five attitude towards learning. Learning becomes interwoven with living and does not stop at the school doors nor at the regular teaching hours. We combine the two for our students, with dedicated hours for joint guided learning activities (for master students approximately one day a week) and for the rest freedom to plan their own and their group's work.

Life-Long Learning Versus Learning at School

On a larger timescale, one can look at the role learning plays during one's life. In the Netherlands, most children go to primary and secondary school, a substantial part to higher education, and some take additional courses and training during their professional careers. But in general, education is seen as the formal activity one does in an educational institute. But with the speed of technological, social, cultural, economic, global change, etcetera, the need for life-long learning is increasing. That brings opportunities and asks for a different attitude of learners, their social context, teachers, educational institutes, government, industry, etcetera. We see life-long learning as a possibility to extend and reframe learning at school, and we have been working towards a life-long learning approach for more than 10 years now.

Offline Versus Online (Digital) Learning

With the advances in technology, specifically in the area of digital media, online learning is becoming more and more popular in higher education, e.g. by using websites (e.g. Khan Academy and Learning Management Systems (LMS) like Blackboard and Canvas), using videos (with platforms like YouTube and Vimeo to share them), social media (e.g. Facebook, Slack, Yammer, WhatsApp) and even dedicated MOOCs (Massive Open Online Course) connect worldwide students and provide access to education at a distance. In primary and secondary education, it is still in its infancy, although the kids themselves learn a lot via informal, online learning. We advocate blended learning that combines the strengths of both worlds and uses both physical media (e.g. books, hand-outs, prototypes, live demos and hands-on workshops) and digital media.

Learning Alone Versus in a Uniform Group Versus in a Diverse Group

In most educational settings, students learn in a group. Groups run the risk of being addressed as one, as Prince Ae pointed out, with learning not attuned to the individual learner. Such groups are generally uniform, its composition based on age (primary schools), age and intelligence (secondary schools) and field of expertise (higher education). In the beginning of this chapter, we looked at the knowledge and transformation paradigm. Especially the latter shows the necessity of being able to work in multi-stakeholder teams. Therefore, we are exploring how to make use of the combination of these three different forms of learning, and finding a balance between working alone and in teams (both uniform and diverse). We are exploring various activities in mixed teams with other schools (from different levels). Moreover, we deliberately facilitate many workshops outside of university for multi-stakeholder groups interested in innovation and design.

Reflection Versus Ongoing Action

Schön's reflective practice is based on the ability of people (in his studies, professional designers and architects) to know, reflect and learn in and on action; to learn by doing, and through reflection gain an understanding that arises from experience (Schön, 1983). Reflection is a motor for knowledge (Hillen, 2017). Moreover, reflection can help to obtain stability and regain order, especially when learning has an equilibrium – disequilibrium – re-equilibrium pattern (Piaget, 1971), where one goes from one stable state to another, in which the disequilibrium is often chaos through which one reaches order. The disequilibrium is a driving force of changing behaviour and development, although the chaos can feel uncomfortable for students (Doll, 1986). We make intensive use of reflection in, on and for action and would advise it as a learning mechanism from a young age.

Four Concrete Examples of Innovative Ways of Learning

In the second part of this chapter, I will provide concrete examples of ways of learning, clustered around four topics: self-directed life-long learning; city-situated learning; embodied ways of learning; and tools to support 21st century skills of children. With these examples, I aim at elucidating the consequences of using a learning approach based on the above-mentioned paradigm shift and the related 10 parameters. I will discuss every example on the basis of four items: the goal, rationale and vision behind this example; the design; the implementation and usage; and the lessons we learned, thus aiming to give you handles to implement your own educational innovations.

Self-Directed Life-Long Learning

The department of Industrial Design at the Eindhoven University of Technology was founded in 2000. It responded right from its start to the societal and technological changes as sketched in the first section, by creating an educational environment and mechanisms to enhance competency development and sharing. For 3,5 years, between 2008 and 2011, I was director of Education, aiming at fine-tuning the system towards a full-fletched self-directed life-long learning approach. In the first example, I will sketch the system and lessons learned during this period.

The Industrial Design Self-Directed Life-Long Learning Ecosystem

Goal, Rationale and Vision

In the Industrial Design (ID) competency-centred learning model used until 2011, learning and working came together. Students learned to learn (what, how and why) and we facilitated their learning. Attitude played an important role; our students needed to develop the ability to reflect, to self-regulate their learning, to learn from experience and to assess themselves. Staff members made a shift from teacher-focused to learning-focused, thus a change from being an authoritative source of knowledge to facilitating students' learning. Pivotal in our approach was the notion of activity, learning by doing, because we believe that learning is an active construction of meaning by the learner in its context.

Design, Implementation and Usage[2]

We aimed at embodying this self-directed life-long learning ecosystem in all our forms of organization, communication, facilitation, etcetera. For example, our students had to create their own individual curriculums. At the start of the semester, they selected their learning activities, depending on their individual learning needs and in compliance with the ID competence framework we offered. They could choose their projects of interest on a market in dialogue with the teachers who were offering these projects.

During and at the conclusion of learning activities, students reflected on their activities and they invited staff members involved to provide them with (written) feedback on processes and outcomes. They had no exams, apart from the final bachelor or master exam, and they received no grades, only only a promoted or hold verdict for every semester. This verdict was based on their showcase, the exhibition and a discussion with the assessor and coach. Through this, they demonstrated the development of their overall competence of designing, vision on designing and their growth as a designer, underpinned with evidence.

The learning was socially situated. For example, coaches were stimulated to set up joined projects with colleagues having different competencies. We created the ID café. We offered at least four identity / self-directed learning weeks per year to stimulate open learning activities for the entire community. We organized four internal exhibitions per year and one large public exhibition during the Dutch Design Week. We developed technological platforms and used social networks to share information such as our Library of Skills, blogs, and Facebook and YouTube.

❯

---

[2] Because the design, implementation and usage took place in the past and are rather interwoven, we discuss them here together.

Figure 9.2   *The self-directed life-long learning ecosystem at Industrial Design.*

What Did We Learn?

I used the past tense for my explanation of the learning ecosystem, since the current system is quite different. In September 2011, Industrial Design became part of The Bachelor College of the University. An educational system based on a different paradigm, was no longer feasible. Trying new systems that challenge the current paradigms and experiment with new forms of learning, can also imply that for that moment, that the solution is too radical for that context. However, several principles of our system, such as having a personal mentor during one's study, were integrated in the Bachelor College.

So what did we learn when we look back at this period? When I posted the link to the Prince Ae video *The people vs the school system* (2016) on the Facebook page of Industrial Design, I received the following comment from an alumnus:

> *Absolutely love this! Thanks for the amazing years of education at ID, it opened my eyes to what education could be like. Every year was different, which made me more flexible for change, and it taught me to reflect and become aware of my own learning process. Seeing this video, I can only hope that educational systems keep developing. Thank you, and your son for sharing.*

We learned through our students and alumni, as well as the official accreditation and assessment procedures, that this new way of learning was successful. Setting up a programme based on self-directed competency-centred life-long learning seems a good way to train design students, and several international schools have followed our model.

That doesn't mean that our approach didn't have drawbacks. The gap between our department and the rest of the university was too big. This requires attention if you want to set up such a programme. Moreover, this system was not suitable for all students. It requires a strong internal motivation and drive to learn. But for those our system did resonate with, they can reach great height, as was often indicated by their employers and clients after their study.

City-Situated Multi-Stakeholder Learning

Almost half of the 10 parameters mentioned point towards a merger of living and learning, by moving learning into the everyday context of a person. Through city-situated multi-stakeholder learning, we explore how we can merge formal and informal learning, using a variety of media. In 2017, we set up the Studio for Connected Society (SCS), where we offer a design programme around social innovation in the 'Designhuis', a creative meeting place in the city centre of Eindhoven. Students from various higher education institutes (TU Eindhoven, Fontys Applied University and Design Academy Eindhoven) can work together with various societal stakeholders on social challenges in context. Results from the pre-edition *Transformative Homes for Sensuous Dementia* can be read in Van Dijk and Hummels (2017)[3]. SCS builds upon the lessons learned from the Learning on the Move project, which I will explain now.

Learning on the Move (LOTM)

Goal, Rationale and Vision

Higher education institutes need to stay up to speed with individual learning pathways, digitalisation, a highly dynamic society and job market, and increasing forms of collaboration. LOTM started in 2014 and aimed at developing an (in)formal learning ecosystem in the neighbourhood, initiated by (applied) universities and vocational education, and supported by societal partners like city governance and healthcare organizations. What kind of infrastructure, approaches and tools are necessary to stimulate cooperative learning outside the standard school environment? The main parameters explored were: formal versus informal learning; learning at an institute versus in society; offline versus online (digital) learning; learning alone versus in uniform/diverse groups, and reflection versus ongoing action.

Design

LOTM has resulted in a combination of physical and digital workspaces both inside and outside the regular educational environment. Next to insights into multi-stakeholder collaboration and developing embodied tools (see next topic), the main deliverable is a digital platform that facilitates project teams with tools to reflect, to share progress updates, to keep in contact with stakeholders and to maintain schedules and deadlines. The digital platform is open for students and stakeholders and integrates seamlessly with existing educational systems, while tempting students to explore more informal ways of learning and keeping a strong emphasis on communication and reflection (Van den Heuvel and Hummels, 2017).

>

---

[3] See also https://vimeo.com/194153765.

Figure 9.3   *The informal learning eco-system of LOTM.*

Implementation and Usage

As of 2014, the platform, tools and approach were developed with a variety of educational and societal partners. At the end of 2016, this building phase was concluded, and the deliverables are as of 2017 being used in various projects, such as the Studio for Connected Society and the European Erasmus+ project Strategy for Change.

What Did We Learn?

It is challenging to set up an (in)formal eco-learning system with different formal education institutes from different backgrounds and levels. Existing systems and curricula are quickly in the way when exploring and experimenting with new forms of learning. In order to succeed, it requires the acknowledgement of all partners that space for experimentation, however small, is crucial.

Embodied Ways of Learning

Competency development makes use of the analytical as well as synthetic skills of the student. Therefore, students would benefit from methods and tools that support them in connecting the abstract to the sensorial, the intuitive to the analytical, imagination to reason, and making to thinking. They would benefit from embodied ways of learning. During my whole career, I've worked on developing such methods and tools, focusing on movement in general (Hummels, Overbeeke & Klooster, 2007), or specific frameworks, such as Designing in Skills (Trotto & Hummels, 2013a), Engagement Catalysers (Trotto & Hummels, 2013b) and The Blue Studio (Jaasma et al., 2017).

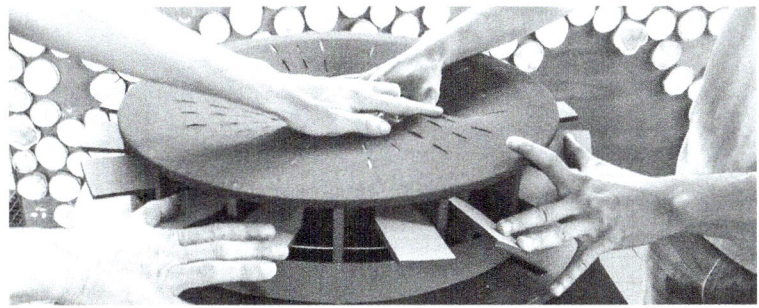

Figure 9.4 *Engagement Catalyser*

Let me explain one of such tools, the Embodied Ideation Toolkit (Smit et al, 2016).

Embodied Ideation Toolkit (EIT)

Goal, Rationale and Vision
Design is becoming more and more a part of multi-stakeholder collaborations that aim for innovation. Given the shift in paradigms, these collaboration networks require new tools that facilitate collaboration, open innovation, rapid co-creation and that support the skills of a wide variety of people. As innovation asks for open-mindedness and inclusion of people not trained in design, we aimed at developing a toolset with objects that stimulate multi-stakeholder creativity in an embodied way without requiring specific training.

Design
The Embodied Ideation Toolkit is a set of tangible magnetic non-descriptive objects, designed as tools to support creative sessions, e.g. through creating scenarios or visualizing concepts and relationships. The objects aim at triggering scaffolding in various ways, by stimulating curiosity and exploration.

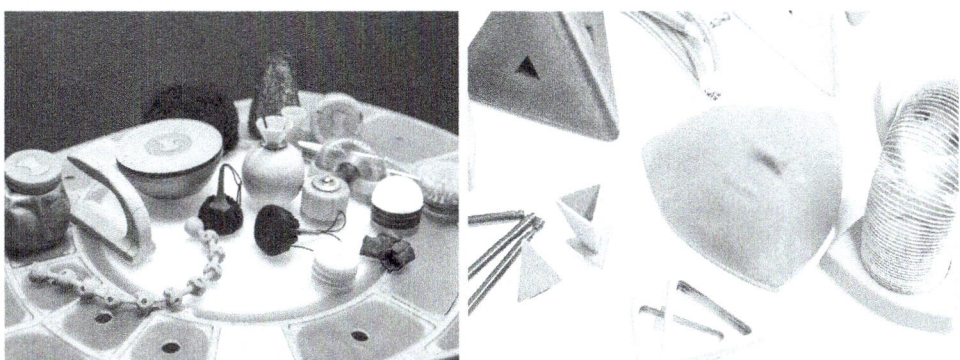

Figure 9.5 *Two of the versions of the Embodied Interaction Toolkit.*

❯

Implementation and Usage

The first version of the set was developed in September 2014, during a two-week Master class at the department of Industrial Design. The set was further developed, resulting in two versions in 2015 and 2016. We are currently developing the fourth interactive set that can sense and display the movements of the objects. Up till now, we have used the set in hundreds of creative multi-stakeholder settings (inside and outside of the university, both nationally and internationally) addressing a variety of topics.

Figure 9.6   *The toolkit in different learning settings. TIAS Business School (left), FabCafe in Tokyo (right).*

What Did We Learn?

When looking at all the sessions, we saw that most participating stakeholders, even those without a design background, were stimulated to explore the richness of the physical and material properties of the objects. The threshold to start interacting with the set is very low, which appears to make it easy for participants to communicate, express themselves and to come up with new concepts for the design cases. By physically examining the objects, their materials and affordances, the majority of users move quickly to an exploratory dimension that enables them to tackle challenges and open up innovative opportunities. For example, a group of 12 business students from Umeå, Sweden, was able to make a tangible business model within half an hour, to their own surprise (Smit et al., 2016). The strength of EIT and related tools is the facilitation to explore different perspectives outside the current frame of reference, help to switch off the usual pattern of thinking, and get into a more creative mode.

Tools to Support 21st Century Skills of Children

The concept of 21st century skills (Binkley et al, 2010) is closely related to life-long learning competencies as discussed above, with an emphasis on competencies such as collaboration, communication, use of ICT, creativity and critical reflection (Thijs et al., 2014). Our students and alumni have already been working on developing products and tools to support 21st century skills. For example, our alumnus Rick de Visser (2014) developed KnapZack in 2014, together with education consultancy Onderwijs Maak Je Samen and four primary schools in the Netherlands. KnapZack is a digital tablet-based portfolio tool that stimulates reflection for children at primary schools using photos, movies and notes. The tool takes an embodied and reflective approach, as do the designs of alumnus Mitchell Jacobs and his company Studio Tast, which I will describe below.

GoedWijzer and IMO-LEARN by Studio Tast

Goal, Rationale and Vision

Studio Tast (http://www.studiotast.com/) is a design firm developing contemporary products, platforms and learning materials centred on the combination of thinking and doing, in which online and offline learning meet. Their designs aim at stimulating the pupils' curiosity, thereby motivating them to learn. The core emphasis is on embodied learning, stressing the importance of doing and sensing, and using the capabilities of the body.

Design

Studio Tast has developed several educational tools, including GoedWijzer and iMO-LEARN. GoedWijzer is a clock-reading experience for children, aged 7 to 9, in primary school education. It enables children to learn autonomously, with their preferred method, in the classroom, combining today's technological possibilities with embodied learning. The product consists of an application which is controlled by a physical clock with tools.

iMO-LEARN combines learning and moving to enable children to learn more intensively and stimulate creativity. The seats are equipped with motion sensors and linked to dedicated digiboard software, thus providing instant feedback to teachers and pupils. The pupils answer questions by moving their seats. Since the platform is open, the teachers can develop their own content.

Figure 9.7 *Learning how to read a clock with GoedWijzer (left) and active learning with the class through iMO-LEARN (right).*

Implementation and Usage

GoedWijzer is a fully working product tested in De Driestam primary school in Eindhoven. It is, however, not (yet) on the market.

The concept of the iMO-LEARN seat was developed at the Southern Denmark University. The client, i3-Technologies asked Studio Tast to redesign the seat, incorporate and develop the electronics, do user research and design the interaction style, in combination with the interface of the digiboard software. iMO-LEARN is commercially available on the global market as of September 2016.

What Did We Learn?

GoedWijzer remained a concept and turned out to be not marketable. One of the reasons for this was the strong link with the overall vision, but insufficient eye for business during the development process. With iMO-LEARN, business focus was integrated in the overall vision from day one. The iMO-LEARN platform appears to be marketable due to its simplicity. GoedWijzer offered a dedicated, content-ready platform and tools. This might be OK for learning how tell time, but the openness of iMO-LEARN stimulates a wide variety of application areas. Moreover, the system can be connected to any learning approach or model. This diversity seems a great advantage in stimulating society to really embrace new tools and methods that are based on a new paradigm. However, this openness demands an active role of the teacher, who should be able and motivated to make appropriate and inspiring lessons.

So, designing the way to facilitate and motivate the teacher in such open systems, should also be part of the development process.

Conclusions

In this chapter, I sketched the major shifts in paradigms, both on a societal and educational level, and described my own position and approach towards education, combined in 10 parameters. The four concrete examples in combination with the parameters, aim at providing inspiration, guidelines and insights into a self-directed, competency-centred, life-long and situated learning approach. They taught us that a paradigm shift in education asks for an innovation attitude and innovative processes and tools to make the difference. To learn, to try, to fail, to try again, to step out of the regular setting and create a context where to explore new approaches and tools. To get your hands dirty, try new things, step out of your comfort zone and to explore new ways of learning. To learn from and with your students and acknowledge that they might know, see or approach things differently, sometimes even better.

You can start small, by altering the setting and approach of your learning activity once by using different tools, have different 'rules' and especially change the physical setting. And if you are ambitious you can envision what your educational setting and underlying paradigm will be in

5-10 year's time and develop your roadmap, for which you might use the 10 parameters and the lessons we've learned. It is not always easy, else it wouldn't be a paradigm shift. But we owe it to ourselves and our children to rethink education.

Key Questions

- Ken Robinson and Prince Ae plea for a paradigm shift in formal education, and I do too. Despite several smaller efforts, a systemic change in primary, secondary and higher education seems still far away. What and who do you consider necessary to enable our children to be educated as lifelong, self-directed and competency-centred learners of the 21st century, fitting a knowledge and transformation paradigm, instead of the industrial paradigm?
- Technology might support us in new ways of learning – blending formal and informal, analogue and digital, local and global – next to enriching learning with different forms of media. What do you see as concrete possibilities of technology to support a knowledge / transformation paradigmatic approach to education, and what are potential risks?
- What would need to change in your own organization to realize a 21st century approach to education, and what could be a first small step to realize educational innovation in your organization?

About the author

Prof. dr. ir. Caroline Hummels is a professor Design and Theory for Transformative Qualities at the department of Industrial Design at the Eindhoven University of Technology. Caroline uses a Research-through-Design approach to explore the transformative qualities of products/systems, including related frameworks, methods and tools, with a focus on embodied interaction. Thereby, she focuses on participatory sensemaking, ethics, aesthetics, multi-stakeholder social design/ innovation, health and wellbeing and education.

Contact: c.c.m.hummels@tue.nl.

References

Ae, P. (2016). *The people vs the school system.* Online movie: last accessed February 28 2017: https://www.youtube.com/watch?v=dqTTojTija8.

Arslan, Y. (2017). *Veldwerk verslag Roadmap Leren 2030: Op welke manieren kan de gemeente innovatie ondersteunen binnen de formele en informele leerdomeinen in Eindhoven.* Internal report Eindhoven University of Technology.

Binkley, M., Erstad, O., Herman, J., Raizen, S., Ripley, M. and Rumble, M. (2012). Defining 21st century skills. In: P. Griffin et al. (Eds) *Assessment and teaching of 21st Century Skills.* Springer Science+Business Media. pp 17-66.

Birenbaum, M. (2003). New insights into learning and teaching and their implications for assessment. In Mien Segers, Filip Dochy and Eduardo Cascallar (Eds.), *Optimising New Modes of Assessment: In search of Qualities and Standards.* Dordrecht: Kluwer Academic Publishers, pp 13-36.

Brand, R. and Rocchi, S. (2011). *Rethinking value in a changing landscape: a model for strategic reflection and business transformation.* Philips Design internal document.

Castells, M. (1996, second edition, 2010). *Volume I: The Rise of the Network Society.* The Information Age: Economy, Society and Culture. Malden, MA; Oxford, UK: Blackwell (second edition: Chichester, UK: Wiley-Blackwell).

Crawford, S. (193). The Origin and Development of a Concept: The Information Society. *Bull Med Libr Assoc. 71*(4) October. pp. 380–385.

Dewey, J. (1938). *Experience and education.* New York: Touchstone.

Dijk, J. van, (1991) *De netwerkmaatschappij: sociale aspecten van nieuwe media.* Uitgever: in Houten: Bohn Stafleu Van Loghum 1991. (English version first published in 1992: *The Network Society: Social Aspects of New Media*).

Dijk, J. van, and Hummels, C. (2017). Designing for Embodied Being-in-the-World: Two Cases, Seven Principles and One Framework. In: *Proceedings of TEI 2017*, ACM New York, USA.

Doll, W. (1986). Prigogine: A New Sense of Order, A New Curriculum. *Theory into Practice, Beyond the Measured Curriculum 25*(1), pp. 10-16.

Dreyfus, H. (1991). *Being-in-the-world: A commentary on Heidegger's Being and Time, Division I.* Cambridge (MA): MIT.

Fleener, M.J. (2005). Introduction: chaos, complexity, curriculum, and culture. In: W. Doll, M. Fleener, D. Trueit and J. Julien (eds). *Chaos, complexity, curriculum, and culture: a conversation.* New York: Peter Lang, pp. 1-17.

Heuvel, R. van den, and Hummels, C. (2017). *Learning on the Move.* Eindhoven University of Technology, The Netherlands.

Hillen, V. (2017). *People Place Process: A self-reflection tool to become a professional in design thinking, based on Pedagogical Action Research.* Eindhoven University of Technology.

Hummels, C. (2012). *Matter of transformation: sculpting a valuable tomorrow.* Inaugural lecture, September 28, 2012. Eindhoven University of Technology. Download available at: https://pure.tue.nl/ws/files/3663176/hummels2012.pdf.

Hummels, C. Overbeeke, K. and Klooster, S. (2007). Move to get moved: a search for methods, tools and knowledge to design for expressive and rich movement-based interaction for design. *Personal and Ubiquitous Computing,* volume 11, issue 8, pp 677-690.

Hummels, C. and Frens, J. (2011). Designing disruptive innovative systems, products and services: RTD process. In: Denis A. Coelho (Ed.) *Industrial Design – New Frontiers.* Intech Open Access Publisher. 147-172. Available at: www.intechopen.com.

Hummels, C. and Vinke, D. (2009). *Eindhoven designs; volume two: Developing the competence of designing intelligent systems.* Eindhoven University of Technology, The Netherlands

Hummels, C. and Lévy, P. (2013). Matter of transformation: designing an alternative tomorrow inspired by phenomenology. *ACM Interactions, 20*(6), pp. 42-49.

Jaasma, P., Smit, D., Dijk, J. van, Latcham, T., Trotto, A. and Hummels, C. (2017). The Blue Studio: Designing an Interactive Environment for Embodied Multi-Stakeholder Ideation Processes. In: *Proceedings of TEI 2017*, ACM New York, USA.

Kuhn, T. (1970). *The Structure of Scientific Revolutions*, second ed. University of Chicago Press, Chicago.

Merleau-Ponty, M. (1962). *Phenomenology of Perception.* C. Smith, trans. Humanities Press, New York, 1962.

Pearce, D. and Turner, K. (1989). *Economics of Natural Resources and the Environment.* Johns Hopkins University Press.

Piaget, J. (1971). *Biology and knowledge.* Chicago IL: University of Chicago press.

Pine II, J. and Gilmore, J. (1998). Welcome to the Experience Economy. *Harvard Business Review*, July-August 1998, pp 97-105.

Robinson, K. (2010a). *Bring on the learning revolution!* A TED2010 talk. Last accessed on February 28, 2017: https://www.ted.com/talks/sir_ken_robinson_bring_on_the_revolution

Robinson, K. (2010b). *Changing Education Paradigms.* RSA Animate talk. Last accessed on February 28, 2017: https://www.ted.com/talks/ken_robinson_changing_education_paradigms.

Sennett, R. (2008), *The craftsman.* Penguin Books, London.

Shelp, R. (1982). *Beyond Industrialization: Ascendancy of the Global Service Economy.* Praeger Publishers.

Schön, D. (1983). *The Reflective practitioner.* New York: Basic Books.

Smit, D., Oogjes, D., Goveia de Rocha, B., Trotto, A., Hur, Y. and Hummels, C. (2016). Ideating in Skills: Developing Tools for Embodied Co-Design. In: *Proc. of the 10th Int. TEI'16 Conference.* pp 78-85, ACM New York, NY, USA.

Stahel, W. (2006). *The Performance Economy.* London, UK: Palgrave Macmillan Ltd

Thijs, A., Fisser, P., and Hoeven, M. van der, (2014). *21e eeuwse vaardigheden in het curriculum van het funderend onderwijs.* Enschede: SLO.

Trotto, A. and Hummels, C. (2013a). Designing in skills: nurturing personal engagement in design. In *Proceedings of the 5th IASDR conferece*, 26-30 August 2013, Tokio, Japan.

Trotto, A. and Hummels, C. (2013b). Engage me, do! Engagement Catalysers to ignite a (design) conversation. In *Proceedings of the DPPI 2013 conference.* Newcastle, September 3-5, 2013, pp. 136-145.

Vinke, D. and Hummels, C. (2010). Authentic assessment for autonomous learning. *ConnectED 2010 – 2nd international conference on design education*, 28 June – 1 July 2010, Sydney, Australia.

Visser, R. de,(2014). *Knapzack.* Internal Master Graduation report Eindhoven University of Technology.

Williams, R. (2002). *Retooling: A Historian Confronts Technological Change.* Cambridge MA, USA: MIT Press.

LATIFA EL BOUMASSOUDI
TEACHER

'YOU'RE NO LONGER THE OMNISCIENT AUTHORITY IMPARTING INFORMATION'

According to senior general secondary education teacher Latifa el Boumassoudi, everyone broadly agrees that education needs to transform. Nowadays, it is much more about guiding students in their learning process and stimulating their curiosity. So what about knowledge? It's definitely still important, but it isn't the main issue.

'As a teacher, you're no longer the omniscient authority imparting information. Of course, students need to have specific knowledge about certain matters, but they also need to be able to make good use of it. I try to motivate my pupils to do this by making the lessons relevant to their own world or by letting them experience the subject matter. I believe it's essential to build a good relationship with pupils so that you can introduce more depth in your lessons and experiment as a teacher. The government has set the final objectives, but you can play around with these as a teacher. For example, you can choose what to focus on and what approach to take. This gives me a lot of flexibility and freedom in the lessons I give. I really appreciate this.'

"Knowledge is definitely still important, but it isn't the main issue."

STUDENTS REMAIN STUDENTS

'The students are well aware that they have to go to school for a certain number of hours each week and need to learn certain things there. As long as we have national final examinations that are graded, it will also be necessary to practise these. Examinations require different skills from practical assignments and other elements.

However, students remain students. In general, they don't want to be made to do things but they want to be able to make their own choices. As a teacher, you try to convert the external motivation of grades into this internal motivation. For example, during flexible learning time we organize different projects with a focus on gaining skills, with students choosing the projects that appeal to them most. Through these projects, students learn a lot about working together and analysing their own performance critically and at the same time we engage their creativity and put their problem-solving skills to the test. This is a different way of learning, not directly related to subject knowledge. Teachers from different subject areas work together to develop these projects.'

CONTINUING DEVELOPMENT

'Next year I will also be teaching laptop classes. For me, using a laptop is not an objective in itself, merely a tool in the learning process. Each pupil's learning needs are different. Some are more focused on deepening and broadening their studies, whereas others' main aim is to practise and repeat the material covered. The use of digital applications and, in particular, differentiating between different pupils' needs, demands an

"You have to keep developing yourself and learning from others."

investment from you as a teacher, but that is a good thing. You need to keep analysing your own performance because you can learn from this as a teacher. No teacher is perfect, even one with twenty years' experience. You have to keep developing yourself and learning from others.' ‹

Chapter 10

Reflecting on the 'Dutch Way' – Observations and Future Directions

Prof. dr. Alma Harris & Dr. Michelle S. Jones,
University of Bath

ntroduction

The global interest in high-performing education systems shows no signs of slowing down. The simple and persuasive argument of 'borrowing from the best' has placed an international spotlight on a select group of education systems (Harris et al, 2016). The OECD report 'Supporting Teacher Professionalism[1]' that drew upon the results from the 2013 'Teaching and Learning International Survey' (TALIS)[2], examined teachers' and principals' perceived professionalism. Thirty-four countries were scored on three measures: teachers' professional knowledge, work autonomy, and access to peer networks. Of those education systems in the survey that scored the highest on the index of professionalism, seven were in Europe and the Netherlands was placed fourth in this group. Yet, despite this ranking, and other external indicators highlighting the success of the Dutch education system, it tends not to feature prominently in the global discourse about system transformation and improvement.

At present, the results of large-scale educational assessments, such as PISA[3], dominate the contemporary discourse about education reform. While there is much that can be learned from cross-cultural comparisons, there is much more to be gained from in-depth county-specific analysis, as the chapters in this book ably demonstrate. Therefore, *The Dutch Way* is both a timely and illuminating text. Through its contributions, from a wide range of experts, the book presents important insights into an education system that undoubtedly deserves more international attention. It presents a rare opportunity to look inside a system and to ask what can be learned from the educational processes and practices within it.

As the editors of this book clearly point out, this book is not an uncritical celebration of all that makes up the education system in the Netherlands. Instead, it is a thoughtful, empirically informed, reflective narrative compiled by those best placed to comment upon what has been achieved and what is still to be achieved within this educational context.

The aim of this chapter is not to comment on each individual contribution as this has been covered, very ably, by the editors in the introduction. This chapter reflects upon the performance of the Dutch education system and highlights areas or features that could be usefully considered by the wider international community. The purpose of this final chapter therefore, is to reflect upon an education system that continues to invest in its improvement with determination and a genuine humility that so characterizes the 'Dutch Way'.

The first part of the chapter takes a glance at the evidence from the latest PISA round and the most recent OECD country report[4]. It argues that, based on this data and other external

[1] http://www.oecd.org/edu/supporting-teacher-professionalism-9789264248601-en.htm
[2] http://www.oecd.org/edu/school/talis-2013-results.htm
[3] http://www.oecd.org/pisa
[4] http://www.oecd.org/netherlands/

indicators of performance, the Netherlands seems to be 'a best-kept educational secret'[5]. While the Dutch education system may not be as visible in international discussions as some other countries, this chapter argues that it has much to offer. The available evidence points to the fact that unlike many other education systems, some of them in the top 5 of PISA, the Dutch system promotes equity alongside excellence and has had considerable success in ensuring that equality of opportunity is prioritized and realized (OECD, 2016).

The second part of the chapter considers why the Dutch system performs as it does, and offers some reflective observations. The aim is not to produce a definitive assessment of the system but rather to highlight some noteworthy features and aspects. The third part of the chapter offers some suggestions about what the international community could learn from the Dutch education system. It proposes that, in rapidly changing and uncertain times, the core values that underpin the Dutch Way will be even more important to reinforce and recognize.

In short, this chapter underlines that Dutch educators should firstly, be proud of their education system, secondly, should acknowledge what it has achieved and thirdly, should celebrate its track record in educational inclusion, diversity, and equity.

The Dutch Way: A Best-Kept Secret?

The latest PISA[6] results came along in December 2016 fuelling the usual set of insecurity, hyperactivity, and hyperbole about the performance of different education systems. There were worries about why certain countries slipped down the rankings and questions about exactly how some East Asian education systems continue to perform so well. Inevitably the PISA results also caused much policy activity and prompted a range of different responses, from policy makers, including the Dutch Ministry of Education[7]. For the Netherlands, the PISA results brought the news that in all subjects the Netherlands scored *above* the OECD average[8]. In science and maths, however, the trend since 2006 was one of decline with reading scores remaining stable.

In terms of measures of equity, the Netherlands scores *better* than the OECD average, the data also shows that, in the Netherlands, the negative impact of poverty and disadvantage on subsequent academic performance, is *lower* than in many other countries participating in PISA. The OECD report (2016:35) states that social background, in the Netherlands, has 'less effect on outcomes' than many other countries. It adds that '9% of students are resilient meaning that they succeed at school despite a disadvantaged background-which is significantly higher than the OECD average of 9% (OECD, 2016; 35)

---

[5] https://internationalednews.com/2016/05/25/leading-futures-alternative-perspectives-on-education- reform-and-policy/

[6] http://www.oecd.org/pisa/

[7] https://www.rijksoverheid.nl/documenten/kamerstukken/2016/12/06/aanbiedingsbrief-bij-resultaten-pisa-2015-in-vogelvlucht

[8] http://www.compareyourcountry.org/pisa/country/nld

The latest PISA results[9] also show that the Netherlands is 11th in Maths in the international rankings, 15th in Reading and 17th in Science. Looking at just the European countries in the PISA rankings, would place the Netherlands 5th for Maths, 9th for Reading and 6th for Science. It *outperforms* Finland in Maths and dramatically *outperforms* the UK in all three subjects. In summary, the Netherlands continues to *outpace* many other countries participating in PISA, in terms of equity and educational performance.

The Netherlands spends far more than the OECD average on education, approximating to 19,000 US dollars per student. Only 6 countries spend more, with Luxembourg at the top of the list[10]. While expenditure is certainly no guarantee of success or better educational outcomes, it is an important factor and a strong indicator of the value placed on education. In terms of the percentages of youth who are not in employment, education or training, the track record is *well below* the OECD average. Since 2005, the percentage of young people in this category has not exceeded 5% and on average has stayed at 3.6%[11]. Compared with the UK, which averages around 10.5% and Ireland, which averages 11%, young people in the Netherlands are half as likely to be out of a job or not in to be in education. This has profound societal consequences and reinforces the importance of equality of opportunity in Dutch society.

The recent OECD (2016) report sheds some additional light on the performance of the Dutch education system. The literacy level of adults in the Netherlands is *high*, the country comes third in international measures after Finland and Japan. This report also states that the Netherlands 'is an equitable system with above-average results' which again reinforces how performance and equity are a powerful combination. As noted already, the Netherlands has a strong vocational system (see Chapter 8) which ensures that only a very low percentage of students do not progress into a job. The report also notes that the education system in the Netherlands has strong school autonomy balanced by strong public accountability. In other words, schools in the Netherlands may have more latitude to make decisions but they are held publicly accountable for their actions.

The OECD (2016) report also pointed to some areas where further work is needed. For example, there is significant variation in performance between schools in the Netherlands, meaning that which school you go to matters a great deal. In other countries, like Finland, this is less of an issue, as most schools tend to perform similarly. The report also highlights that there are fewer 'excellent students' in the Netherlands than might be expected indicating that perhaps those very able students are not being pushed sufficiently or targeted for specialist support. Like many other countries, the Netherlands is facing a challenging and interesting time as many experienced teachers and school leaders are due to retire. This is an opportunity to invest, in a large-scale way, in a renewal of the profession and in light of this the Onderwijscoöperatie (a professional

---

[9]   https://www.oecd.org/pisa/pisa-2015-results-in-focus.pdf
[10]   https://data.oecd.org/eduresource/education-spending.htm
[11]   https://data.oecd.org/youthinac/youth-not-in-employment-education-or-training-neet.htm

teachers' body) has released a strong policy agenda focused on teacher quality. There is a huge amount of energy and resource, at the moment, directed at enhancing the professional status of teachers and leaders in the Netherlands. This is undoubtedly another positive aspect and important dimension of the Dutch Way.

To summarize, based on the OECD (2016) report it can be concluded that the education system in the Netherlands is *good* by a range of external measures and it is suggested that it is perfectly possible to move the system into the next category of 'great'. The introductory section of the OECD (2016:11) report states:

> The Dutch school system is one of the best in the OECD... It is also equitable with a very low proportion of low performers. Basic skills are very good on average while the system minimises weak basic skills among teenagers effectively as the East Asia champions of Japan and Korea. This is supplemented by a strong vocational education and training system with good labour market outcomes. The system is underpinned by a high level of decentralisation, balanced by a national examination system and a strong Inspectorate of Education, school financing which supports disadvantaged students, experimentation and innovation, and good data and research.

The report also notes; 'in many respects the Dutch education system stands out from the crowd' (OECD 2016; 17).

So here is a question, do most educators in the Netherlands think about their system like this? In short, if they do, they rarely vocalize it. Possibly, this is part of the Dutch Way?

Exploring the Dutch Way

Unlike many other education systems, the Netherlands appears to be delivering both educational quality and equity. Yet, as highlighted earlier, the Dutch education system is not necessarily on the radar of international policy makers seeking ways to secure better performance. The Dutch seem to be remarkably quiet about their educational successes and accomplishments. Possibly this is because unlike some of their near European neighbours, they are less convinced about the merits of their system. Yet, they have a track record in educational equity that should be the envy of many countries in Europe and beyond.

For example, fewer Dutch 15-years-olds scored below the PISA performance level 2, which is believed to mark the basic competency which enables active participation in a society. The impact of student socioeconomic background on performance in mathematics was less pronounced in the Netherlands than at the OECD average. The Netherlands also has an *above-average* proportion of resilient students i.e. students who manage to overcome difficult socioeconomic circumstances and exceed expectations, when compared to students in other countries[12] (see Chapter 7 for more details).

In terms of equity, the Netherlands is a particularly *strong* system example. It is the only country participating in PIRLS[13] where all students achieved, at least, the low international benchmark of performance in reading. In addition, 99% of Dutch students achieved at least the low international benchmark in mathematics and science in TIMSS. Young people in the Netherlands, up to the age of 18, must attend school until they attain a basic qualification and there is a strong policy on truancy and absenteeism. The Ministry has signed performance agreements on student drop-out with municipalities and schools in 39 regions, which ensures that the most vulnerable young people are supported[14]. In 2006, the government introduced a successful program (Aanval op de uitval) with a regional approach to promote school success and to avoid early school drop-outs.

The OECD (2016) report shows that, in terms of the percentage of low-performing students, the Netherlands is far *below* the OECD average. In the Netherlands, students from low socioeconomic backgrounds are 1.72 times more likely to be low performers than their peers with high socioeconomic status which is below the OECD average (2.37)[15]. A higher proportion of Dutch disadvantaged students[16] attend schools with students from better-off backgrounds than the OECD average.

The Netherlands is one of the OECD's most devolved education systems, with schools enjoying a high degree of autonomy. This particular brand of autonomy, however, is not to be confused with increased privatization of schooling or the erosion of local control of schooling. Rather, this particular brand of localized empowerment is based upon the principle of *freedom of education*[17] (see Chapter 1) where public and private schools are on an equal footing and all schools receive public funding, provided that they meet the requirements for schools in their sector. In the Netherlands, all teachers receive high quality teacher training at bachelor's and master's[18] level plus there is a great emphasis on teacher autonomy and professionalism (see Chapter 4). The Onderwijscoöperatie (Education Cooperative[19]), which involves over 200,000 teachers, is run by teachers for teachers with the chief aim of safeguarding the quality of the profession.

---

[12] https://internationalednews.com/2016/05/25/leading-futures-alternative-perspectives-on-education-reform-and-policy/
[13] Progress in International Reading Literacy Studies
[14] http://www.oecd-ilibrary.org/education/equity-and-quality-in-education_9789264130852-en
[15] http://www.oecd.org/netherlands/49603617.pdf
[16] http://www.oecd.org/netherlands/49603617.pdf
[17] https://www.government.nl/topics/freedom-of-education
[18] https://www.european-agency.org/country-information/netherlands/national-overview/teacher-training-basic-and-specialist-teacher-training
[19] https://onderwijscooperatie.nl/

Before rushing headlong to conclude that the Netherlands is some educational utopia where schools and teachers are blissfully free from any interference, think again. As noted in the OECD (2016) report, central government sets learning objectives and quality standards that apply to both publicly and privately run schools. The Inspectorate of Education[20] monitors school quality and compliance with central rules and regulations. Unlike many other education systems, the Dutch system balances support and pressure in a positive way (see Chapter 5). While there is a framework of standards, with broadly formulated goals, there are also additional resources and teaching support in schools that need it the most. If schools improve, they are rewarded with more autonomy and freedom to innovate, if they are considered high-performing they can apply for 'Excellent School' status[21].

Also of note is the fact that the Dutch education system is not overly encumbered with overzealous accountability, prescription and standardization. There is no national curriculum in the Netherlands. However, certain learning objectives are stipulated by the Ministry of Education, Culture and Science[22] and are expected to be met at the end of primary and lower secondary education. There is testing in the Netherlands and notably, the system stands out internationally for its high-quality standardized assessments[23]. While the issue of testing remains for some Dutch educators somewhat controversial, on balance, the pressure to compete and perform is not as acute or demoralizing as in many other countries[24].

The norms and values of the Dutch society are collaborative and this is threaded through the very fabric of schooling and education, more generally. Competition hardly plays a role in Dutch educational culture; students are seldom graded against each other or expected to compete against one another. It would appear that Dutch children are 'the happiest in the world'[25] and that young people in the Netherlands feel less stress than, for example their Asian counterparts. External research undertaken by the University of Utrecht and the Sociaal en Cultureel Planbureau (Netherlands Institute for Social Research)[26] similarly found that out of 39 countries, Dutch children say that they are the happiest as they feel less pressure to perform in tests and examinations.

A comprehensive UNICEF report[27], that has looked at socioeconomic differences among children in different countries and the relative effects upon well-being, concludes that the Netherlands has the *lowest* relative life satisfaction gap for children. This measure indicates how far those with the lowest levels of life satisfaction fall behind their peers. The Netherlands is at the top of a group of OECD countries with Finland coming 11th and the United Kingdom located in 20th

---

[20] https://english.onderwijsinspectie.nl/
[21] http://nltimes.nl/2016/01/18/130-dutch-schools-deemed-excellent
[22] https://www.government.nl/ministries/ministry-of-education-culture-and-science
[23] http://www.cito.com/we-are/the-story-of-cito
[24] http://www.findingdutchland.com/five-impressions-of-the-dutch-educational-system/
[25] http://www.findingdutchland.com/five-impressions-of-the-dutch-educational-system/
[26] http://www.scp.nl/english/
[27] https://www.unicef-irc.org/publications/pdf/RC13_eng.pdf

position. Essentially, this data reinforces that for young people in the Netherlands, socioeconomic differences are not affecting their well-being and happiness as profoundly and acutely as in many other countries.

The Netherlands also performs well in terms of special educational needs provision and inclusion. A recent report by the Dutch Inspectorate of Education[28] states that '1 August 2014 saw the introduction of inclusive education. School boards are now responsible for providing inclusive education to every pupil. Boards that collaborate within an alliance are free to apply funds reserved for additional support for this purpose and to determine which pupil is to receive which care. It is expected that more pupils will be placed in mainstream education and that separate facilities will increasingly be of a temporary nature'. The emphasis on *every* pupil is both notable and commendable.

In summary, the education system in the Netherlands reflects a strong commitment to collective and equitable development[29]. Dutch educational policy making reflects power sharing and consensus in decision making. Such strong cultural norms and values are at the heart of educational practice and largely, it is suggested, explain the consistently good performance of its education system. The national belief in fairness, equity and justice not only drives the education system but also, at a practical level, translates into a powerful collective effort to ensure success for every child in every setting.

What Can We Learn from the Dutch Way?

So, what can the international community learn from the Dutch education system? Essentially, there are three things. First, that the Netherlands does not rely on school competition or market forces to secure better educational performance. Conversely, it relies on strong collaboration between teachers, schools and municipalities to raise achievement and attainment (see Chapter 2, in which the three domains of education – qualification, socialization and subjectification – are discussed). Second, it does not exclude students from its education system who are disadvantaged, marginalized or are refugees from another country. Instead, it makes every effort to ensure that young people, from all backgrounds, do not leave school early and that they enter the workforce qualified to participate. Third, the Dutch system shows that it is perfectly possible to combine educational equity and quality. While some may argue that there is more work to be done in this area, compared to many other countries the Dutch education system is undoubtedly moving in a positive direction.

For those interested in navigating the slopes of quick-fix, high performance, the education system in the Netherlands is categorically off-piste. The Dutch Way emanates from a long history and a

[28] http://the-state-of-education-in-the-netherlands-2013-2014%20(1).pdf
[29] https://www.cgdev.org/commitment-development-index

proud tradition of building civic society around democratic values that continue to define both an education system and a country. In years to come, when the high-octane remedies for better educational performance have been over-sold to the point where they have lost their lustre and attraction to policy makers, Dutch educators will still be striving, in their quiet but determined way, for educational excellence through equity[30].

Currently, dark clouds are rolling over many countries and education systems. The shadows of bigotry, fear, prejudice, and discrimination are threats to children who are different, marginalized, poor or simply fleeing from war-torn places. The future currency of educational excellence will be access and in some countries, barriers are already being erected to exclude rather than include, those in most need. In sharp contrast, the education system in the Netherlands continues to exemplify its firm belief in fairness and inclusivity, coupled with the collective commitment to social justice, equality, and educational access for all.

While the Dutch education system, like many others, has its shortcomings, its core educational values remain firmly fixed. The twin pursuit of excellence and equity cannot be celebrated or reinforced enough. In the future, there will be major social, economic, and political challenges (see Chapter 6). The fact that the Dutch education system continues to demonstrate that excellence *through* equity is both imperative and achievable, is not only profoundly hopeful but also captures the very essence of the Dutch Way.

[30] The phrase 'excellence through equity' is attributed to Professor Andy Hargreaves, Boston College USA

About the authors

Prof. dr. Alma Harris, FRSA, has held Professorial posts at the University of Warwick, Institute of Education, University College London, the University of Malaya and latterly, the University of Bath. She is internationally known for her research and writing on educational leadership and school improvement. In 2009–2012, she was seconded to the Welsh Government as a senior policy adviser to assist with the process of system-wide reform. She co-led the Professional Learning Communities (PLC) programme with Dr Michelle Jones, and also led on the development and implementation of a Master's qualification for all newly qualified teachers in Wales. Since 2009, she has worked for the World Bank contributing to development and research programmes aimed at supporting schools in challenging contexts in Russia. Professor Harris is a Visiting Professor at the Moscow Higher School of Economics. Dr Harris is Past President of the International Congress for School Effectiveness and School Improvement (ICSEI), which is an organisation dedicated to enhancing quality and equity in education. In January 2016, she received the ICSEI honorary lifetime award. She was appointed as an international adviser to the First Minister (Scottish Government) in 2016.

Dr. Michelle Suzette Jones is an internationally recognized expert in school leadership, professional learning communities and blended learning. Before taking up her most recent academic post at the University of Bath, she was Associate Professor and Deputy Director of the Institute of Educational Leadership, University of Malaya, where she led on Academic Development and Internationalization. Dr Jones' commitment to educational excellence has driven her entire career. In 2008 she was seconded to the Welsh Government, UK as an Education Adviser and co led the national implementation of the 'Professional Learning Communities' programme in over 2000 schools in Wales. She has been an Education consultant for the World Bank since 2010 assisting schools in challenging circumstances. Most recently, she has been working with government agencies in England, Russia, Singapore, Australia and Malaysia to contribute to the design and delivery of their leadership and professional learning programmes. Dr Jones is a Research Fellow of the 'Hong Kong Institute of Education' and a Senior Research Fellow at the Moscow Higher School of Economics. She is currently the principal investigator on a research project that is exploring instructional leadership practices in Asia and is also the project lead on a Head Foundation funded project that is exploring 'turnaround schools' in Malaysia and Indonesia.

References

Harris, A., Jones, M., & Adams, D. (2016). Qualified to lead? A comparative, contextual and cultural view of educational policy borrowing. *Educational Research, 58*(2), 166-178.

OECD (2016) 'Review of National Policies on Education: Netherlands, Foundations for the Future. OECD Publishing.